Critique of Information

Theory, Culture & Society

Theory, Culture & Society caters for the resurgence of interest in culture within contemporary social science and the humanities. Building on the heritage of classical social theory, the book series examines ways in which this tradition has been reshaped by a new generation of theorists. It also publishes theoretically informed analyses of everyday life, popular culture, and new intellectual movements.

EDITOR: Mike Featherstone, *Nottingham Trent University*

SERIES EDITORIAL BOARD
Roy Boyne, *University of Durham*
Mike Hepworth, *University of Aberdeen*
Scott Lash, *Goldsmiths College, University of London*
Roland Robertson, *University of Pittsburgh*
Bryan S. Turner, *University of Cambridge*

THE TCS CENTRE
The Theory, Culture & Society book series, the journals *Theory, Culture & Society* and *Body & Society*, and related conference, seminar and post-graduate programmes operate from the TCS Centre at Nottingham Trent University. For further details of the TCS Centre's activities please contact:

Centre Administrator
The TCS Centre, Room 175
Faculty of Humanities
Nottingham Trent University
Clifton Lane, Nottingham, NG11 8NS, UK
e-mail: tcs@ntu.ac.uk
web: http://tcs.ntu.ac.uk

Recent volumes include:

Individualization
Ulrich Beck and E. Beck-Gernsheim

Virilio Live
John Armitage

The Sociological Ambition
Chris Shilling and Philip A. Mellor

The Tourist Gaze
John Urry

Reading Race
Norman K. Denzin

Critique of Information

Scott Lash

SAGE Publications
London • Thousand Oaks • New Delhi

SAGE Publications Ltd
6 Bonhill Street
London EC2A 4PU

SAGE Publications Inc
2455 Teller Road
Thousand Oaks, California 91320

SAGE Publications India Pvt Ltd
32, M-Block Market
Greater Kailash - I
New Delhi 110 048

British Library Cataloguing in Publication data

A catalogue record for this book is available from
the British Library

ISBN 0 7619 5268 3
    0 7619 5269 1

Library of Congress Control Number available

Typeset by SIVA Math Setters, Chennai, India
Printed and bound in Great Britain by Athenaeum Press,
Gateshead

Contents

Acknowledgements

I am grateful for discussions with Dan Shapiro, Jeremy Valentine, Andreas Wittel and Jakob Arnoldi. I want to specially thank Celia Lury for discussions about intellectual property, the brand, forms of life and the nature of information in general. The idea of 'proprietary forms of life' is explored in much greater depth in Franklin, Lury and Stacey (2000). I want to thank the late and sadly lamented Dede Boden for initiations into the intricacies of phenomenology and Marshall McLuhan, and for general discussions on what indeed is 'reflexivity'. I have been working with Lury and Boden for over five years now on research projects on global cultural products and new media. I want to thank Mike Featherstone for innumerable discussions on a range of issues in the technological culture which has been a main focus of our work at *Theory, Culture & Society* for the past half decade. I am grateful for the comments of Mark Poster, Nigel Thrift and Alain Touraine who served as publishers' readers of the book. I want to dedicate this book to my little daughter, Eva.

Introduction

A mirror would do well to reflect before it sends forth its images

(Jean Cocteau, *Le sang d'un poète*)

This book asks the question: is a critical theory possible in the contemporary information society? The initial chapters thus address central dimensions of this global information order that has come rapidly to displace the older national manufacturing society. The middle chapters focus on the question of critique and critical theory. And the final chapters more directly focus on how critical theory might be reconfigured to come to grips with this information order. The point I want to make is that critique has always involved a transcendental, another separate space from which critical reflection can be launched. My argument in this book is that such critique is no longer possible. The global information order itself has, it seems to me, erased and swallowed up into itself all transcendentals. There is no outside space any more for such critical reflection. And there is just as little time. There is no escaping from the information order, thus the critique of information will have to come from inside the information itself.

Chapter 1 gives a rather full introduction to what I mean by critique of information. Chapter 2 lays down basic elements of the information order. It is entitled 'technological forms of life'. It begins by discussing the notion of 'forms of life'. It then asks what happens when these forms of life become technological. Chapter 3 argues that power in the information order works less from a principle, less of exploitation than exclusion. It works from principles of exclusion and inclusion into what may be called 'live zones and dead zones', into 'tame zones' and 'wild zones'. The national manufacturing society involves power as exploitation. The global information culture depends on power as exclusion. This means mostly exclusion from the 'loop', from the means of information, from the global flows of information and communication. The principal actors in the national manufacturing society were nations, institutions and organizations. In the information order key relationships are less within a country than between global cities in different countries. The importance of relations of production internal to organizations is now paralleled by new relations of production and communication between smaller and more amorphous 'disorganizations'. It is such disorganizations that are addressed in Chapter 4. A critical theory, with or without a transcendental, must also be a theory of power. Too many analysts limit themselves to enthusing over expanding post-industrial horizons of innovation and choice. A major aim of this book is to explore the contours of an emergent informational regime of power.

Chapters 5 and 6 address the products of the information society. The national manufacturing society focuses attention on 'the subject'. The global information culture for its part witnesses a new autonomy for *objects*, which in their global flow tend to escape from the intentions, from the sovereignty of the subject. This applies to the global movements of such varied objects as images, communications, finance. Highly branded and fast-moving consumer goods also share informational qualities in their ephemerality, their quick turnover, immediate impact and quick movement. They too spin out of control of subjects in their movement through global networks. Chapter 5 thus addresses these objects as they move with speed through global networks. The information society is, as Manuel Castells (1996) argues, a 'network society', and this book returns repeatedly to the issue of networks. The basic argument here and throughout the book is that as forms of life become informational, they shake off their 'organic' qualities and take on the form of networks. That is, forms of life in the network society are somehow lifted out, disembedded. Being-in-the-world is transformed, as it were, into 'being-in-the-globe'. To be sure there is in this the logic of commodification. But the spread and ubiquity of the information and communication networks cannot be reduced to commodification. Indeed, in a very important sense both organic forms of life and the commodity are subsumed into the general informationalization of the networks. The information order is at the same time a 'media society'. This is the topic of Chapter 6. Media work through interfaces, and the media society witnesses the general spread of interfaces to the point at which consumer goods themselves become interfaces (Manzini, 1989).[1] The media society's paradigmatic unit of culture is the 'communication', which in its brevity, speed and ephemerality is taking over from narrative and discourse as the axial principle of culture. Indeed theory itself is swept up in this logic of communication, and in an important sense becomes 'media theory'.

Chapters 7–10 leave for the moment the noise and operations of the information order and address the issue of *critique*. This book is as much about critique as it is about information. To an older generation critical theory meant 'German theory' of the Frankfurt School – the work of Theodor Adorno, Max Horkheimer, Herbert Marcuse and Jürgen Habermas. To a somewhat younger generation it means 'French theory' – Michel Foucault, Jacques Lacan, Emmanuel Levinas, Jacques Derrida. The thread connecting older and newer generations is Martin Heidegger, and some dimension of 'Being' that is transcendental to the empirical order of commodification, linearity and instrumental rationality. For the Frankfurt School thus, 'system', identity and instrumental rationality constitute the realm of the empirical, while lifeworld, negation and communicative rationality comprise the transcendental. For French theory the empirical is 'the same' or 'presence', or the metanarrative and the transcendental is 'the other' or *différance*.

This said, there are two types of critical theory. These are 'aporetics' and 'dialectics'. In aporetics the transcendental and empirical are irreconcilable, unbridgeable, undecidable. Aporetics has its origins in Kant. The other type of critical theory insists on grounding the transcendental in the empirical. This second type of critical theory is in a significant sense Hegelian. It is

Hegelian, however, not in promising any resolution in an absolute, or triumph of reason, but instead in grounding every transcendental. Thus Chapter 7 registers a disagreement with the aporetics of Emmanuel Levinas and his ethics of the unknowable other. Such an ethics, I argue, refuses to ground this transcendental in any notion of tradition or community and hence remain incomprehensibly abstract. It seems to me that some form of limited translatability is necessary for any sort of living with the other. Chapter 6 interrogates the limits of Jacques Derrida's notion of *différance*. Derrida's notion of the 'sign', I argue, depends on a transcendental differance, ungrounded in any empirical. What is needed instead is a more situated semiotics, grounded especially in forms of sociality. Chapter 8 is similarly a challenge to the critical theory of Emmanuel Levinas, and specifically of Levinas's ungrounded (undersocialized) notion of 'the other'.

Chapter 9 continues these explorations in critical theory with considerations of the work of Henri Lefebvre. Lefebvre launched a critique of the abstract rationalism of both Cartesian space and structural semiotics from the point of view of a radical materialism of everyday life. His materialist metaphysics begins from the metaphor of the body of 'the spider', which through mimesis weaves a web in the production of space. I ask the question: what sort of production of space would this lead to in the heart of the global information society? It would lead it seems to a spatialization in which the spider took on attributes of the machine, of the technological system, and the web took on attributes of a network. 'Web' and 'network' stand in juxtaposition in a Lefebvrian, a potentially radical materialist, critique. This is critique of informational capitalism from the point of view of a very grounded notion of urban space. Chapter 10 begins where Chapter 9 ends, again with the 'web', now not that of Lefebvre's mimetic and tactile spider, but instead of Walter Benjamin's 'storyteller'. The storyteller's web begins from 'far away and long ago'. As a ladder, its rungs stretch from way above to far below. The storyteller and his memories are disrupted by modern temporality – of Newtonian time, of the novel, whose pacing brings the being of the protagonist into brutal juxtaposition with his own mortality. But what happens to the being of this protagonist in an age after time, an age of speed, of shock-experience (*Chokerlebnis*)? What happens to Being when there is little time for thinking? What happens when death is no longer consigned to the realm of the other, but occupies the same immanent plane with technology and profane culture, in which Being becomes just another terminal in the network, just another being? Contemporary time for Benjamin is flattened out into the immanent space of technology and *Chokerlebnis*. Yet Benjamin's critical theory retains a dialectical materialism; a dialectical materialism in which the empirical world of technology and shock experience and speed has levelled Being and Reason into a wasteland, but in which the transcendental moment is preserved as memory and mourning.

Chapters 11–13 return to the immanence, the indifference of information. Chapter 11 explores the twofold nature of information society. Here there is, on the one hand, production, consisting of design-intensive, information-intensive labour, of informational forces of production and digital products. There is, on the other hand, the circulation of informational goods. Here the most highly rational production can lead to the most irrational circulation and distribution. In this context it makes sense to speak of a 'dis-informed information society'. The contradiction is that as the information society leads ever more to a 'smartening up', it at the same time brings with it a certain inevitable 'dumbing down'. These informational goods are particular types of cultural good. Unlike narrative, information compresses beginning, middle and end into a present immediacy of a 'now-here'. Unlike discourse, information does not need legitimating arguments, does not take the form of propositional utterances, but works with an immediate communicational violence.

The global information order is a 'technological culture'. Here previously existing dualisms of technology, on the one hand, and culture, on the other, collapse into the same immanent plane. What previously was a representational culture of narrative, discourse and the image which the reader, viewer or audience encountered in a dualistic relation, now becomes a technological culture. Culture is comprised no longer primarily of such representations but instead of cultural objects as technologies that are in the same space with what is now less the reader, viewer, spectator or audience than the user, the player. Chapter 12 addresses this collapse of representation. Here we first consider the idea of 'play' as an immanent world of symbolic exchange, a world indeed more 'primordial' – in the sense of older than, and a condition of existence of, than the dualistic culture of representation emerging with the world religions and their rationalist/humanist heirs. In this the immanent activity of symbolic exchange hardens into the rigidity of a separate sphere of the symbolic cut off from and transcendental to the profane practices of everyday life. If McLuhan and Baudrillard are right and the slow expansion of a previous linear order undergoes a sudden implosion of 'reversibility', then perhaps play is once again coming to the fore as a modal activity of the technological culture.

The collapse of representation into the immanence of the information order is also reflected in the phenomenological challenge to positivist dualism. Husserl broke with positivistic subject-object thinking by re-locating the subject in the world with an intentionality, an attitude to objects. Husserl however brought back the transcendental through the back door, in the special kind of bracketing of a transcendental reduction that would reveal the ontological structures of things-in-themselves. The sociologist Harold Garfinkel, however, has followed through the phenomenological revolution to its radical conclusions. He breaks with both the transcendental attitude and ontology for a radical empiricism of the 'natural attitude'. Garfinkel also discards the mentalism of Husserl's philosophy of consciousness. For Garfinkel the entity that possesses intentionality, the entity that makes sense of the world is not consciousness, but instead forms of social life. It is forms of life that have attitudes, that possess intentionality. Making sense of the world takes place without a transcendental subject but through the very external and *empirical* communications between members participating in a given form of life. In Chapter 12 we will address this radically empiricist, yet resolutely anti-positivist, phenomenology of communications. Here 'reflexivity' – with the disappearance of the space and time for reflection – is the immediate tying of sense-making to forms of life. This mode of reflexivity is paralleled, we will see, in the cybernetics of technological systems. What we are speaking about is a phenomenology of communications (Luhmann, 1997), indeed a 'technological phenomenology'.

The implications of all this is a new, non-linear regime of power. This is the subject of Chapter 13. We address non-linearity via the work of Marshall McLuhan. For McLuhan the subject is not just immanent and in the world with technological objects, but merges with them as his 'extensions'. In the contemporary post-societal framework of movement and flows (Urry, 2000), at centre stage are technologies, less of production than of communication. This is communication in its broadest sense comprising any sort of movement of people and things. Technologies of communication, whether of people transport, goods transport or transport of messages and other immaterial things, presume their own substrate. These substrates, McLuhan argued, tended once to be linear and continuous and take the form of 'roads'. Now they tend to be rather non-linear and discontinuous and take the form of 'ports', from international airports to mobile tele-ports. The older, national, 'imagined community' worked from linear and hierarchical 'road' type communication from centre to provinces, in for example the 'making of peasants into Frenchmen', and from institutions of centre–periphery linear communication, from national telephone grids to hierarchical bureaucratic firms. In contrast, contemporary 'networked' communication, say between global cities, is non-linear and discontinuous. Indeed networks, unlike classical institutions or states, are by definition discontinuous and non-linear.

This shift brings with it new constellations of power that any critique of information must engage with. Post-structural theory (Foucault, Derrida, Lyotard) tends to treat power – whether as discourse, 'metaphysics of presence' or meta-narratives – as linear and continuous. Resistance for its part is non-linear, complex. Even for Foucault, who sees power as circulating at a micro-level in the capillaries of society, it is a knowledge-power regime of linear and discursive power that works at such a local level. Power, it seems to me, has become a lot more elusive in the information order: it has itself become non-linear and discontinuous. I draw on the work of Donna Haraway to interrogate this. Here we would be moving to a regime of power-knowledge, whose ethos is not discursive but informational. In this, 'life' becomes a question no longer of organic systems but instead technological systems. And capital accumulation becomes also accumulation literally of forms of life as information in the databases of, for example, the human genome project. Now not just ICT but life itself is becoming increasingly 'proprietary', increasingly inscribed in types of intellectual property.

In the older representational culture of the manufacturing society, the principle of causality predominates in the linking of objects and indeed subjects with one another. In the technological culture such causality is displaced by 'additivity'. Linear cause is displaced by non-linear adding on.[2] This has crucial implications for critique. Critique itself must now be connected to today's social and technological forms of life though additivity. With the disappearance of transcendentals, critique and the critic can no longer occupy the transcendental, but must instead add on, must instead be a 'supplement' to the immanent and global actor-networks of the information age. The disappearance of the transcendental leaves only the empirical: the information age is radically empiricist. Critique can be no longer transcendental but must become, while equally anti-positivist, empiricist. As empiricist critique becomes *modest*. The third millennium's critic is Haraway's 'modest witness'. In the place of the transcendental other or transcendental difference, stands the modesty of the 'and', of what Gilles Deleuze calls 'the conjunction'. The information order is inescapable. It gives us no longer an outside place to stand. But as supplement and operating inescapably in the media of information, critique can contribute to the reconfiguring of the information, to the re-fashioning of the technological object and its boundaries, to reworking the boundaries of the proprietary and non-proprietary. In an age of generalized informational indifference, the critic can make a difference. In the guise of a conclusion, Chapter 14 ties a number of the book's themes. It starts by suggesting that the information society is perhaps primarily a *communications* order. It uses the idea of communications to understand the deterritorialization of the institutions, structures, organizations and systems of the national manufacturing order. Then it looks at how the logic of information flows reterritorialize into new formation of the brand, the platform, the standard, intellectual property and the network. It then understands the information order in terms of the crisis of reproduction of the social and of the symbolic order. The information flows, we see, run counter to all logics of reproduction, forsaking these for consumption, excess and chronic production.

Note

1 This idea of the interface is Celia Lury's. She introduced me to the work of Manzini.

2 Such 'adding on' is at the same time a hypercausality: more causal than the causal, an autopoetic and recursive *self*-causality. This also is reflexivity.

1

Informationcritique

How is critical social science, critical theory or critique possible in the information society? Critical theory in Germany in the nineteen sixties, seventies and eighties was often and largely understood as '*Ideologiekritik*'. This is critical theory so expanded as to encompass Adorno and Habermas and Marxism. But what happens in an age in which symbolic power is no longer ideological, that is, an age in which symbolic power no longer takes the forms of the systems of ideas that constitute ideologies? What happens when symbolic power instead is largely *informational*? Ideologies were extended in time and space. They claimed universality. They were extended often in the temporal form of 'metanarratives'. They entailed 'systems of belief'. They incorporated reflection and indeed needed time for reflection. Information is compressed in time and space. It makes no claim to universality but is contained in the immediacy of the particular. Information shrinks or compresses metanarratives to a mere point, a signal, a mere event in time. There is an immediacy to information that has little in common with systems of belief like Christianity or the Enlightenment. The very speed and ephemerality of information leaves almost no time for reflection. The question then becomes what sort of future for critical theory in an age in which there is little time for reflection? Critical social science grew up in the age of *Ideologiekritik*. What will happen to critical social science in an age of *Informationskritik*? Indeed, is such a thing as informationcritique possible? Can critical thought operate in an information age?

Information

What is Information?

Let me start by discussing what might be the main parameters of the information age. I would understand contemporary times very much in terms of the information society, rather than postmodernism or the risk society, late capitalism etc. Information society is, first, preferable to postmodernism in that the former says what the society's principle is rather than saying merely what it comes after. Postmodernism primarily in this sense comes after modernism. Second, postmodernism deals largely with disorder, fragmentation, irrationality, whilst the notion of information accounts for both the (new) order and disorder that we experience. Indeed, as we will see below, the disorder (irrationality) is largely the unintended consequence of the order (rationality). Third, architects such as Robert Venturi understand postmodernism in terms of 'complexity' and 'contradiction', and in particular from the contradiction of juxtaposition of elements of style, and of the contradiction of decoration and structure. In comparison, information is preferable and more powerful as a notion because it operates from a unified principle. Thus an 'informational architecture' is an architecture of flows, of movement, encouraging real time relations over distances; it is an architecture of disembedding, of the compression of time and space (Koolhaas et al., 1997).

I think we should understand the information society – in contrast to other analyses of it from say Bell (1973), Touraine (1974) and Castells (1996), is a focus on the primary qualities of information itself. Here information must be understood sharply in contradistinction from other, earlier sociocultural categories such as narrative or discourse or monument or institution. The primary qualities of information are flow, disembeddedness, spatial compression, temporal compression, real-time relations. It is not exclusively, but mainly, in this sense that we live in an information age. Some people have called some of such qualities late-modern (Giddens, 1990), others postmodern (Harvey, 1989), but these concepts seem to me to be too amorphous. Information is not.

I would understand the information society somewhat differently than it usually has been understood by sociologists.[1] The information society has often been understood in terms of knowledge-intensive production and a post-industrial array of goods and service that are produced. This needs to be broadened. First and foremost perhaps is to look at the paradox of the information society. This is, how can such highly rational production result in the incredible *ir*rationality of information overloads, misinformation, disinformation and out-of-control information. At stake is a *dis*informed information society. The key to understanding this is to look at what is pro-duced in information production not as information-rich goods and services, but more or less as out-of-control bytes of information. This is a theory of unintended consequences (Beck et al., 1994).

Information production involves an important compression, indeed several important compressions. Perhaps pivotal would be a perverse reading of McLuhan's dictum; and to read 'the medium is the message' in the sense that the message is the paradigmatic medium of the information age. Previously the dominant medium was narrative, lyric poetry, discourse, the painting. But now it is the message: the message or the 'communication'. The medium now is very byte-like. It is compressed. The newspaper already gave us the model for the information age. Only now it has become much more pervasive and has spread to a whole series of mostly machinic inter-faces. Unlike, say, narrative or discourse or painting, the information in newspapers comes in very short messages.[2] It is compressed. Literally compressed. Narrative as in the novel works from a beginning, middle and end. The subjective intentions of the protagonist are the motor of the plot and events follow from one another as causes and effects. Discourse – as in say philosophic or social scientific texts – is comprised of conceptual frame-works, of serious speech acts, of propositional logic, of speech acts backed up by legitimating arguments. Information is none of these. Once the medium becomes the message, or the byte (quite short but of various lengths) of information, the stakes are radically altered. The value of a discursive book will last 20 or more years; the informational message in the newspaper will have value for only a day. After a day we throw it in the garbage. The message, as German sociologist of science Knorr-Cetina (2000) has shown, for international currency traders sometimes has validity (or value) for a mere 20 seconds. At that point your interlocutor is free to change the price spread on the currency deal at hand. Discourse or the narrative novel or painting is produced with great time for reflection, say three to four years for a social science discursive text. The message, the information bite, the match report that is written for the *Sun* after Manchester United v. Arsenal must be ready for transmission in about 90 minutes. There is no time for reflection. It must be produced pretty much in real time, a time contiguous with the event, separable with difficulty indeed from the event, and in this sense 'indexical'. This is another way in which time is compressed in informationalization. It is very different from narrative or discourse. The bit of information has its effect on you without the sort of legitimating argument that you are presented with in discourse. Information here is outside of a systematic conceptual framework.

Power

I have just alluded to the non-discursive, illegitimate, preconscious nature of informational power. In this sense the work of Michel Foucault may no longer have as much purchase on the social world as it once had. Power was once largely discursive; it is now largely informational. Power is still very strongly, as Foucault suggested, tied to knowledge, but informational knowledge is increasingly displacing narrative and discursive knowledge. Power is indeed still very importantly tied to the commodity, in an age that is more than ever capitalist. But in a very important way it may no longer be commodification that is driving informationalization, but instead informationalization that is driving commodification. Information explodes the distinction between use value and exchange value, as Mark Poster (1995) suggests in *The Second Media Age*. But then it is recaptured by capital for further commodification. Fast-moving consumer goods and branded consumer products are also informational in their quick obsolescence, their global flows, their regulation through intellectual property, their largely immaterial nature in which the work of design and branding assumes centrality, while the actual production is outsourced to Malaysia or Thailand.

Power in the manufacturing age was attached to property as the mechanical means of production. In the information age it is attached to intellectual property. It is intellectual property, especially in the form of patent, copyright and trademark, that put a new order on the out-of-control swirls of bits and bytes of information so that they can be valorized to create profit. For example, in biotechnology, patents on genome techniques and forms of genetic modification allow specific firms exclusive rights to the valorization of genetic information (Rabinow, 1999; Franklin et al., 2000). In the IT sector itself, copyright (again the right to keep everybody else out) in, say, operating systems software allows firms to realize super profits. In fast-moving consumer goods and designer goods, the trademarking of brands, which are already in the public domain, such as McDonald's, Nike, but also Versace and Boss, establishes other monopolies and reconfigurations of power around the otherwise anarchy of information. There is a sort of twisting dialectic involved in the information society. It moves from order to disorder to new order. Highly rational and knowledge-intensive production results in a quasi-anarchy of information proliferation and flows. This disorder of information produces its own power relations. These comprise the immediate power/knowledge of bytes of information on the one hand, and the reordering of information in categories of intellectual property, on the other. This seems to be the context of capital accumulation on a world scale in the information age.

Inequality: From Exploitation to Exclusion

In the information order inequality tends to be less and less defined by relations of production between capitalists and workers in a given firm or factory. This is the paradigm for inequality in the industrial order. In the information order central is less exploitation than *exclusion*. And exclusion is first and foremost something that is defined in conjunction with the information and communication flows, with information and communication structures. What emerges here is a 'loop' of relatively disembedded (hence increasingly global) elites. The information order is a society of 'the and' connected by networks. These networks have mobile human–machine interfaces as terminals that are connected by lines of communication. Through these interfaces flow finance, technology, media, culture, information, communications and the like. There is something 'generic' (i.e. not national, a-contextual and non-identity) about being in the loop of such networks. The man–machine interfaces at issue are communication interfaces, including perhaps above all regular air travel for business purposes facilitating face-to-face communication. Important here is the occupation of expensive space in the central districts of the increasingly generic global cities, again opening up the array of face-to-face communications and transactions (Koolhass et al., 1997). In the global city you can meet face-to-face without flying. And partake of generic networks that regularly interface others.

The consequence is the emergence of a global elite, whose point of identification is the global elite in other such cities. Thus in the global culture industries, the elite in Saõ Paulo (journalists, TV presenters, curators, architects, film distributors, pay television producers, advertising, pop music sector etc.) have more in common with their counterparts in Tokyo, New York, London, Paris, Milan and Los Angeles than they do with their own compatriots in Brazil. Their identification tends to be outward, they compete increasingly in international or transnational labour markets. To self-include and self-identify in the context of the *global* information and communication flows is to self-*exclude* and *dis*-identify from the *national* flows. And the result, in say the UK, is what Will Hutton (1998) calls 'overclass' and 'self-exclusion'. Where there was social health care, schooling, pensions and security now there is 'contracting out' into private schools, health insurance, pensions and policing. Ulrich Beck (2000) calls this 'Brazilianization'. Everything equal the closer the country is to the core, say Germany, France, Japan, the less of this self-exclusion there will be. The less it will lead to vast inequalities. The greatest inequalities are produced on the periphery. If what Samir Amin (1970) called 'accumulation on a world scale' led to surplus exploitation, then 'informationalization' on a world scale leads to a massive surplus of exclusion. In the USA, UK, Japan, Germany, Holland – especially in highly branded and informationalized firms, the work of design is carried out in the core, the work of production being increasingly contracted out to say Indonesia and Thailand. In the core the previously exploited, semi-skilled and ethnic minority working classes become increasingly irrelevant to informational-accumulation, which now takes place not on their backs but behind their backs. A self-excluding overclass leads to a forcibly excluded underclass. Such is the way of the global information order. Power and inequality are if any-thing nastier and more violent in the information order and informationcri-tique must deal with this.

A critical theory in the information age must also be affirmative and not just negative. This is the nub of 'post-colonial' theory. Post-colonialism goes beyond the simple dualism of earlier notions of world system and develop-ment. At issue is never simple 'roots' on the one side versus domination on the other. Instead these roots are at the same time 'routes' (Gilroy, 1993, 2000; Clifford, 1997). At issue in post-colonial theory are 'third spaces' (Bhabha, 1994; Soja, 1996; Spivak, 1999) that are ωiasporas of 'performa-tivity' and not 'pedagogy', whether this is a pedagogy of simple domination or a counter-pedagogy of resistance. Yet there is something fixed to these ideas of a third space, something that has to do too much with a culture perhaps without origins, but that is still a sort of static layering. It is this sort of 'layering' at issue in the layering of ethnicities that we are given in US-American multiculturalism (Hall, 1999). Even if these layered ethnici-ties occupy a third (frontier or border) space of hybridity, and are engaged in performativity in this space, we still have a layering of hybrid ethnicities. The problem is the fixedness, the staticness. Informationcritique is much more based on movement; on diaspora rather than hybridity, because the former entails movement. This is a radicalized diaspora where terminus is not fixed, but shot through with contingency, with accident, with spaces to dis-identify as well as re-identify. This is a post-colonialism of movement, of contingency, of flows (Appadurai, 1996), disjunctures and junctures, of objects as well as subjects, of communications. It is an information order which is at the same time a disordering: a chronic dialectic of disordering, re-ordering and again dis-ordering.

Critique

The Universal or the Transcendental?

Critique is surely something that happens in thought. It integrates theory and practice but it is something that somehow primarily involves the dimension of thought. Critique has normally taken two forms. One is the critique of the particular through the universal. This is the sort of critique of the late Marx, in which capitalism is seen as a particular criticized from the universalism of Marxian theory. This is also the idea of critique we have in Habermas (1984), in which the particularism of 'strategic rationality' is criticized from the universalism of communicative rationality. Habermas proffers critique through discourse; through the legitimation of speech acts that are at the same time validity claims, through a set of legitimating arguments. This I think is difficult in the information age because of the very speed and immediacy of sociocultural processes. Universalism involves very much the opposite of the information age's space–time compression. It involves instead spatiotemporal, not compression, but *extension*, taking the form *inter alia* of metanarratives. The information age compresses not just metanarratives but also narratives.

The more widespread notion of critique is not of the particular by the universal. It is the critique of the universal–particular couple itself. Here reason or thought becomes something that evades the logic of universal and particular, that is, something that moves outside of propositional logic. It rejects propositional logic as the space of 'the same', and operates instead from a critical space of 'the other'. Thus Kantian critique establishes limits for the operation of pure reason. The sphere of pure reason, of logic, is the sphere of necessity. It is here that we have understanding of nature. Outside of the limits of this realm and the condition for its possibility is the realm of practical reason, the sphere of freedom. Its rules are not at all the rules of logic. Inside the sphere of pure reason, the laws of nature, of necessity – cause, effect, syllogism, identity are operative. Outside there is the unknowability of the moral law, of freedom, of God, infinity and of things-in-themselves. We can know things, said Kant, according to the above stated laws of nature, but we cannot know them as they are in themselves. We cannot know things according to their own ontological structures. All this takes place in the idiom not of the understanding but of praxis, of practical reason.

This is the dominant notion of critique from which the critical social and human sciences come. The logic of necessity, of pure reason, is also for Kant, and later Hegel, the logic of instrumental reason, in which nature becomes a means not an end. It is also positivism, hence the uncomfortable positivist echoes in the late Marx and late Habermas, something not present in the Habermas of *Theory and Practice* (1963) or Marx's earlier writings. Thus basically for Hegel, reason is only in its first beginnings identified with Kantian pure reason. For Kant the concepts of the understanding (*Verstand*) had to do with such mathematical knowledge and physics's knowledge of nature, while the ideas of reason (*Vernunft*) were the ungraspables through logic of freedom, infinity and things themselves. Hegel started his *Encyclopaedia* thus with nature (i.e. the understanding and pure reason) before moving to mind, which needs to be otherwise explored, and finally on to the state, religion, art and philosophy. Reason thus ultimately points less to science (in the Anglo-Saxon sense) than the critique of science.

Descartes bequeathed to us – in place of religion and the *ancien régime* – the centrality of the subject, of subject-object thinking. The Enlightenment extended this to the moral and political realm in which science – on a natural science model – would be the universalist motor of history on the way towards the good society, morally and politically. Kant, an *Aufklarer*, was as importantly a critic of the Enlightenment. He wanted to preserve a very important place for reason. Kantian critique is a critique in the first instance of the *ancien régime*, speculative reason, and of Humean scepticism to establish a sphere of reason as knowledge on the model of physics, maths and logic. But more importantly, critique established the critique of instrumental reason. The morality and politics involved here, unlike the Enlightenment (the late Marx, Durkheim and sociological positivism) do not have to do with the application of science to existing particulars, but with the moral law, something that lies outside of the knowable, of the understanding, outside of the relationship of universal to particular.

Aporetics and Dialectics

Subsequently we have had two traditions of critique: one of dialectics and the second of aporetics. Dialectics comprises most of the German tradition from Hegel to early Marx to Lukács to Adorno, Marcuse and the young Habermas and now, for example, Seyla Benhabib (1987), Gillian Rose (1981) and Fredric Jameson. Aporetics comes from Kant and informs Heidegger and most of the French post-structuralist tradition. Aporetics speaks of an 'aporia of reason'. This pertains to Kant's distinction between two types of reason. One is the understanding, science and logic. The other is 'pure practical reason', focusing on the moral law, the condition of possibility of moral action. The first sphere is the sphere of 'the same' and instrumental rationality. And the second, the 'outside', though it governs the sphere of practice and relations between humans, is more than just this. It includes God (religion), noumena, that is, the knowing of things, not according to the principles of science (nature), but in-themselves, according to their own ontological structures, infinity (including death) and finally the aesthetic. Some critical theorists have understood this 'sphere of freedom' in terms of not instrumental but substantive rationality. In any event, for Kant and for Hegel not just the inside is reason, but so is the outside. The outside, the realm of practical/substantive reason is somehow more fundamental (more 'primordial') than the inside. It is the condition of possibility of the inside. Enlightenment as distinct from *the* Enlightenment, and surely critique, begin to be primarily identified with this 'outside'. These two types of reason underlie the subsequent battles between positivism and hermeneutics (interpretative social science) in sociology.

This Kantian distinction between the two spheres of reason, in which the second is defined by a major dimension of unknowability, underlies both dialectic and aporetic traditions of critique. The 'aporetic' tradition speaks of irreconcilables, whereas in 'dialectics' there is either a resolution or at least an interpenetration of the two spheres. Dialectics, at their best, have little to do with the *resolution* of the particular into the absolute, whether the latter is the Prussian state or philosophy. They have more to do with a correction of the unhappy abstraction of aporetics. At their best, dialectics are not about reconciliation or absolutes but a recognition that the way we lead our lives – cultural experience, ethical activities, social relations, relations to place, the way that we live our bodies – cannot be approached through such abstraction. Most of Hegel's *Philosophy of Right* (1967) is addressed not to resolution in the absolute, but to the necessary appearance of the moral law (i.e. the sphere of 'the other', of freedom, of substantive reason) in the grain of social life in 'the same'. This is not a relation between universal and particular, but between the *transcendental* and the particular. Between the way that 'the Other' (or 'Being') manifests itself in the particular.

Kantian aporetics would have ontology, on the one hand, and things, on the other, as unbridgeable antinomies. Thus if Husserl and Heidegger can talk of the ontological structure of things, in this sense they are on the side of dialectics. Similarly, Adorno's 'negative dialectics' wants to understand the aesthetic in a much more grounded way than Kantian aesthetics, in terms of the materiality of art. Yet for Adorno this transcendental moment grounded in the particular does not lead to any kind of reconciliation. Thus should be understood also Gillian Rose's (1981, 1992) and Seyla Benhabib's (1987) excursions into critical theory. Again there is no necessary reconciliation. But the transcendental moment of reason or 'being' is manifested in the conventions of everyday ethical practice (Benhabib) or in the law, love and religion (Rose).

Informationcritique

What I am arguing is that both German dialectics and French post-structuralist aporetics are legitimate heirs to the mantle of critical theory. Both aporetics and dialectics are legitimate critique. Both dialectics and aporetics, both forms of critical theory, are based in a fundamental *dualism*, a fundamental binary, of the two types of reason. One speaks of grounding and reconciliation, the other of unbridgeability. But both speak in terms of such a fundamental dualism. Both presume a sphere of transcendence. In critique it is *thought*, whether philosophic, sociological/hermeneutic, whether manifested in art, cinema or the novel, that occupies this transcendental realm. But as long as we have a transcendental realm of thought, and this transcendental realm is identified with truth, being, the primordial and the like (and this goes for Heidegger as well as Marx, for Gadamer as well as Habermas), we are still in the realm of *Ideologiekritik*. This ideologycritique has been effective. But it is suited much better to the constitutive dualisms of the era of the national manufacturing society. The problem is that the global information culture tends to destroy these dualisms, tends to erase the possibility of a transcendental realm. It tends to destroy the fibre of the ground as we are lifted out from the grain of social relations into networks. It tends to erase differences between the same and the other, as national boundaries are questioned and the boundaries between human and non-human nature and culture are challenged. The point is, informationcritique must be critique without transcendentals.

Ideologiekritik and informationcritique are both first and foremost a question of thought. And what happens to thought in the information society? As transcendentals disappear, thought is swept up into the general plane of *immanence* with everything else. In the information age, cultural experience is displaced from the previously existing transcendental dualisms of the reader and the book, the concerto and the audience, the painting and the spectator. Culture is displaced into an immanent plane of actors attached or interfaced with machines. Now we experience cultural things not as transcendental representations, but instead as immanent things: as objects, as technologies. In this generalized immanence, superstructures collapse as the economy is culturalized, informationalized.

The older manufacturing capitalism was very much driven by the contradiction between use-value and exchange-value, in which use-value occupied the space of 'the transcendental' (substantive/practical reason) and exchange-value the space of 'the empirical' (instrumental rationality). The couple use-value/exchange-value is the instantiation of the transcendental/empirical pair in goods. Manufacturing capitalism was driven by the logic of commodification (exchange-value) and its critique (use-value). At points it must have looked like commodification would completely subsume critique (Marcuse). But the logic of informationalization is altogether different. Unlike the logic of commodification, it is not dualist, but immanentist. It explodes and partly marginalizes the exchange-value/use-value couple. In its place is an immanent plane of actor-networks: of humans and non-humans, of cultural objects and material objects, that are generally disembedded and not at all necessarily re-embedded. The actors, the networks, the non-humans, the interface of humans and machines are disembedded. The information is disembedded. This is a society of the 'and', not a society of 'the there'. A society of the 'conjunction', not of the 'adverb'. *Ideologiekritik*, as Cartesian critique of the *ancien régime*, foregrounded a problematics of the 'I', of the substantive, of the subject on the one hand and object on the other. This was a problematics of beings, of the noun. *Ideologiekritik* as critique, not of the *ancien régime* but of instrumental reason, posits a problematics of 'the there' (world or life-world), of the adverbial. But now we have the network society, the society of the 'and', denoted by neither noun nor adverb, but the conjunction.

How does critical theory work in this general informational immanence in which there is no outside any more? In which nothing is the primordial or transcendent condition of possibility of anything else. This general immanence of informationalization is not the old 'same' of instrumental rationality and the commodity. As it erodes the transcendent it also erodes the instrumental (empirical). It is instead something else entirely. The old 'same' presumed the 'other' of critique and practical reason. All this disappears now. Without an other there is no same. Everything that used to be in the other is now part and parcel of this informationalized and networked general immanence. Even death; even what Max Weber called theodicy; even, for that matter, 'life'. So which way for informationcritique, for critical social science in the information age? First it is only critical social science that will even problematize the information age. While the philosophers, anthropologists and aestheticians will speak in absolutes, ignoring the centrality of socio-cultural change, the proper study of sociologists is the understanding of social change, and the transition to the global information culture. Second, we need to break with the dualist notions of critique. And here, we might turn for inspiration to Nietzsche; to Nietzsche's idea of *amor fati*. This means to embrace your fate. This means no longer to deal with the dualism of necessity and freedom, but the more primordial fate. It is not to live fate like habit, but to seize it. For Nietszche, all dualisms (from Plato to Christian spirit and matter to Kant's aporia and logically on to Adorno, Hegel's and Marx's dialectics as well as Heidegger's unbridgeable 'ontological difference' of beings and Being) would constitutively be 'slave moralities'. Truth on the other hand is immanent. Truth is neither 'out there' nor 'in here'. The 'out there' and 'in here' no longer make sense in the information age's Nietzschean problematics of immanence.

Informationalization opens up a new paradigm of power and inequality. It opens up as well infinite opportunities for a whole array of innovations and creativity. The critique of information must deal with these emergent constellations of power and inequality. But perhaps most important is that in the age of general informationalization, critique itself must become informational. There must necessarily be an informationalization of critique. This is very different from the older *Ideologiekritik*. *Ideologycritique* had to be somehow outside of ideology. With the disappearance of a constitutive outside, informationcritique must be inside of information. There is no outside any more. Critique, and the texts of critical theory, must be part and parcel of this general informationalization. Here the critical theory text becomes just another object, just another cultural object, consumed less reflectively than in the past, written (and often not just written, as CD-ROM, installation and Web presentation become increasingly prevalent), under conditions of time and budget constraint much more than in the past. Informationcritique itself is branded, another object of intellectual property, machinically mediated. Through your laptop, PDA, your movement from interface with auto and mobile phone to aeroplane to television to pager to the streaming-enabling baseline software in your TV set-top box.

Texts of informationcritique are part and parcel of these flows, these 'economies of signs and space'. Perhaps with a bit more duration, a bit more time for reflection, but none the less part of the global information and mediascapes.

Notes

1 The interface of post-industrial and postmodern is addressed in the work of Mark Poster (1990, 1995), Kevin Robins (1996), Andrew Feenberg (1993) and Frank Webster (1995).

2 At the same time newspapers are increasingly the site for discursively justified and analytic expert opinion. Thus our information environment comprises increasing proportions of both stock experience and discourse experience. This too is part of the phenomenon of a disinformed information society. I am grateful to Jakob Aruoldi on this point. His empirical work on this will be submitted as a London University PhD thesis in 2002.

2

Technological Forms of Life

Forms of Life

We think so naturally in terms of the notion of 'forms of life', that it is difficult to obtain any distance on the notion. Ludwig Wittgenstein made the concept of 'forms of life' rather common currency across a range of scholarly disciplines. Indeed, in academic talk and everyday talk we speak incessantly of life and forms of life. We speak of '*life*-sciences', psychologists look at the '*life*-course'; we organize our identities in terms of '*life*-narratives'. We 'lead' our lives. Political philosophers speak of the 'good life'; molecular biologists of 'artificial life'. Conservatives in abortion debates, call themselves not pro-God or pro-Christ, but 'pro-life'. We talk about life styles, and, rather differently, about the 'meaning of life'. We ask are there forms of life on such and such a planet, in such and such a desert, at the bottom of such and such a sea? We are obsessed with life and *the organic*. We worry about GM foods with their modification of the organic. Middle class liberals shop in the '*organic*' section of our supermarkets, if they can afford it. Poorer liberals may want an *organic*, holistic medicine. And conservatives will view the nation as an *organic* whole: as an organism.

We encounter thus lots of chatter, lots of worry about 'life'. 'Life', however, is different from '*forms* of life'. What might *forms* of life be? A form of life is a 'way of life', a mode of doing things. A culture, in the anthropological and the everyday sense, is a form of life, a way of doing things. Hence *multi-culturalism*, promoting a plurality of forms of life, is seen by some as a threat to the integrity of French or British, German or Austrian culture. Multi-culturalism is seen as a threat to 'the American way of life'. Forms of life embrace both natural or biological forms of life, on the one hand, and social, or cultural forms of life, on the other.

We think so naturally in terms of 'life' and forms of life that it is strange to consider that this was not always the case. Michel Foucault (1966), in *The Order of Things*, wrote that we only began to understand nature and society in terms of 'life' in Modernity, in the nineteenth and twentieth centuries. Previously, we understood things in terms of 'classification'. Hence in regard to the natural world, there was the predominance of natural history, in which the idea was to *classify* natural things into genera and species. In regard to culture and the study of language the idea was to use the classification categories of grammar. In pre-modern economics there was mercantilism, the 'analysis of riches', in which again things are classified by words. But where there was once classification, in nineteenth-century modernity there is 'life' and the organism. In the life sciences, there is no longer primarily genus–species and anatomical classification but in modern biology the organism, the living organism and its functions that become the field of study. In language, it is no longer classification according to the elements of grammar that is dominant. It is now the philological study of natural languages, in which a language is studied as a living organism at the root of a national culture. In the economy, there is a move from the classification principles of the older mercantilism to modern political economy and the labour theory of value of Ricardo and of Marx. Here the economy is an organism, with labour at its heart. At stake is the 'reproduction' of an economic unit or, as Marx put it, 'accumulation', which is the expanded reproduction of the economy as organism.

The adoption of the life, or organic metaphor spread in the twentieth century to emergent sociology and anthropology. Thus the functionalism of Talcott Parsons and the early Emile Durkheim saw society as an organism; and Radcliffe-Brown and Malinowski saw culture as a self-reproducing physiological system. This organic model was a re-assertion of the positivist tradition. But the idea of forms of life – the lineage of Wittgenstein's notion – is intrinsically anti-positivist. Life here is not organicist but vitalist; it is phenomenological. Thus the centrality of 'life' or life-force in *Lebensphilosophie*: of Nietzsche, Bergson, Dilthey and Georg Simmel (and in the novel, Proust and Joyce). There is a shift here from the disembodied Cartesian ego to the 'life' of the body, from cognition to perception; from Newtonian time to the time of experience. The governing concept in this is Husserl's notion of *'intentionality'*. In phenomenology, we make sense of things through not neutrality, but 'intentionality'. We have knowledge, no longer from the neutral position of objective observer, but from a position of 'interest', from an 'attitude' to something. With intentionality, with an attitude, we are in the world, in the *'life*-world', with whatever we are investigating. Phenomenological enquiry makes sense of the world less through 'intellection', but through what Husserl and Bergson called 'intuition'. We have knowledge, not through the abstraction of judgement, but through the immediacy of experience. Intuition is more bodily and organic than intellection; experience more life-like (Er*leb*nis in German) than judgement. The time of judgement is abstract, Newtonian time, while the time of experience is the stream (the flow) of sense-impressions; it is the stream of consciousness or unconsciousness. One knows, one imposes an order on things, not through judging and classifying from above. Knowledge instead comes through experience, 'below', in the same life-world with people and things.

To make sense of (natural and social) things is to ascribe meaning. The sense-maker in the regime of classification (which is still with us in the various guises of positivism) attributed logical meanings to things. This is true not just in the human sciences, but also of classical narrative and perspective painting. The regime of classification made sense of the world thus through *epistemology*. 'Epistemology', as Hans-Georg Gadamer (1976) notes, is preoccupied with the status of knowledge, with what constitutes valid scientific knowledge, with indeed objective knowledge, with the correspondence between representations and things. But in phenomenological engagement, we make sense less through logic and epistemology than through *ontology*. We experience or interrogate things and people less in regard to their logical meaning than their *existential* meaning. We are looking for ontological meaning. The neutral and detached space of the scientific observer can yield epistemological knowledge, as Kant noted, of the *appearances* of things – that is, cause and effect, explanation. But experiencing things, through being in the life-world with them, can open up knowledge of *things-in-themselves*. To know things-in-themselves is to know them not epistemologically, but in their ontological structures. This sort of knowledge of deeper, ontological structures is also central to Freud, where the thing-in-itself was the unconscious; and for Marx, where it is social class (*Klasse-an-sich*). Thus in forms of life, knowledge takes place in the life-world, through the subject understood as life (the body, class interest, the unconscious, the will to power). Through being no longer above things, but in the world with things, we come to grips not with epistemology and appearances, but with deeper ontological structures.

Technological Forms of Life

What happens when forms of life became technological? In technological forms of life we make sense of the world through technological systems. As sense-makers, we operate less like cyborgs than interfaces. These interfaces of humans and machines are conjunctions of organic and technological systems. Organic systems work on a physiological model. Technological systems work on a cybernetic model. Cybernetic, self-regulating systems work through functions of intelligence, command, control and communication. We do not merge with these systems, but we face our environment in our interface with technological systems. As such an organic-technological interface, I say, 'I just can't function without my WAP mobile phone. I can't live without my laptop computer, digital camcorder, fax machine, automobile. I can't function without Ryanair, Amazon.com and my digital cable and satellite channels.'

I operate as a man–machine interface – that is, as a technological form of natural life – because I must necessarily navigate through technological forms of social life. As technological nature, I must navigate through technological culture. And technological culture is constitutively culture *at a distance*.[1] Forms of life become forms of life at-a-distance. Because my forms of social life are so normally and chronically at-a-distance, I cannot navigate these distances, I cannot achieve sociality apart from my machine interface.

I cannot achieve sociality in the absence of technological systems, apart from my interface with communication and transportation machines. Technological forms of life are life at-a-distance: not just culture, but also *nature*-at-a-distance. The Human Genome Project and the various human DNA databases are nature at a distance. What was previously internal and proximal to the organism is stored in an external and distant database as genetic information. What was previously internal to my mental life is also storable in a distant information database. In technological forms of life, what were more or less closed systems, my body, the social body, becomes more or less open constellations. My body cannot interface with technological systems unless it is more or less open. Social bodies cannot interface with one another unless they are to a certain degree open. When individual or social bodies open up, their organs are often externalized at a distance. This is true of the institutions of nation-states as well. Technological forms of life, whether natural or social, are like Deleuze and Guattari's (1983) 'body without organs'. As they open, they externalize their organs, and open up to flows of information and communication.

I will argue in what follows that with technology, forms of life are *flattened*. I will argue that they become *non-linear*. I will argue that forms of life become *lifted out*.

Flattening

Harold Garfinkel is a theorist of technological forms of life. He takes the 'awe' of the within, of interiority, and he externalizes it onto the everydayness of the 'without', onto the technical, the practical. He takes the depth of ontological structures and flattens them out into what is a radical empiricism of technological forms of life. In both classification and forms of life, there is a focus on the vertical. In both there is a certain verticality. With classification, there is the verticality of subject and object, of classifier and classified, of universal and particular. Forms of life, however, give us a new verticality, new dualisms. For epistemological dualism is substituted ontological dualism. Both these models of verticality are based on a transcendental term, on the one hand, and an empirical term on the other. The forerunner of this is of course the dualisms of religion, of the sacred, as the transcendental term, and the profane, as the empirical. In already secular classification, the transcendental comprises the categories of classification. And the empirical comprises the things to be classified. In classification (or epistemology), the transcendental stands 'above' the empirical, as subject to object. In forms of life and ontology, the transcendental term stands 'below' the empirical (for example, the unconscious, ontological meaning Marx's infrastructure). Dualism 'from above' is displaced by dualism 'from below'. A dualism of height by a dualism of depth (hence, 'deep ontology', 'deep structures'). In *technological* forms of life, the transcendental term is flattened into the empirical. The dualism of epistemology and ontology is flattened into the radical monism of technology.

In the world religions, the transcendental entailed the cosmological privilege of the priest (Parsons, 1968). In classification, the transcendental implied the epistemological privilege of the scientist, the philosopher (Durkheim and Mauss, 1963). In forms of life, we have the ontological privilege of the psychoanalyst, the proletarian party and the artist. In technological forms of life, these privileges are thrown into crisis. Now the unconscious surfaces into the everyday; as the transcendental of the economy collapses into culture of everyday life; and as art becomes just another mode of communication. Technological forms of life suggest not positivism, which is the subject-object type thinking of classification, but *empiricism,* in which the observer is in principle not fundamentally different from the observed. Look closer at phenomenology: at the shift from the transcendental and philosophical phenomenology of Husserl/Heidegger to the socio-technical and empiricist phenomenology of Garfinkel. First, the transcendental reduction disappears. The transcendentally reducing philosopher is himself reduced or flattened into an empirically observing actor, who is neither better nor fundamentally different than the social processes he observes. By definition, intentionality needs an ego and an object. With the disappearance of a transcendental ego (and Heidegger's *Dasein* is a variant of this), there is no sense any more to ontological structures. Deep meaning disappears. What remains is empirical meaning. Empirical meaning is neither logical (as in classification) nor ontological, but everyday and contingent.

This entails a transformation of reflexivity. Reflexivity was always a question of going beyond classification and epistemology, in order to gain some kind of, however opaque, knowledge of ontological structures. Thus Kant spoke of 'reflective judgement', which – unlike determinate judgement – was aimed at deep, ontological meaning: Hegel similarly spoke of 'reflection' and Husserl of the 'reflective attitude'. In each of these cases there is a distancing of the 'reflector' from the everyday, a move into a separate space for reflection. Meaningful (as distinct from trivial) knowledge, on the one hand, and forms of life, on the other, are still separated. Now, consider Garfinkel's empiricist phenomenology. Reflexivity is now no longer separate but 'incarnate' in activities. Knowledge is 'reflexively *tied*' to activities, expressions, events. In such an empiricist phenomenology there is no longer any distance between knowledge and practice; knowing no longer reflects on doing; instead, doing, is at the same time, knowing. Logical and ontological knowledge no longer have a separate status from trivial everyday or empirical knowledge. Such reflexivity is closer to a 'reflex' than the distance of reflection. Reflexivity in technological forms of life does not involve a dialectic of theory and practise. Dialectics presumes two levels. Technological reflexivity assumes a *fusion* of theory and practice. Theory is 'incarnate' in practice.

In this empiricist phenomenology, sense-making loses its interiority. There is a flattening of the interiority of the subject. The expressive subjectivity of the artist, the analysand, the philosopher, the interiority of proletarian consciousness are eroded. Expressive subjectivity presumed consciousness as an interior monologue. Meaning was somehow in consciousness. One made meaning for oneself. In technological forms of life, sense-making is for *others.* Sense-making is account-giving, it is 'glossing', it is *communication.*

Sense-making or knowledge is the glossing, the account-giving of everyday activities that is inseparable from those activities. Reflexivity in the technological culture is not a separate process of reflection. There is no time, no space for such reflection. There is fusion of words and things, of thought and practice. To think is not just at the same time to do; to think is at the same time to communicate. In the technological culture, reflexivity becomes practice; it becomes communication.

Non-Linearity

Technological forms of life are non-linear. This involves:

1 Compression Technological forms of life are non-linear first, as units of meaning. This entails compression. Linear units of meaning, such as narrative and discourse, are compressed in the technological age into abbreviated, non-extended and non-linear forms of meaning such as units of information and communication. We make sense through abbreviated units of information. Note that I am not speaking about information overloads. I am not saying that there is so much information about that we cannot attach meaning to all of it. The constant bombardment by signals, the ads of consumer culture and the like does not constitute information. It is chaos, noise. It only becomes information when meaning is attached to it. Information only happens at the interface of the sense-maker and his/her environment. Or at the interface of the environment on the one hand, and the interface of sense-maker and his/her attached information and communication machines on the other. If there is no meaning, then there is no information. Out there otherwise is just chaos or noise. Richard Sennett (1998) has argued that meaning is drained from life with the decline of life-narratives. I disagree. Meaning just changes. It becomes informational.

2 Speed-up As regards time, the break with linearity involves speed-up. In 'simple' forms of life, we have narratives and metanarratives. A certain pace of movement of time is conducive to such narratives and metanarratives. Just about the right pace for reflection. Technological forms of life are too fast for reflection and too fast for linearity. They not only compress linearity; they outpace it. In speed-up culture becomes increasingly ephemeral. The monument lasts for centuries, if not millennia; the novel for generations; a scholarly book a decade. The newspaper article has value for just a day. The pyramids took centuries to build; the scholarly discourse of a treatise – entailing reflection – takes say, four years. The newspaper report on the latest soccer match must be written and wired within 90 minutes after the match. This leaves no time for reflection, and scarce dedicated space as we compose messages in trains, on planes and read our email on mobile phones.

Superman, who was an extra-terrestrial, was faster than a speeding bullet. Technological forms of life are quick too. They are sometimes as fast as the speed of light. They are faster than a metanarrative. Cyclical time, as Max Weber noted, is really slow. Narrative time – whether that of the novel, the life narrative or the metanarrative of progress, is quite a lot faster. Technological time doesn't so much refuse metanarratives; it outpaces them. Technological time does not so much question progress; it is too fast for progress. It believes in progress, yet is too fast for it. Now we get better and better, even faster than in the Whig notion of history. We improve so fast in technological time that improvement itself is thrown into question.

Technological time is too fast for the cause-and-effect of Newtonian time. Invention is so fast that we outpace the logic of cause-and-effect. The torpid slowness of cyclical time meant lots of security. The quicker time of cause-and-effect meant that we needed to organize our own security. Technological time outpaces the determinacy of causality; it leads to a radical indeterminancy, to radical contingency; to a chronic insecurity. This breakdown of linear time gives us the risk society. When the linearity of Marxist blueprints disappears in Eastern Europe, there is sudden insecurity. Outpacing the predictability of causal logic, we are thrown into the unpredictable logic of consequences. Sociology, classically in Weber, Marx and Durkheim, was obsessed with the causes of modernity. Technological speed-up puts focus on modernity's *consequences*. The language of consequences is non-linear; if they were linear, we would not worry about them. And it is not the failure but the success of linearity that is at fault.

In cause, we look to the past to explain the present. In consequences, we look at the present as causing risks in the future (Arnoldi, 2000). Our gaze is firmly on the future in technological forms of life. In a distant past we invested in landed property, that was the basis of security and continuity (*Blut und Boden*) over the generations. Here value formed a link with the past. More recently, we invested in shares in manufacturing firms whose assets and turnover were approximately equal to its market capitalization. At that point, value was in the present. In the technological age, value is in the future. We find our security by investing in the most radical insecurity, by investing in contingency. Hence Microsoft, on turnover of approximately $23bn has had a market capitalization of some $225bn, some 10 times its assets and turnover.[2] In the technological age, capital accumulates in the future. What is true for capitalism is true for welfare. The classical welfare state was about social engineering to make life better in the present. Genetic engineering is about welfare in the future. The new generation is not the 'now generation', but the 'not-yet generation'.

3 Stretch-out: Discontinuity Technological forms of life are stretched out. The mediaeval city had organic, almost natural, almost familial social bonds of apprentice, journeyman and master craftsman. It had winding and meandering streets, following the natural gait of cows and sheep. The modern nation-state has linear bonds. Relationships, and hence the social bond, are more role-specific than diffuse, as the linear contract replaces organic status. This is already a stretching out and thinning of organic bonds. The 'imagined community' of the modern nation-state displaces the mediaeval, real community. This is an imagined community because the people in it cannot possibly know one another face-to-face. The imagined community of the nation-state is already the beginning of culture at-a-distance. Not just social bonds, but spatial links straighten out and become linear: in national roads, railroads, telephone land-lines and electricity grids. As stretched out and linear there is, however, a continuity of spatial links, a continuity of social bonds.

But technological forms of life are *really* stretched out. They are too long, stretched out too far for linearity. They are so stretched out that they tear asunder. Spatial link and social bond break. They then reconstitute as the links of non-linear and discontinuous *networks*. The technological culture is a network society. The links of networks are so thin that they occupy almost no breadth at all. They are, to cite Bruno Latour (1993: 119), 'topological' rather than 'topographical'. They are connected not by the social bond *per se*, but by socio-*technical* ties. They are joined by links that are as much technical as they are social. Networks are somehow *inorganic* at the same time as organic. There is something artificial, not life-like at all, about networks. They are culture at a much greater distance. If social bonds (of nation) are held together by myths of origin, the socio-technical links of networks are held together by far more tenuous units of meaning. They are held together by *communications* (Luhmann, 1997): the telephone call, the globally televised football match, the last exchange of emails.

In a sense, transportation is just another form of distanced communication. In each case there is a symbolic exchange between A and B at a distance. Forms of life are so stretched out in the age of technology that the linearity of roads and lines are no longer long enough. Hence, communications are increasingly via non-linear and discontinuous 'ports': through airports, 'teleports' of mobile phones, modem ports, through Internet portals. To move from port to port is to move, not in a straight line but to hop about, to move discontinuously. Networks in this sense are non-linear and discontinuous. The movement along networks is often in several directions at once, and not along a straight path. Things get 'diffused' through networks. The network society is a society of flows, a society of global communications. Flows are of many things, prominent among them is information. But all flows are also flows of communications. Marx's manufacturing society was based on the machines that transformed nature. Today's machines are less about the transformation of nature, or even the transformation of culture (information), but about the *transmission* of culture (communications). The society of flows, the network society, is less an information society than a *communications* society.

National communities are linear and continuous. The links between global cities are non-linear. Multiculturalism and cosmopolitanism are non-linear. The idea of integration into a national, imagined community – whether in the American 'melting pot', French republicanism or German Constitutional Patriotism (Habermas's *Verfassungspatriotismus*) – is linear. They work from pedagogic narratives of integration. But technological forms of life are less linear than 'mosaic'. They involve a mosaic of networked communities. Cosmopolitanism is a question of citizenship, and universalist citizenship rights. But it is also a question of culture, of *multi*culture, instead of the uniform culture of the melting pot. Assimilation means making the same, that is, a certain 'endoticism'. Multiculturalism and cosmopolitanism presumes a mutual exoticism, yet the opening of a conversation. They presume a mutual 'going native'. They involve not assimilation to a Western norm, but Hannah Arendt's putting oneself in the place of the concrete and particular other. Multiculturalism here refers to not just the (mosaic) character of a given geographical territory. It refers also to the plural identification of mobile and transnationally networked individuals. When the Turkish diaspora stretches from Ankara to Berlin to London's Hackney, and communications to all of these places become ever cheaper, then plural identification means a more tenuous link to any one culture.[3] It means more space for strong elements of *dis*-identification with the diaspora altogether. The tenuousness of the networks of technological forms of life leaves space for individualism, for contingency, for nomadic subjectivity. Multiculturalism is also culture at a distance. It is a given single culture spread or stretched over a distance. It also means that different cultures – previously at a distance – come face to face with one another.

Lifting Out

Technological forms of life are disembedded, they are somehow 'lifted out'. As lifted out, they take on increasingly less and less the characteristic of any particular place, and can be any place or indeed no place. This lifted-out space of placelessness is a generic space. It is not any particular space, but a generic space (Koolhaas et al., 1997). It is characterized not so much by a multiple of identities, but by an absence of identity (Augé, 1995). Its context is no context at all. Its difference is indifference. Airports and indeed aeroplanes are such generic spaces. So are the branded spaces of department stores, one Ralph Lauren section is interchangeable with another, one Boss with another, one Tommy Hilfiger with another. The department store could be in Tokyo, London, Chicago, as could the airport. Many theme parks – Disney, Universal – are such generic spaces. One McDonald's is interchangeable with another; one Benetton with another; one Warner Village with another (Franklin et al., 2000). The Internet is a generic space. It is no particular space. Indeed networks are themselves by definition lifted-out spaces. CNN and the world of the Teletubbies are generic spaces. Generic spaces are disembedded and never really re-embed (Knorr-Cetina, 2000). Sometimes this involves a literal lifting-out, as in air transport, mobile telephony and digital satellite television. Sometimes there is a 'digging in', as in cable television and underground broadband Internet connections. In all cases, social interaction is on a different level from ordinary forms of life.

The 'laboratory' is such a generic space. The laboratory is 'lifted-out' from normal life. It consists not of men in blue collars, but people in white coats.

In normal life, people do routine things. In laboratory life, they discover things; they invent things. The laboratory produces not goods, nor services, but knowledge; it produces research. The laboratory is a generic space. Whether in Tokyo, Paris or Los Angeles people wear white coats. Laboratories are filled with similar equipment and the same scholarly and professional journals. In laboratories people must know English and be digitally literate. There is a certain context-lessness about the laboratory. Twenty years ago Bruno Latour and Steve Woolgar (1979) wrote *Laboratory Life*. Twenty-three years later, more and more of normal life is becoming like laboratory life. When Latour and Woolgar wrote, the laboratory produced scholarly papers. Now it just as often produces *prototypes*. Research has become increasingly research & *development*. Laboratory science becomes increasingly techno-logical, as bio-technology scholars and computer science whiz-kids from the universities produce prototypes, set up their own small firms. There is a double movement here. First, science 'descends', so to speak, from its pure autonomy to become techno-science. Second, there is the rise, so to speak, of everyday social relations to become, themselves, forms of laboratory life. At the same time, science and society become technological.

The same happens in the arts with the phenomenon of 'the studio'. The studio was a space of creativity, lifted-out from routine forms of life as pure art. Pure painting, sculpting, composing music went on in the studio. But now the new media wings of global publishers like Bertelsmann have become 'Bertelsmann Studios'. London multimedia firms like AMX Digital have renamed themselves AMX Studios. Successful architects agency Libeskind in Berlin is Studio Libeskind. The biggest digital media university research and training site in Europe is Malmo Studios in the new Malmo University. What is produced in the new studios (and laboratories) seriously flies in the face of the idea of genius of the autonomous artist and scientist. This is because it is collectively produced. The model for the new studios of 'techno-art' is of course Hollywood cinema. What the laboratory and the (Hollywood and new) studio make are *prototypes*. This is unlike the factory, which makes copies; and the office, which circulates those copies. The laboratory and the studio make prototypes. And when consumption gets increasingly specialized, and product markets increasingly unpredictable, competition becomes a question less of 'copies', than of prototypes. Progressively more people work in prototype production. 'Laboratories' and 'studios' spread to more and more economic sectors. Life itself becomes increasingly like laboratory life. Like science, art descends from its autonomy to become techno-art and sell its prototypes on the market.

Laboratories and studios produce prototypes. The difference is that laboratories get their prototypes patented. Studios (including of course software firms) get their prototypes copyrighted. Patent and copyright are forms of intellectual property. Material prototypes are patented. Symbolic prototypes are copyrighted. Laboratories make prototypes of material goods for patent. Studios make prototypes of symbolic goods for copyright. Note: studios do not just involve symbolic labour, as do offices. Studios invent symbolic goods. All intellectual property is lifted-out, is disembedded in comparison with real property. Real property is based on the accumulation of capital; intellectual property on accumulation of information. Real property is based on accumulations of the same: as Marx said, 'homologous congealed labour time'. Intellectual property is based on the accumulation of difference. Every prototype must be different than the one before. Intellectual property is based on the accumulation of symbols, of meaning. To have meaning, there must be intelligible difference. Today, the production of prototypes (of intellectual property) has become routinized. Today production entails chronic invention, the chronic repetition of difference. Patent is the chronic invention of the real; copyright, the routine invention of the imaginary.

Brand environments are lifted out, generic spaces. This involves the third category of intellectual property, the trademark (Lury, 1993). If you copyright a material (technological or natural good) and you copyright a symbolic good, then what do you trademark? You trademark a logo or a name (like McDonald's or now Mick Jagger). What is trademarked are '*marks*', be they colours, names or the logos (Franklin et al., 2000). To trademark is to make these marks intellectual property. It is to award exclusive rights in these marks. These marks, and the meanings attached to them, are known as 'brands'. In French and in German the word for brand is indeed *Marken*. And in English, or at least American English, we brand a steer by marking him with the logo of our ranch. Whereas patent and copyright presume the invention of a prototype, trademark does not. For marks (like those of Boots the Chemist or Virgin or Ford) to be trademarked they – the marks and the goods and services associated with the marks – must already have a presence in the public domain. In some case there is trademark protection awarded to a mark, for which there is not yet a range of goods and services – For example, Mick Jagger, who now, it seems, intends to bring out a range of products under this mark. Whereas you copyright a book, record, bit of application software that is new and you want to *get it* out in the public domain, trademark is already in the public domain.[4] Let me give an example. When I make a bit of money from writing a wonderful and innovative book, it is through copyright. When I subsequently write a bad book and it still sells, then it must do so from my name as brand and effective trademark. When I write a third, pretty good book, which then doesn't sell at all, it may be because my brand value has declined.

Trademark as intellectual property, and the work of branding seems to be increasingly central to 'studios'. Like other work in studios, it is not so much work of production, as *design*. But unlike other work of design, it does not create new units of intellectual property. It instead *valorizes* existing units of intellectual property. These existing units are the marks or brands (Lury, 1999). In new media studios it seems that there has been a shift in the direction of trademark oriented work and branding. New media firms were at one time primarily oriented to producing CD-ROMs, Web-graphics and computer games, that is, prototypes as symbolic goods that would come under copyright. They were producing new bits of intellectual property. Now they seem to be spending a lot more of their time doing branding work for other firms. They are now thus increasingly a business service, valorizing trademark, as existing intellectual property. New media firms are increasingly designing sites and e-commerce facilities (i.e. making a marketplace). Furthermore, classical advertising is now doing online brand valorization. E-commerce is buying at a distance; consumer culture at a distance. It is forms of life at a distance. What is happening here is terrestrial brand valorization of technological forms of life.[5]

'Platforms' are lifted out spaces. Microsoft Windows Operating System is such a platform. It comes under intellectual property law, the law of copyright. But platforms are not necessarily proprietary. The dominant European platform for mobile phone communications is not proprietary. No one has intellectual property rights in it. Neither is Linux operating system, or Unix as an operating system for servers. Platforms are very special kinds of intellectual property. Without them, one cannot gain admission to participate in various forms of technological life. Platforms may or may not be 'standards'. There is no standard yet for set-top boxes for digital television. The platform for European mobile phone voice communications is a standard. In the US there are competing platforms and not yet a standard. Where there are competing platforms, the issue of proprietary or non-proprietary is important. Where there is a standard it is crucial. If you own a proprietary standard you are in fact a gatekeeper for the world. Unless they pay you a licence fee, they are excluded from technological forms of life. Other platforms for technological forms of life are airports, and space in the right districts of global cities. You often need capital for access to these platforms, these generic spaces. They are expensive. You need cultural capital as well as economic capital. You need the 'social capital' of the right networks (Leadbeater, 1999). At issue may be a new type of social stratification, in which social class depends on relations to intellectual property and rights of access to the lifted-out spaces of technological forms of life.

Conclusions, Politics

I already have started my conclusion. I have shifted from what might appear as celebration to critique. In technological capitalism, power works perhaps less through exploitation than exclusion. Real property in the means of production carries with it the right to exploit. Intellectual property carries with it the right to exclude. The ownership of trademark prohibits anyone else from valorizing that trademark. This is how modern sponsorship works. The valorization of patents of human and plant DNA from the third world is the stake in the struggles around globalization at the WTO in Seattle. The ownership of copyright in a platform, which is a standard, is the stake in the continuing power struggles between the US Department of Justice and Microsoft. These are struggles involving not just questions of who owns the

DNA database and who owns the platforms, but about pushing back the boundaries of the proprietary as such. Social class becomes a question of access to the platforms, access to the lifted-outness of technological forms of life. It becomes a question of access, to not just the means of production, but the means of invention.

In technological forms of life, not just resistance but also power is non-linear. Power itself is no longer primarily pedagogical or narrative but instead, itself performative. 'Nation' now works less through 'narrative' or 'pedagogy' but through the performativity of information and communication. Power works less through the linearity and the reflective argument of discourse or ideology than through the immediacy of information, of communications. Power works not perhaps primarily neither on the level of the reflective intellect nor on the level of the unconscious, but on the level of tacit knowledge. Power may be less disciplinary than it is itself, nomadic in the shape of multinationals, footloose to move from country to country. Politics in technological life is also a politics in which those at the interface of technology and forms of life, the already significant and increasing numbers employed in the laboratories and the studios, will play an ever more important role. Finally, politics in technological forms of life will increasingly problematize the future. This is the case, of course, in the politics of nature: in environmental politics, and the politics of DNA and GMOs. Capital itself increasingly accumulates in the future.

Notes

1 I am indebted to Kevin Robins for this concept.

2 This is as of June 2001, 15 months *after* the NASDAQ crash.

3 I am indebted on this to conversations with Kevin Robins.

4 The ideas in this paragraph are taken from Celia Lury. I am responsible for any misinterpretation.

5 Thanks to Andreas Wittel on this. This chapter and the book is informed by research done on new media with Wittel, Lury, Deirdre Boden and Dan Shapiro as part of the Economic and Social Research Council Virtual Society? Programme.

3

Live Zones, Dead Zones: Towards a Global Information Culture[1]

Towards a Global Information Culture

What are the new political stakes in today's transition from a national manufacturing society to a global, informational culture? What are the implications for politics in an era whose fundamental and axial principles are being replaced by three new governing logics? An era in which (1) the principle of the national is being displaced by that of the global; (2) the logic of manufacturing is displaced by the logic of information; and (3) the logic of the social is being displaced by that of the cultural. Let us consider these one by one.

1 From the National to the Global National economic, political and cultural relations are in decline and being displaced by global flows. These include flows of finance, technology, information, communication, images, ideas, immigrants, tourists and business travellers. Politically, supra- and sub-national institutions begin to threaten the hegemony of the institutions of the national state.

2 The Logic of Manufacturing Gives Way to a Logic of Information In the economy, the objects produced take on an increasingly informational nature. This is true both in the services and for the composition of material objects – such as children's computer games, consumer electronics items and their associated software. The means of production become progressively more information-alized, with an ever-greater proportion of micro-electronic components. Finally, the production process itself becomes no longer labour-intensive, but more information- or knowledge-intensive, more 'design-intensive'. This is true especially in cutting edge sectors like microelectronics and biotechnology. These flexibly made products take on increasingly the character of entities that are constructed: they seem no longer so much to be 'objects', but instead to be 'artefacts'.

3 The Social is Displaced by the Cultural This follows from the erosion of the national 'society' by the logic of the flows. Nearly all of these flows are comprised of symbolic or *cultural* goods – from images to money to ideas to communications to the 'travelling cultures' that travel with immigrants. The 'disintegration' or decline of the social comprises, on the one hand, a decline in social institutions and, on the other, a progressive demise of social structures. The decline of institutions involves a less important place for organizations such as the political party and institutions such as the church and more of a place for less permanent and more intense forms of social relations. It involves a decline in the prominence of social norms and a rise in the importance of cultural values. The social has always been a matter of *Gesellschaft*, whilst the cultural bears important traces of the *Gemeinschaft*. Consider, for example, Max Weber's juxtaposition of the 'sect' which is *gemeinschaftlich* with the *gesellschaftlich* 'church'. Contemporary new social movements – in which the middle classes predominate – bear, in the most positive ways, strong resemblance to the sect. The church, like Michels's organized or bureaucratic political party, is governed by formal and procedural rules. They are means to ends in which, as often noted, the means will tend to become the ends. In the sect, in the informally networked and affectively intense new social movement, the means are not so easily separable from the ends. At stake, in the sect and the grass-roots social movement, are surely not procedural norms, but instead cultural values. At stake are the sort of values that inform the 'good life'.[2]

The issue is not so much post-material values, but values *tout court*. The issue is just the opposite of the sort of intersubjectivity endorsed by Jürgen Habermas in communicative action or discursive will formation. Habermas's communicative action is based very much on procedural and *gesellschaftlich* norms. It avowedly will not and cannot address the issue of cultural values. The *critique* of modernity puts no longer social and procedural norms, but now cultural values very squarely on the agenda once again. This book deals with the contemporary era, not so much in terms of postmodernity, but instead more broadly as an informational order. Yet it is helpful to think in terms of a contrast of modernization and 'postmodernization'. Here postmodernization witnesses the decline of institutions, which are by definition *gesellschaftlich*. Even the family to the extent that it becomes contractual and regulated by law is a *gesellschaftlich* institution. Postmodernization witnesses the rise of forms of sociality that bear a closer resemblance to *Gemeinschaften*. Only these are somehow 'post-traditional' *Gemeinschaften* (Berking and Neckel, 1990). They are small, mobile and flexible groupings – sometimes enduring, often easily dissoluble – formed with an intensive affective bonding – even when electronically mediated. And most global networks of communication and exchange are indeed extra-organizational, as relations of production are situated increasingly not within the firm but between firms; as communications proceed increasingly between firms and between individuals in networks.

It should be noted, however, that many of these 'electronic communities' are in fact not communities at all. It should be noted that many of these electronic communities comprise social relations even more *gesellschaftlich*, even more impersonal, even more distanced than those within the classic, 'modernist' bureaucratic industrial firm. What kind of electronic community is involved in the internationally linked networks of futures and commodity traders on the world's major stock exchanges? What sorts of public spheres are at stake here? On the one hand, the postmodern displacement of modern institutions leads to forms of social relations even more emptied out of meaning than in modernity. It leads to a state of affairs that Heidegger in his critique of technology would have seen as even more technological than modernity. On the other hand, postmodernization involves the displacement of normatively regulated, more or less unwieldy societal institutions and organizations (in the economy, politically, in leisure) by smaller, value-inscribed, intensively bonded more flexible cultural forms of life. Heidegger represented a current of German thought that approvingly counterposed 'Kultur' to technological civilization. In this sense, postmodernity speaks in large part the idiom of Kultur. These smaller scale intensive social forms can form the basis, I shall argue below, of a contemporary and truly radical political culture.

Information Structures: The Zones

I mentioned just above that the disintegration of the social also involves a decline in importance of social structure. Indeed postmodernization would seem to entail the decline of social structures and their replacement by a structure of flows. Postmodernization means the replacement of social structures by *information and communication structures*. Information and communication structures frame the above-mentioned flows of information, communications, images, money, ideas and technology (Lash and Urry, 1994). One can map these flows literally as do some communications geographers. One can trace the flows of money, books, of other cultural products, of images as they move on a world scale. One can look at their enhanced concentration, the unusually high levels of 'wiredness' in places like the City of London, Silicon Valley, science parks in Germany and Japan, the vicinity of selected and high-powered higher education institutions. But the structure of the flows, the displacement of social structures by information and communication structures leads to new patterns of inequality. Now no longer is social class determined by access to the mode of production, but by access to the 'mode of information' (Poster, 1990). Social inequality is then decisively now a question of access to the global flows. Social inequality, determined now by the flows, takes on a determinately spatial form. The determination of today's social classes may be a question less of location in production than location in space. The determination of class today may, in particular, be a matter of *zones*. Where the flows are particularly heavy, there are what Tim Luke (1995) has referred to as 'live zones'. Where they are relatively light, we have 'dead zones'. Where there is a high density of the flows we tend to find 'tame zones'. Where such density is diminished one tends to find 'wild zones'. But 'live zones' and 'dead zones' do not exactly map onto 'tame zones' and 'wild zones'. Live zones and dead zones refer most of all to economic spaces (though of course to an increasingly 'semiotic' economy), whereas tame zones and wild zones refer most of all to 'identity spaces'. In an important sense the live and dead zones of economic spaces refer to the presence (or relative absence) of the flows and the identity spaces refer to what social actors do with them.

Thus, at the risk of being overly formalistic, we can distinguish four types of zone. First there are zones which are 'live' and 'tame'. Thus many of the spaces of the advanced producer and consumer services of advanced-sector manufacturing, of upper and middle class suburbs, are an economic space of live zones because of the ubiquity of the flows. But they are at the same time, in terms of identity space, tame zones in the sense that identities are relatively stable. These live and tame zones are the space of one fraction of the 'new new middle class'. This is the post-industrial middle class, the 'informational bourgeoisie', in Pierre Bourdieu's (1984) sense, the new 'economic-capital' fraction of the bourgeoisie. If the live and tame zones are filled by this more utilitarian wing of the postmodern bourgeoisie, then the live and *wild* zones tend to comprise Bourdieu's 'intellectuals', though now we may be speaking of new-media culture intellectuals, as the *'cultural* capital' fraction of the post-industrial middle classes. The spaces here are exemplified in neighbourhoods in Chelsea and in downtown New York City in contradistinction to live but tame 'uptown culture'. These are people living in deserted buildings, and other 'found spaces', often with 'found objects'. Live and wild zones are often sited in areas around universities, art schools, alternative cinemas and restaurants, avant-garde pop music and dance venues and the like. These live and wild zones comprise spaces in parts of east and increasingly south London in comparison to the more orthodox high culture of Westminster, Bloomsbury and the West End. Here the fibreoptic might be a bit thinner on the ground and buildings may be not quite as 'smart'. But the flows – and especially ideas and images – are more fleeting, contingent, unpredictable, the population mix is more multi-ethnic, and identity-formation is far less stable.

Similarly there are two types of 'dead zone' in the global informational culture. First there are the dead and wild zones. These comprise many of those made downwardly mobile by the flows, for example those members of the industrial working class in the earlier manufacturing society, who are unemployed, underemployed or homeless in the global informational culture. These individuals fill the places – they include both whites and blacks and other ethnic minorities – of what is coming to be known as the 'underclass'. Here identities are fluid, disintegrated, social disorganization is the rule. These zones, in comparison with those of the expressive middle classes mentioned above, are *seriously* wild, in a number of senses of the word. The other set of dead zones are those, not so much excluded by as passed over by the information and communication structures. In these are found stable identities: identities that feel *threatened* by all this change. These dead and tame zones are often in unfashionable suburbs, small towns and the countryside. They comprise farmers, midlevel white-collar workers and skilled manual workers, almost always of the majority ethnic group. Ideologies here tend to be traditionalist, systematically the most conservative of our four post-industrial socio-spatial classes.

We must remember that the emergent and now increasingly established global informational culture is a *world* system. It is a world (dis)order. And it may also be possible to speak of cores, semi-peripheries and peripheries in this world order in terms of live and dead zones. It is true that there will often be more similarity between global cities in core and periphery than between 'built up' and 'emptied out' spaces of a given core or peripheral country (Sassen, 1991). Yet it still may make sense to speak of nations in the world system in terms of the zones. Thus the USA and say Japan have for a long time now been core and hence live zones: the USA a mixture of wild and tame and Japan predominantly tame – but with increasing identity de-centring and multiculturalism becoming increasingly wild. A country like Saudi Arabia would be mainly dead and tame, while the Palestinian spaces of Jordan, Syria and Israel tend to be dead in terms of economic exclusion from the information flows, yet wild in terms of identity change, flows of ethnicity and disruption by movements of weaponry. Often there is a sort of 'socio-spatial mobility': a movement from zone to zone in a country's recent history. That is, some formerly dead zones come to life or 'go live', and some formerly live zones go dead. Live zones going dead are found perhaps in significant parts of Britain, but also in parts of Russia and for the moment in eastern Germany, in which there has been rapid economic marginalization, quick growth of an un- and underemployed underclass. The result has often been racism, social disorganization and the skinhead culture of the football terraces. Other countries like South Korea, perhaps other NICs like Brazil and countries like Poland, the Czech Republic and Hungary, engaged in a more successful post-socialist transition, will be making the move from the dead zones to those of a relatively high density of information and communication structures. Here it might be expected that identity de-centring on a significant scale will follow some time after large-scale economic growth.

Cultural 'Development'?

What are the implications of all this for such nations – NICs, export oriented 'little dragons' and their import-substituting bigger counterparts? What are the implications for such nations that are as much 'semi-core' as semi-peripheral today – nations such as Brazil,[3] South Korea, Taiwan, Singapore, Argentina and Turkey? What sort of 'cultural development' will parallel economic and political development? It is interesting that a social-scientific literature once based around economic development – from the old modernization theory of mainstream American sociology to Gunder Frank and Wallerstein – can turn to Habermas and critical theory in talking about 'political development': the political creation of public spheres. The question is what happens if we start looking at *cultural* development? And are we not implying a model of cultural development when we speak of a shift from traditional culture to modernization and then to 'postmodernization'?

There are some very major divergences between economic and political development, on the one hand, and cultural development, on the other. Whereas economic and political change can be understood in terms of development, of a 'learning process' according to Habermas, cultural change in today's age of 'global difference' and reflexive negotiation of identities between and within cores and peripheries is surely anything but a learning process. With the refusal of the 'metanarratives' – and especially those of Marxism, of the West, of reason versus nature etc. – cultural change may be just as much a 'forgetting process' as a learning process. Cultural change dissolves institutions as, or more, often than it builds on them. It disintegrates and re-forms power blocs rather than building on or learning from their foundations. Indeed it may not make a lot of sense to speak of cultural *development* at all. Cultural change involves perhaps as much *Abwicklung* (winding down, liquidating) as *Entwicklung* (development). Cultural change would not seem to follow the rhythms, the temporality of homogenous clock time, the time of economic cycles and long waves. Cultural change does not follow a temporality of accumulation – either that of economic growth via the accumulation of capital, or public sphere growth, via the learning process and accumulation of democratic political resources. It follows a different sort of temporality – one moving in fits and starts, without clear and distinct moments and instead with moments as overlapping and hazy images. Cultural change comprises not clear and distinct ideas, rational choices or discursively legitimated speech acts but instead comprises an arsenal of symbols – sometimes empty, sometimes affectively charged, often operating at the level of the unconscious or at best a pre-conscious of tacit background assumptions of an unspoken horizon. Its logic is vastly different from the logic of economic and political change. Indeed, its logic is perhaps not logic at all but may have more in common with *rhetoric*, in the most positive sense of this word. That is, cultural 'development' takes its cues less from logic's idiom of identity, difference, syllogism, cause and substance and more from rhetoric's language of metaphor, metonymy, synecdoche and oxymoron.

Thus where economic and political development are comfortable in the language of rational choice, decisions, preference schedules, strategic interests, steering mechanisms, rational actions and the like, cultural change cannot speak that kind of idiom. Culture does not operate at that sort of level. Its symbols provide the images of dreams, the unspoken myths of communal and national identities, the unarticulated horizon of actions, the habits and tacit technologies of bodies. Culture indeed forms a background to economic and political life. Economic and political change is embedded in cultural practices, embedded in the tacit knowledge, the unarticulated assumptions of culture.

So what has happened in cultural *change* here? Let us, for the purposes of this specific argument, define culture in terms of symbolic practices, and *a* culture as a set of more or less coherent, more or less loosely held together symbolic practices. Let me stress these two terms, first 'symbolic', and then 'practice'. Here I am using 'symbolic' in contrast to 'semiotic', and 'symbol' in contradistinction from 'sign'. A symbolic practice is also we shall see vastly different and perhaps opposite to a 'communicative action'. By symbolic I am referring to full symbols, to affectively charged symbols, to meaning-laden symbols, to what might be called 'heavy symbols'. 'Semiotic', on the other hand, refers to the lighter symbols, the emptied-out symbols that are signs. In traditional societies we get symbolic practices. Only later do we get the emptier, semiotic signs. Symbols are always inscribed in practices, in forms of life, in a 'world', a 'being-in-the-world'. Signs, in contrast, are typically attached to referents, to entities, to things that have been differentiated and separated from the practices of forms of life. With modernization and differentiation, signs become differentiated from forms of life, from being-in-the-world, and become attached to things, to entities. Signs become, like capital, one of a whole set of abstractions of modern societies (Baudrillard, 1994a). Regarding signs and symbols, where we once lived in primarily a local and symbolic order, we now live in a global and largely semiotic (dis)order.

Symbolic practices are also vastly different from 'communicative actions'. Symbolic exchange – and here I would draw on Bourdieu and Baudrillard's understandings of Mauss's idea of gift exchange – may be a phenomenon that is richer than 'communicative action' (Baudrillard, 1994b; M. Gane, 1991). In communicative action, what is communicated is an utterance, a speech act, a statement, a 'clear and distinct idea' that can either be accepted or rejected as valid in the light of the better legitimating argument. What is exchanged in symbolic exchange is laden with affect; it is a gift, an insult that will govern the rhythm of lives until repaid. Symbolic exchange operates at a more pre-conscious and unconscious level than does communicative action, affecting the bearing of our bodies. Symbolic exchange governs forms of life. It sets the standard in practices of what constitutes the good life. This has implications for politics in what is, not a national manufacturing society, but a global informational culture. It suggests a politics, not of communicative action, civil society and the public sphere; but instead a politics of symbolic practices taking place on the margins of public and private spaces.

To define culture as a symbolic practice is to emphasize *practice* in contradistinction to *action*. Action is individualistic, it is a question of the 'I', or at best a collection of atomized 'I's. Practice is communal; it is of the 'We'. Action takes place at the level of consciousness, practice foregrounds the unconscious and preconscious. Action is of the mind; practice is bodily. Action wields clear and distinct ideas, practice works in regard to symbols. Action deals with preference schedules and choice on the marketplace, practice with background assumptions, horizons and habitus. Action takes on the assumptions of positivism, practice of hermeneutics. Action speaks of political decision-making, practice of political culture. Action has to do with individual choices in the context of decided-upon procedural rules; practice is inseparable from the very real concerns of the good life.

The problem in the global semiotic order is that culture has become detached from practice. This already happened in the national manufacturing order, with the differentiation of culture in the modernization process. Once differentiated, culture then operates as ideology and is functional for the accumulation of manufacturing capital. Even worse, in this context, is post-modernization. What happens here is that culture itself comes under the logic of accumulation. This is partly a matter of informational (or semiotic) economic sectors attaining dominance in the economy and in the accumulation of capital. But the worst is that culture itself, analytically distinct from its economic form, comes under the principle of accumulation. Culture becomes what Heidegger (1977) understood as technology. Now no longer is culture just a differentiated and separate sphere, taking up the position of the sacred (in juxtaposition to 'the profane' of everyday life) as it was in 'high modernism', but culture itself becomes what Heidegger called the 'standing reserve'. Culture itself comes under the heading of *Gestell* or enframing. The German *Gestell* (frame) shares roots with *be*stellen (ordering), *vor*stellen (representing) and *her*stellen (producing) each of which involve a *Gestell* or frame. Once framed as representation, ordered like the purchasing order in a factory, once produced: once constituted through these three different types of framing as empty signs, then culture as a stockpile of signs, as a 'standing reserve', can itself become accumulated.

Thus technology in Heidegger's sense is a matter of the accumulation of frames. These frames are, at the same time, emptied of symbolic affect and are instrumentalist or proceduralist. They follow a logic of not reception but production; a logic of neither indexicality nor silence, but representation. Marx understood the accumulation of capital – in the shape of the commodity, of exchange-value – in a similar sense as such an accumulation of empty frames. The accumulation of 'political competences' (or 'civilizational competences') can also be so understood. Such political accumulation, via a learning process, is matched by the development of what Weber called the legal-rational order, the *Rechtsstaat*, which itself, in an important sense, is a frame, a set of instruments, of procedures.[4] This political accumulation of frames, this 'political technology', is a very special sort of technology. It is (and this is a very good thing) the guarantor of individual rights and the rights of minorities. But it is still a matter of an accumulation of 'external goods', in MacIntyre's (1981) sense, rather than a question of the good itself, or the good life.[5] Other accumulations of frames as instruments, as standing reserve, other accumulations of external goods, which one can 'valorize', include the acquisition of symbolic, cultural and social and bodily capital (Bourdieu, 1984). If modernization meant the introduction of such 'technology' into the economic and political realms, then *post*modernization takes the principle of accumulation into every sphere of social life. What were meaningful forms of life become then mere 'lifestyles' and strategies for accumulating the various forms of Bourdieu's capital, themselves all valorizable external goods. Now culture itself can come under the principle of accumulation. And now develops the possibility, the nightmare scenario, of cultural resources as empty signs being accumulated alongside political and economic resources in what appears to be a final triumph of instrumental reason. To the extent that this is true, it is possible for the media itself to occupy the place of power (Han, 1995). Increasingly, industrial capital may come to function in the reproduction of the mediascape, if media are understood to cover all sorts of communications. Now the manufacturing economy functions to reproduce the informational economy. Now the mode of production functions in the interests of reproduction of the information and communication structures.

Public Spheres: Civil Society or Ethical Life?

What are the implications here for the formation of public spheres, for the *Strukturwandel der Offentlichkeit* that Habermas spoke of in his benchmark work of that title published almost 40 years ago? What are the implications of all this for the development of a civil society, understood to be the basis of resistance to the state by the democratic regimes of the eastern and central countries of Europe? Could the formation of such public spheres also be a basis for challenging the sort of power increasingly lodged in the mediascape, in the information and communication structures? I am not sure that there is reason for much optimism here. I am not sure that a genuinely radical political option lies in the development of a set of micro- and 'subaltern' public spheres comprising civil society. Civil society does, as Cohen and Arato have argued, have communicative action as its 'steering mechanism' (Cohen and Arato, 1992). But that indeed – and I have argued this at length above – may be not the solution, but the problem. Let me be clear that I do not want to undervalue the importance of the *basis* of civil society. The basis of civil society and the democratic state is what Germans have called the *Rechtsstaat*, what Anglo-Americans understand under the general notion of legality, what Max Weber understood in terms of legal-rational governance. Here, legality, the legal-state or the *Rechtsstaat* is itself the *limit condition* (in Derrida's sense) between the state and civil society. Legality is a 'limit condition' in the double sense, first, of a 'limit', a porous and complexly configured limit, separating state and civil society; and second of a 'condition', a condition of the existence of both constitutional state and civil society. Legality (the *Rechtsstaat*) is at the same time the condition of existence of, on the one hand (procedural) constitutionalism in the state and, on the other, civic rights or *Bürgerrechte*, that is, rights of citizenship in civil society.

This said, however, there is a problem with the notion of civil society. Civil society is what Hegel (1967) in the *Philosophy of Right* called *bürgerliche Gesellschaft*. And these two words, *bürgerlich* and *Gesellschaft*, signal two very important problems with the idea of civil society. First, it is *bürgerlich* or bourgeois. It is, among other things, the place of constitution of the bourgeois subject, with his (her) individual property rights and his own interests to be played out in the context of civil society's norms and the procedural rules. Second, it is *gesellschaftlich*. It is not *gemeinschaftlich* but *gesellschaftlich*. Third, it is structured through associations. Social movements in the global informational order would seem to be rooted in a political culture that has little to do with civil society. This political culture seems to foreground less civil society's 'I' of individualism, and more the 'We' of communal solidarity. It foregrounds less the *Gesellschaftlich* than *Gemeinschaften*; albeit, of course, post-traditional *Gemeinschaften*. It is made up not of *associ*ations, but of much less formal and more affectively bonded *soci*ations. Associations are based on individuals and membership. Sociations are based on mutual recognition and not membership, but belonging. Hegel in the *Philosophy of Right* spoke not only of civil society or *bürgerliche Gesellschaft*, but of *Sittlichkeit*, which is translated in English as 'ethical life'. *Sittlichkeit* is based on *Sitten* or customs, habits. Its meaning is very close to 'habitus', to 'forms of life'. But ethical life is a good translation, perhaps even better than the original German *Sittlichkeit*, because Hegel is always defining it in contradistinction to the abstract morality, the abstract ethics of Kant's categorical imperative. What we are addressing in *Sittlichkeit*, in ethical life, is the coupling of ethics with forms of life. We are talking about a 'situated' politics. Korea, Japan and Russia, among other countries, have precursors of this in the village communities. In sociations in village communities on which, some, for example, argue, Japanese workplace collectivism is based. These forms of sociation can also be found in mediaeval guilds in the West.

Is this public? Is this private? Perhaps this sort of either/or distinction has little purchase on this phenomenon. It might make sense to think less in terms of either/or than both/and. Sociations violate the boundary of public and private. They form on the margins, in the 'limit' that separated the public from the private. It is based not so much on rationally choosing individuals or the granting of validity to discursively redeemed speech acts. Its basis instead is affective bonding, the innovation of ritual and shared meanings, it is recognition based on the co-production of horizons. The Korean precedent of the pre-modern Confucian intellectual is especially instructive here. The point is that not civil society and public spheres, but ethical life and immediate and local forms of sociation would seem to be a better basis for a radical political culture under conditions of postmodernity. The global informational culture and the logic of the flows are eroding the national – organizational and associational – bases of public sphere and civil society. Thus a radical politics of public sphere and civil society may be increasingly untenable.

There has been considerable debate between communitarian ethics and the more liberal, deliberative democratic ethics of thinkers such as Rawls and Habermas. The notion of ethical life and an ethics of, not action, but practice, just discussed, shares a number of themes with the communitarians. This has become a three-sided debate between liberals, communitarians and deconstructionists. Postmodern and post-structuralist ethics – from Bauman to Derrida to Levinas – are an ethics of deconstruction, an ethics of difference. Many discussions of post-*colonial* politics advocate such a postmodern politics of difference (Bhabha, 1994). There is, I think, a one-sided emphasis on difference and deconstruction by post-colonial analysts – from Said to Spivak to Bhabha – that they share with the ethics of deconstruction of Levinas, Derrida and Bauman. The point is that the critique of Western metanarratives is not only possible via this political ethics of difference, but is also involved in the notions of community, ethical life and practice. These ideas are present not just in the work of some communitarians, but also in life-world phenomenologists such as Heidegger and Schutz. Gadamer, also a life-world phenomenologist, is often cited as a communitarian and Charles Taylor, a leading communitarian thinker, has his roots in life-world phenomenology. Life-world phenomenology shares important assumptions with eastern doctrines and experience (Jung, 1989; Hahm, 1994). It shares assumptions with student movement politics in countries like Korea, for instance, where there is an effective neo-Confucian 'left'. For life-world phenomenology and these sorts of new Eastern politics there is the importance of relations rather than atomized individuals, the importance of community, the validity of traditions and a focus on practices. Paul Gilroy's (2000) focus on 'belonging' has brought these sorts of notions into post-colonial theory.

Influential social theorists such as Ulrich Beck and Anthony Giddens (Beck et al., 1994), who share fundamental assumptions with Habermas, are critical of such communitarian and neo-traditional life-world ethics, on the grounds that they do not take into account the extent to which today's societies have become individualized. But today's Korean neo-Confucians and the 'neo-traditionalists' in the new social movements in the West choose – in a highly individualistic manner – the radical political communities they are entering. They 'innovate' the traditions of those communities. Indeed, those who join them tend to be the *most* individualized people in contemporary societies. It is the younger generation of students in Korea who are neo-Confucianist. Their middle-aged fathers and professors are likely to be 'modernists' or liberals in some important sense. Yet in terms of social and cultural life practices, it is the sons and daughters who are more individualized. In, for example, Barcelona, again it is the younger generation, the students, who are 'neo-traditional' Catalan nationalists, which is a left anti-racialist nationalism. Their professors and fathers, on the other hand, will tend to be social democrats, Marxists or liberals. The more individualized sons and daughters again are the *more* communitarian, the more neo-traditionalist. Indeed this sort of ethos is found in today's anti-globalization movements at WTO protest. Much of postmodern politics and ethics tend surprisingly to have the same anti-community assumptions as the sociologists of individualization. The implications of this, especially in the analysis of non-Western countries (in post-colonial theory), are one-sided. There is a focus on difference and deconstruction to the neglect of forms of life; to the neglect of the invention of traditions, the creation of communities. I think that the experience of student politics outside the core at the turn of the millennium and the theoretical input of life-world phenomenology can bring a significant corrective here.

Conclusions: The Problem of Solidarity

What are the implications in terms of the live zones and dead zones – the zones that arise with the rise to dominance of the information and communication structures of the global informational culture? New social movements, it seems, may form more easily in the wilder zones, zones of indeterminate identity, rather than the stable identity of the tame zones. Key perhaps are the live and wild zones of the economically advanced countries. I have tried to suggest in this chapter that the sort of solidarity that makes contemporary radical politics possible may have little to do with civil society, public sphere formation and communicative action. These notions tend to presume individualism, rational choice, disembedded actions and proceduralism. These assumptions seem to be unacceptable to many actually existing new social movements and make solidarity unlikely. Further, they themselves share many characteristics with the instrumental rationality they seek to combat. Contemporary political movements seem instead, I have suggested, to be for smaller scale, more local, groupings with higher levels of affective bonding. These are groupings that have more in common with the sect than the church, with *Gemeinschaft* than *Gesellschaft*. These are post-traditional communities, which in the legal framework of the constitutional state, struggle to create the good life. They embody in microcosm the good life itself, hence transgressing distinctions between means and ends. Pre-modern social forms such as the Confucianist-inscribed village solidarity in Korea can be very instructive in the reflexive construction of these new forms of political sociation, these new forms of political culture.

It is nearly four decades since Alexander Gerschenkron (1962) wrote *Economic Backwardness in Historical Perspective*, which addressed the advantages of not being first in economic development. It makes sense perhaps in this context also to talk about *political* and *cultural* backwardness in perspective. With all of the caveats I entered above about the notion of cultural development, this is perhaps worth considering. It may be worthy of consideration especially in today's context of countries like Korea, the other NICs, the post-socialist countries, other Western 'boundary' countries like Finland. These countries seem to be making – in the economy, politics and culture – an intensively sped-up transition from a pre-modern and traditional social ordering directly to postmodernization, skipping over, as it were, the stage of the modern. The disadvantages to this of course are that the bases of democratic politics, the legal underpinnings of the constitutional state and citizenship rights, are not very secure. The advantages are that the more vivid memory of pre-modern and communal forms of sociation may well have unanticipated advantages in the global informational culture.

Notes

1 This chapter was originally delivered as a paper at a conference on postmodernization at Seoul National University in South Korea.

2 Seyla Benhabib, in *Situating the Self* (1992) contrasts substantive values with procedural norms in this context. I think in this she fundamentally breaks with Habermas's views for a more communitarian standpoint. She would disagree with this and see herself as a Habermasian. Benhabib already departed substantially from Habermas for a sort of neo-Aristotelian position in her *Critique, Norm and Utopia* (1986) in which she used Hegelian Sittlichkeit as a place from which to launch critique against the excesses of Enlightenment identity thinking. Habermas seems to attempt this in *The Philosophical Discourse of Modernity* (1987), but to my mind he was unable to sufficiently situate his more abstract version of intersubjectivity.

3 An OEDC report in 2001 showed that South Korea had the highest penetration of broadband connections of any country in the world.

4 This is more a virtue than a shortcoming.

5 I am indebted to Russell Keat for this understanding of MacIntyre. Any shortcomings in interpretation are mine.

4

Disorganizations

Sociology has a very acute and very alive tradition of addressing questions of organization and of power. A number of these theories foreground structure, and a number foreground agency or action. For structuralists, organizations are 'hierarchical systems of normative rules'. For action-analysts, organizations are 'playing fields of interacting, strategically acting and negotiating agents'. Very often structural analysts of power and organizations will find themselves locked in conflict with action theorists. Indeed, structuralists will argue that their perspective has more validity than the action perspective, while action theorists will argue that their perspective has the greater validity. I want to claim instead that the structure and systems theoretical and action-oriented theories of power and organizations are not just perspectives. I want to claim that they are true. They are both right. Both structure and action theories describe very much the truth that is 'out there'. Organizations are 'hierarchical systems of normative rules'. They are at the same time 'playing fields of interacting, strategically acting and negotiating agents'. Organizations and the 'power resources' that reside in organizations stand thus in no way in contradiction to the individualization process of high modernity. Indeed, individualization is the complement, the other side of this organizational power. Organizational power is the condition of existence of individualization, and individualization is the condition of existence of organizations. That is, without individualization and its accompanying strategic action and interaction, without the rational choice that individualization presumes, no organizations on the sort of scale we have witnessed would have been possible.

What I want to argue, however, is that organizations and their accompanying power, and indeed individualization as we know it, are decaying social forms, decaying *Formen der Vergesellschaftungen*. What is emergent is not so much organizations as *dis*organizations, not so much individualization as sociality, and not so much power as violence. I want to focus in this chapter on disorganizations, and in coming to some idea of what disorganizations are I want to discuss sociality in contradistinction from individualization, and violence as opposed to power.

What then are disorganizations? Disorganizations are not the absence of organization, but the decline of organizations. The decline of organized capitalism does entail a decline in organization and a rise in individualism. But it also entails a rise in certain forms of sociation that are non-organizational, indeed often non-institutional. So disorganizations are not the absence of sociation but particular forms of sociation. They are not chaos, not chaotic. Indeed they may be more strongly structured by ultimate values than are organizations. Disorganizations are neither formal nor informal organizations; they are something else. Disorganizations are less local, less fixed, more often globally dispersed, constantly changing and literally on the move than are informal organizations. Disorganizations are neither traditional, or *Gemeinschaften*, nor modern, *Gesellschaften*. They seem at first glance to resemble *Gemeinschaften* more than *Gesellschaften*: and to the extent they do we can understand them as forms of *nachtraditionellen Vergemeinschaftungen* (Berking and Neckel, 1990). Disorganizations presume a certain level and a particular mode – or should we say singular mode – of individualization, though they are somehow at the same time much more collective than are organizations. Disorganizations presume a different mode of individualization than organizations, they presume a non-utilitarian, non-strategic, non-self-identical mode of individualization. Organizations and institutions make rational choices (usually) with unintended consequences (side effects). Disorganizations operate from a different logic. They often *are* the side effects, are the unintended consequences of the rational choices of organizations.

What examples are there of these disorganizations? Youth cultures, say BritPop subcultures or Brazilian skateboarding and surf wear culture. The *new* new social movements. Ghetto youth gangs, excluded from the information and communication structures of the global information culture. The tribes of gangster capitalism involved in today's illegal circulations of drugs, weapons, immigrants and body parts. The neo-families of our transformed intimacy. The flexibly networked work sociations in the new sectors – bio-tech, software, multimedia. None of these emergent forms of sociation fits exactly to the ideal type of disorganizations. And this chapter is devoted to the development of this ideal type.

Durkheim, though perhaps not Marx nor Weber, would have had an instinctual understanding of what disorganizations are. Disorganizations have little to do with power resources residing either in legitimately consecrated class or status groups, or in the means of production or even power resources residing in institutions of surveillance. Disorganizations may well be the unintended consequences of Marxian, Weberian or Foucauldian power resources but they are not them. Disorganizations are neither Marxian nor Weberian but Durkheimian. They are profoundly *cultural* creatures. They *are* elementary forms of religious life. Durkheim (1947) meant by this not churches but pre-institutional religion. He meant not even sects, which presume schisms from churches as institutions. These are, literally, *elementary* forms – that is, pre-institutional forms.

Let us start from the definitions of organizations from the point of view of both structure and agency in order to look at what these emerging disorganizations are. From the viewpoint of system and structure, organizations are 'hierarchized systems of normative rules'. Disorganizations are perhaps less hierarchical than horizontal. They are anti-systemic: not just anti-structure but anti-system – they are too open to interference and invasion from the environment to be systems; further, they are not involved in reproduction as are systems. They are instead involved in production. Disorganizations are finally not normatively but *value* co-ordinated and are perhaps more unruly than rule bound. From the standpoint of agency we perceive that organizations are 'playing fields of interacting, strategically acting and negotiating agents'. Disorganizations are too temporal to be captured by the spatial assumptions of the field analogy. They are rarely in the field, but always on the road. Their agents are anything but strategic. The notion of agent connotes the 'unit act'. Participants in disorganizations are involved typically not in unit acts, but in activities.

Norms and Values

Organizations are about norms. Disorganizations are about values. Norms are procedural. Western constitutions, based on norms, are procedural in the sense that they establish a level playing field of general procedural rules within which, first, individuals can pursue their own private utilitarian interests and, second, individuals can pursue their own forms of life and values. Modern organizations and institutions are similarly procedural. Even Habermas's discursive will formation is procedural. When Hegel criticized Kant's categorical imperative he criticized it because – like procedural norms – it was impossible to apply, too empty to apply in the absence of a *Sittlichkeit*, in the absence of values.

Disorganizations deal with substantive values rather than norms. But they are unlike pre-modern forms of sociation, for example, ancient constitutions and their inscription in values ('virtues'). There is a fixity to the pre-modern sociation of the polis. A fixity within the walls of the *cité*. Disorganizations for their part are fluid and mobile. They form, they de-form, they break up and come together again in different places. Their existence is one of being on the move. They cross borders, and like rhizomes put down rootless roots. Their roots are at the same time routes (Clifford, 1997). Disorganizations are reflexive about values. They are neither traditional communities (*Gemeinschaften*) nor *gesellschaftlich* bodies like organizations and institutions. They are instead reflexive *Gemeinschaften*. Reflexive communities. Organizations abstract from values.

Traditional sociations are inscribed in a *doxa* of values, that is, they are unquestioning about values. For their part, disorganizations practise chronic value heterodoxy. Disorganizations consist not of hierarchs but of heresiarchs. Disorganizations, unlike traditional *Gemeinschaften*, do not *re*produce values, they continually innovate and *pro*duce values (Wiewiorka, 1991; Touraine, 1995). This is part of their not institutional but anti-institutional reflexivity. Traditional communities recognize only their values. Disorganizations are further reflexive in their recognition of the finitude of their values. They subscribe to their values, but recognize that they are one finite set of values alongside those of the values of many other communities. Participants in disorganizations are 'philosophical anthropologists'. They are aware of humankind's deficit of instincts (*Instinktarmut*). They know that values and institutions are the way that particular sociations of human beings cope with their environment. They are aware that though we need values, their particular set of values is finite. Disorganizations can thus live in multi-culturalism. They are also reflexive in their awareness of our *Instinktarmut*, of this 'gap', this fundamental *lack* at the basis of our values. They are thus reflexive in terms of their instability, their undecidability. Traditional socia-tion is based in value consensus. Organizations are sociations based on the abstraction from values. With disorganizations values come back again, but this time as an ongoing and chronic value *dis*sensus.

Means and Ends

Organizations are means to ends. Surely those ends can incorporate more or less ultimate values, such as socialism. Yet commonly the means take over from the ends. Organizations are utilitarian in this way, as means to ends. The 'iron law of oligarchy' – in the case of trade unions for example – suggests that the means, the utilitarian means and procedures, attain promi-nence at the expense of the substantive ends. In sociations where this law of oligarchy did not set in, such as in the French trade union confederations, the CGT and CFDT, fully fledged organizational status (in the sense of impera-tive co-ordination and legitimate control) was never achieved. Organizations then are means. Simmel even more than Marx understood capital as means. In the course of modernity, like capital or exchange-value, organizations accumulate. Disorganizations, like use-value, do not accumulate.

Disorganizations are not means to ends. They follow a logic of ends more than a logic of means. Even in the economy they tend to depart from the utili-tarian assumptions, the means-consciousness of instrumental rationality. Designers in today's design-intensive post-industrial economy heavily invest affect in the tools of design (be it CAD, etc.) and in the artefacts, the things that they design (Molotch, 1996). But this has not a lot to do with a utilitar-ian calculus. Indeed, though a tool of design is a means, the more it is invested with affect, the more we live with these tools and artefacts in our everyday activities, the less these objects are utilitarian commodities, and the more they become not commodities but 'singularities' (Appadurai, 1986). These tools of production and objects produced are increasingly bound up with existential questions of what it means to be a designer. Or to be a sociologist. The socio-logist who has just put his or her book – even if it is a book in rational choice theory – into press has a lot more than a utilitarian investment in that book. It is almost more than metaphorically his or her 'baby'. These artefacts, these tools are not means to ends. They are also not classical ends, but are finalities (*Zweckmäßigkeiten*) without ends that are external to themselves. The logic of production in these new design-intensive disorganizations is increasingly a question of existential meaning and decreasingly of utilitarian calculation.

This was, of course, also the case with the Classical virtues, which are ends not means, that is, 'internal goods' not 'external goods' (MacIntyre, 1981). It is further exemplified also in the traditional and distinguished *Meistermodell* in craft training in Germany. But disorganizations are more complex than such more or less traditional communities of practice. If they are not governed by a logic of means, as are organizations, then they also are not governed by a classic and traditional logic of ends. Disorganizations are not fixed enough, do not have sufficient fixity to be governed by an end- or value-rationality. Their economy is neither clearly an economy of means nor ends. Disorganizations are not so much rule (i.e. means or norms) followers as rule innovators, and as often rule breakers.

In the Workingmen's International, the 'organizationalists' would have been alongside Marx; the 'disorganizationalists' alongside Bakunin. But disorganizations are not primarily the *'ni dieu, ni maître, ni patrie'* anti-structure of Bakunin and Spanish anarchism. They are not a question of anarchism or even anarcho-syndicalism, but of the revolutionary syndicalism of the *ouvriers du livre* of say Rouen in 1906. Disorganizations like *les ouvriers du livre* entail skill. Proletarians can work in organizations: you need skill to work in a disorganization. Unlike, however Rouen's *ouvriers du livre* or even the skilled leather and textile craft workers in the Emilia Romagna, disorganization workers are not fixed but mobile. Disorganizations are rhizomes spreading across borders. They are a Swedish building-electronics firm working with a computer systems installation firm in Manchester on the wiring and interior architecture of a new 'smart building'. They are a small post-production digital editing firm in London Soho liaising with Pixar Productions in the Bay Area.

Much of the work that goes on in disorganizations is not just utilitarian management, but involves creativity. This sort of innovation is not typically a question of aesthetic genius, but instead of cutting and pasting, it is brico-lage, or *basteln*. The same is true for biographies or narratives of the self, per-haps typical of their participants. These are not utilitarian self-identical calculated constructions but again bricolage, *'Bastelbiographien'* (Hitzler and Peters, 1998). At issue is neither the means logic, the utilitarian cognitive reflexivity of organizations, but the aesthetic reflexivity of design-intensive disorganizations. Disorganizations transgress the ends and means distinction. If (traditional) communities followed a logic of ends and organizations, a logic of means, then disorganizations follow a logic in which ends are insep-arable from means, in which the ends are internal to the means. In which the means (whether artefacts made or tools used) are themselves finalities.

Power and Violence

Organizations like Max Weber's political parties 'live in a house of power'. Disorganizations for their part live mainly in a house not of power, but of violence. Power depends on rules. It depends on legitimacy. It depends first on hierarchical and imperative co-ordination within the organization (or institution). And second on rules of interface between the organization and individuals in its environment. For example, the police and the citizenry. Or hospitals and the medical profession and the ill. Or the political institutions of a nation-state and its citizens. Power is surely exercised through both ideology and coercion, yet there is a crucial, indeed pivotal dimension of legitimacy to both ideological and the broadest sense of coercive power. For organizations there is *Macht* and *Herrschaft*, in which *Herrschaft* is legitimate *Macht*. The most important dimension of *Macht* in organizations is *Herrschaft*. With organizations, relations of domination are legitimate and either intra-institutional or between the institution and its environment. Illegitimate *Macht* is the exception. Fully extra-institutional domination is the exception.

Disorganizations operate in a sea of violence. The relation of domination with the excluded underclass – who are not only not inside the institutions but are also excluded from their environment – is one of violence. It is not legitimate. It is not accepted. Being beaten by police and thrown into prison in very large numbers is what happens when power relations do not work. It is social control – and there may not be a lot of control – by violence. The gangs, personal loyalties and warlords of the old Yugoslavia and the ex-USSR may well be based on relations that are personal rather than general and diffuse. But they are not personal in the sense that traditional legitimation was also personal loyalty to the body of the king or the lord of the manor. Succession here does not breed legitimation. Neither is alter's activity at the command of ego legitimized by the fact that alter always has done what ego commanded, that is, that it was based on a mass of precedents. Command in many disorganizations is *pre*-traditional and has to do with the violence that ego is prepared to exercise over alter. If legitimate at all, its legitimacy is neither legal-rational (modern power) nor traditional but more likely to be charismatic, and routinely or chronically charismatic. Charismatic – including non-routinizable – charismatic domination is unpredictable, inherently unstable. So is governance not through power but violence. The idea is to shoot first, warn later.

Death itself takes on a different significance with disorganizations. In the traditional and ancient city the generations of the dead were buried just outside the city walls, thus bequeathing a symbolic, a cosmology – based on the continuity of generations – to life and life activities within the city. With the rise and hegemony of organizations, death itself becomes part and parcel of the rational calculation of institutions, of actuarial statistics of insurance companies, old age care homes, of medicalised calculations. Death here is subsumed, it is compartmentalized, it is kept under control. With disorganizations death is everywhere. No longer subsumed and compartmentalized under rational calculation, death bombards us irrationally from all angles. It is no longer under control. And the affect connected to death is also not under control. It occasions uncontrollable weeping, revenge. It is exemplified in the contemporary sensibility in the films of David Cronenberg in which sex, death, microbes, technology, viruses intermix in a swirling vortex. There is a ubiquity of death, warlords, gangs and drug subcultures here. In this sense disorganizations are surely neither modern nor traditional. They are in very important ways less postmodern than *pre*-traditional.

Governance through ideology was based on power, on symbolic power of, say, manager over worker inside an organization. Governance in disorganizations, to the extent that it is effective, and often it is not, is no longer based on ideology. There is a sort of end, or at least diminution, of ideology. Governance is based now on not symbolic power but symbolic violence. Symbolic violence is different from symbolic power in its illegitimacy, its extra-institutional and extra-organizational nature. A smaller and smaller proportion of productive relations takes place inside organizations, and even inside nation-states. Productive relations take place increasingly between organizations, as academics connect electronically and through the air more closely with their colleagues in New York and Berlin than with those in their own departments; as ever fewer tasks inside the firm have to do with the line activities and imperative co-ordination of subordinates.

The old power relations of capital itself seem to have been altered. Max Weber's Protestant capitalist was an individualist, but he was a rule bound individualist. Weber contrasted him with 'booty capitalism'. For Protestant capitalism rules on the inside, an *innerlich* categorical imperative that transmuted itself into an analytics of the finest utilitarian calculation. Nineteenth century capitalism was bound by legal-rational *Herrschaft*, by a set of laws over an extended territory which made economic transactions predictable. Legal rational domination depended on an attitude, an orientation of individuals to the validity of a given law. Without this, and without the sort of trust that the market itself (as expert system) creates, it is difficult to speak even of the market as an institution. This legitimacy and rule-boundedness become, if anything, even more prominent in organizations.

Oliver Williamson (1985) has rightly shown how markets are institutions. Contemporary economic growth is often not just disorganizational, but extra-institutional. What kind of market as institution is involved in the billions made on futures markets and currency markets speculation? In bribing British MPs to ask parliamentary questions? What about Mafia involvement in Russian banks and in Russian football? What about the increasing billions on billions in world trade in people, drugs and illegal arms? Why the breakneck development for much of the nineteen eighties and nineties in India, China, parts of Brazil and Indonesia in a setting in which the markets come least close to their ideal type as institution? What sort of rule-boundness for Rupert Murdoch and Oracle? Could (and can) Steve Jobs trust Bill Gates? How much extra-institutional capital accumulation is going on in the age of disorganizatons? How much accumulation outside of the normal legitimate relations of power and legal rationality? If Weber's early capitalism thrived on the emergence of predictability, might not disorganized capitalism thrive on unpredictability? Is the legitimated and predictable power relations of capitalism being displaced by a casino or new booty capitalism (Strange, 1996)? The old capitalism of real estate was based on the state providing infrastructure as a sort of level playing field on which capitalists could compete. The new booty capitalism is about owning the playing field, owning now largely virtual infrastructure, owning the means of communication.

In this sense, the sense of violence, disorganizations are not only pre-modern, but pre-*ancient*. They are instead archaic. They are neither de-traditional, nor traditional, but *pre*-traditional. They befit the age before the polis, before the walls of the city. That of course is the meaning of tribalism. It is *pre*-ancient. It is before the age of either modern (legal rational) or traditional legitimation. Tribalism is an age of illegitimation. Not of power, but violence. That is why disorganizations are not Marxist, nor Weberian, but Durkheimian (or Mauss-and-Durkheimian).

Ego and Id

Organizations presume an economy of rational choice and the ego. Dis-organizations operate in media of affect, of libidinal economy, of an economy of desire. Churches are organizations (institutions). Sects are not. Organizations and institutions like the church are carriers of symbolic structures, apparatuses of the symbolic. Sects on the other hand operate out of not a symbolic economy, but an economy of desire, of affect: operate not from the symbolic, but the real. Sects de-sublimate but still produce culture. Culture need not work from the symbolic. Ideology, discourse and the symbolic address the 'I', the ego: they are affectively neutral. Sects and disorganizations are loaded with affect. They de-sublimate. Charismatic Christians speak in tongues. Luther before Lutheranism spoke in the basest tongue.

Organizations are the props, the struts, the joists that sustain ideology, that sustain the symbolic. Organizations sustain the symbolic itself, contributing to the reproduction of economic and social relations. Disorganizations are the enemies of reproduction. They are involved in the *pro*duction of economy, of culture.

It would be a mistake to understand America's worship of Ronald Reagan in the 1980s in terms of 'ideology'. This was not ideology. The Americans *loved* Reagan. They invested affect in him. He was affectively charged. He was integral to the American libidinal economy. They cathected him. Commentators in New Labour's Britain came to curious conclusions regarding the public reaction to the death of the Princess of Wales. They understood Diana-mourning not in terms of an Iranian-like or Argentina-like hysteria, but in terms of the long overdue final victory of modernity. It was the triumph of popular sovereignty, in which even the royalty had to have popular support for legitimacy. But why not take hysteria for what it was. There was an immense investment of desire in the figure of Princess Diana. After all, she was not a ruler, so the issue of legitimation and sovereignty is a bit of a red herring. Like Ronald Reagan, only immeasurably more than Ronald Reagan, she was more a *star* than anything else. She was a star on the level not approached by the Spice Girls or Madonna, or perhaps even Elvis or Marilyn Monroe. Diana had a lot less to do with organization and institutions (hence legitimacy) than with disorganizations, with the de-stabilization and re-routing of our economies of affect.

What were once called ideological apparatuses of the state, like the family, sustained the symbolic by passing values from generation to generation. They were involved in the reproduction of culture and the social bond. But what happens with the rise of such disorganizations as the 'neo-family': the product of divorces, never-marrieds, not necessarily heterosexuals and a number of such re-combinations. The neo-family does not operate in a medium that is more affectively neutral than the family. It does not entail a move to contractuality, a contractualization, or parliamentarization of intimacy. No. Intimacy becomes unstable. It is loaded with affect, loaded with emotional crises. Which is why we always *try* to contractualize it. Intimacy itself produces culture, it does not reproduce ideology. At stake is not ideology, is nothing at all super-structural. At stake are processes that are not super-structural but baser than the base. Processes of the investment of desire.

These processes may include sub-politics, but they are a lot more than sub-politics. In very large measure they are not political at all, but, for example, economic. A great number of disorganizations – indeed even putatively political disorganizations – have very little to do with politics in the more institutional sense of *die Politische*, or '*la politique*'. They bridge on but are also fundamentally other than Hannah Arendt's anti-utilitarian and polis-influenced notion of *das Politische*. They go a lot deeper than politics. They connect with death, existential meaning, childbirth, fundamental bonding, affect and symbolic investment. They go a lot deeper than *any* kind of politics.

Sub-politics are not about the 'publicization' of the private. Sub-politics are not primarily about displacing public processes like citizenship, contractuality and rights, decision-making and genetic engineering to the private realm of intimacy and love relations. Sub-politics is perhaps more a process of the privatization of the public: of the colonization of the public sphere by private. The new prominence of values, mentioned above, previously a matter of 'pattern maintenance' (the public was regulated by norms, not values), to be passed down from generation to generation. With disorganizations, value-transmission becomes a matter of 'pattern *interference*' and takes place also in public space (in environmental, multicultural, gay and feminist sub-politics).

The colonization of the public by the private is exemplified in the cult of revelation in public of private lives, as in the Oprah Winfrey show and its many clones in many countries. And the Royal Family. The 'star' is fundamentally a phenomenon of the private, or the colonization of the public by the private. Publicity-hungry politicians try to take on the role of stars. The statesman and responsible minister was once, in Weber's formulations, to preside over normative conservation and change as subject to the legal rational framework of the nation-state. The head of state, be it prince or president, was to incorporate national values. Now both are stars – international, global stars – who are not only just national. As stars they become part of the economy of affect, the libidinal economy. This may have always been the case. One would die for the affect-invested, value-incorporating head of the nation, one would not die for the spirit of legality or the welfare state. But is it is more than ever the case now? With stars it is their private lives that count, that sell the tabloid newspapers. The private here is converted into the accumulation of capital. This is at the same time the most superficial and the deepest phenomenon. Unlike the head of state, who was national and public, the new politicians are at the same time global and private.

5

Unruly Objects: The Consequences of Reflexivity

Chapters 3 and 4 addressed primarily forms of sociation – political, economic and cultural – in the global information order. If the working class political party and the small avant-gardes of political and aesthetic intellectuals were carriers of critique in the national manufacturing order, then the forms of sociation discussed in the above chapters are often at the same time the carriers, the vehicles potentially of the critique of information. This chapter turns our gaze to the conditions of existence of these sociations, to what might be called the structural principles of the information order itself. But these conditions are not perhaps primarily structural. In place of the old social structures of the manufacturing order is a configuration of flows: flows of signs, media, migrants, technology and money. To a great extent these flows are comprised of objects, though these are themselves often in the form of information and communications. This suggests a certain 'disinformation' involved in the information society, that we have a disinformed information society.[1] The contradiction here suggests itself as a sequence of unintended consequences. That is, that an increasingly information-rich and intelligent production process has as its consequences such anti-knowledge effects as information overload, ephemerality, 'dumbing down' and the like.

Such increasingly information-intensive production presumes very high levels of reflexivity. The knowledge society is also the reflexive society, the society at issue in 'reflexive modernization'. The precursors of such reflexivity lay in Immanuel Kant's idea of 'reflective judgement'. Kant's late and famous statement *'Was ist Aufklärung?'* means clearly not what is *the* Enlightenment, but simply what is enlightenment.

Enlightenment for Kant – after he had written the Third Critique, i.e. *The Critique of Judgement* (1952), often read as the 'aesthetic' critique – surely was not *the* Enlightenment. At stake surely was not the Enlightenment's emphasis on the cognitive moment of reason. Kant understood the latter in terms of determinate judgement. Determinate judgement meant the subsumption of the object under the concepts of the subject. Great stretches of Kant's critical work were devoted to demonstrating the limits of determinate judgement. Cognitive reason and determinate judgement had very specific limits. Enlightenment for Kant meant coming to terms with those limits. This entailed not determinate but 'reflective' judgement. In reflective judgement it is impossible to subsume the object under a concept for the subject. Aesthetic judgements are for Kant a matter of reflective judgement. Here the subject is no longer able to subsume the object under a concept or a pre-given rule. Subjectivity must instead find the rule. Here, the object as a thing-in-itself is never grasped directly, it becomes inaccessible to the subject. It is instead only perceived as if through a glass, darkly, via 'empirical' experience with nature, art, or other cultural objects. What Kant is saying is that in enlightenment the object tends more or less to escape from the grasp of the subject. It tends to take on a greater or lesser autonomy. If *the* Enlightenment made legitimate the emergence and autonomy of the subject, then the much less Faustian, the much more modest enlightenment makes it legitimate to speak of the autonomy, not of the subject but of the object.

This sort of idea takes on temporal characteristics in the process of reflexive modernization. Here reflexivity involves the reflexive monitoring of the object by the subject, in which the subject subsumes the object under rules. This accounts for only part of the theory of reflexive modernization. The other part, which can be more or less prominent, is the dimension of unintended consequences, the dimension of risk and uncertainty. That is, the more we monitor or self-monitor, the more we subsume cognitively, the more gets out of control, the more risk, uncertainty we bring about. The more we monitor the object, the more the object escapes our grasp. The more we strive calculatingly to minimize risks, the more we produce a whole other set of uncertainties. The more we try reflexively to order and make a coherent biography of our life narratives, the more they spin out of control. This moment of contingency, this moment where the object, or the self, escapes the cognitive categories of the subject, is indeed somehow 'aesthetic'.

In this, authors who are more or less 'modernist' tend to give priority to order and the subsumption by the subject, while those who are more or less postmodernist speak rather of the autonomy of the object. Thus, for example, Baudrillard speaks of seduction by the object, of *stratégies fatales* of the object. Kant's notion of Enlightenment in *Was ist Aufklärung?* has been seized upon precisely by postmodernists such as Derrida, Lyotard, Foucault. The notion of enlightenment here is neither modern nor postmodern but instead quite traditional. I think enlightenment entails not just that the subject come to grips with 'his' limits and recognizes the autonomy of the object. That it entails not just a coming to grips with the subject's limits for a politics of the anarchy of the object, for the anarchy of global economies of signs and space. To be enlightened means more than just coming to grips with the future, when the world of the contingent object tells us there may be no future. Enlightenment means also a recognition of the past, of tradition, of memory, of history, of the political and the good. It involves a hermeneutics not of suspicion, but a hermeneutics of retrieval. And this too must find its place in the theory of the object. I want to start from this statement of the theory of reflexivity and move towards such a notion of the object. And I want to do this drawing on the work first of Bruno Latour, then Paul Virilio and finally Walter Benjamin.

Quasi-Objects

'Where', Bruno Latour laments in *We Have Never been Modern* (1993), 'is the Levinas of animals, the Mounier of machines, the Ricoeur of facts?' Where indeed? What Latour is lamenting is the absence of spokespersons for the object in contemporary social thought. Latour himself is such a spokesperson in this important book. *We Have Never Been Modern* is a book about objects, or what Latour calls 'quasi-objects'. Indeed, the human sciences in his view should be about tracing these quasi-objects, looking at their movements and the networks they build. For Latour we should not be talking about subjects and objects at all, but about quasi-subjects and quasi-objects, both being 'actants' in the networks of his 'actor-network theory'. Let us focus on Latour's theory of the object.

Latour (NM: 29 ff.)[2] understands modernity in terms of what he calls a 'constitution' with three central 'guarantees'. The first is that nature or the object is 'transcendent', that is, it is something we don't construct, but discover. The second is to understand society (the subject, the state) as immanent. That is, citizens are free to construct themselves and society (and the state) as it were, 'artificially'. And the third is to assure this separation of powers. This modern dualism, he argues, has always been a myth. Nature (i.e. things, technologies etc.) has always also been immanent, through its construction by communities of scientists, but most importantly through its mobilization by societies and states. Societies and states have enrolled – as they modernize – ever more non-humans. Societies for their part are not just immanent but also transcendent. To the extent that they are durable, that they solidify, that they have *durée*, they too are transcendent. If the object in modernity is transcendent, then these real existing non-humans are not full objects but only 'quasi-objects'. And to the extent that collective and individual subjects are not just eternally constructed but are at the same time transcendent, they become not subjects but quasi-subjects.

This mosaic of quasi-objects is the reality of even the highest modernity. Hence we have never been modern. We have always been enveloped and connected into a 'third kingdom', of neither pure immanence not pure transcendence, but a mediating and medial kingdom which ranges between the poles of immanence and transcendence. It is in this third kingdom that the networks of 'actants' exist. What is called modernity, which Latour dates from the eighteenth century, has carried out a 'work of purification', denying the existence of impure quasi-objects and quasi-subjects and purifying them into the dual poles of society (culture) and nature, of subject and object. The point is that this legislation of sharply differentiated dualistic thinking has instead paradoxically *encouraged* the creation and proliferation of quasi-objects, from vacuum pumps to milling machines, to semiconductors, to a host of other technologies on a scale never before imagined. Thinking in terms of the purified simplicity of nature as transcendent and society as immanent, and 'banning translation networks' has allowed the massive innovation, the creation of a host of 'hybrids', of quasi-objects. It has also enabled the spatial extension of the networks joining these quasi-objects and quasi-subjects on an increasingly global scale. Despite our rhetoric, Latour notes, we have always created these quasi-objects, so we were never modern. The point is, we told ourselves we were modern, which itself permitted the proliferation of these innovations (NM: 46–8).

Thinking dualistically in terms of immanent subject and transcendent object has proliferated the quasi-objects. And it is the quasi-objects that are the concern of Latour's book. He does not speak very much about quasi-subjects as actants but almost always about quasi-objects, about non-humans. Latour observes that the eighteenth century saw the extension of citizenship rights to the middle classes and the nineteenth, to the working classes. Now he says is the time to give citizenship, to redistribute agency to things, to create a 'parliament for things', to speak of the rights of things. What, however, do objects do? What do quasi-subjects do in Latour? Quasi-subjects or humans do carry out the sort of 'work of purification', the sort of reduction and differentiation into dualisms that Latour says corresponds to the modern constitution. But we also, and more importantly, carry out the 'work of mediation and translation': we 'sort', we 'delegate' and 'pass' to create networks. For Latour (NM: 137–8), actants in networks, whether humans or non-humans 'measure and interpret'. We and objects are 'weavers of morphisms'; we and they are 'analogy machines'.

Latour is not so interested in the work of purification as in this work of mediation. It is this, this 'weaving of morphisms' that most closely corresponds to what we do. There is almost, but not quite, a theory of reflexivity and unintended consequences in Latour. For Beck/Giddens we reflexively monitor, that is, engage in subject-object thinking, to attempt to limit and control hybridity/contingency, but this leads to the proliferation of a set of risks, of uncertainties. For Latour, we say we are engaging in subject-object thought, or Kantian determinate judgement; but in fact we perhaps are mostly engaging in 'morphism weaving', that is, Kantian reflective or aesthetic judgement. Only we repress this in modernity. The result is inventions: it is technologies which are also hybrids. The unconscious of modernity is this repressed morphism-weaving and hybrid creation. We refuse to call these hybrids hybrids ('monsters', or quasi-objects). No. We call them objects; we classify them under nature. But they are not exactly unintended consequences. Further they are not – unlike the unintended consequences in Beck's risk society – 'bads', but are clearly goods. Latour's (NM: 41–3) hybrids, his 'monsters', are goods. They are the repressed unconscious of modernity. The unintended consequences, the hybrids, the monsters of reflexive modernity are bads. Latour does not have a theory of bads. His objects are always goods.

The work of mediation is the weaving of morphisms. It is something both people and things do. To weave a morphism entails three steps. First, the creation of the morphism, of an analogy, to measure or judge or 'sort' or classify one entity by another. People do this routinely. So do many machines, like computers, like Boyle's seventeenth century vacuum pumps, the paradigmatic example in *We Have Nevas Been Modern*. He speaks of quasi-objects as measuring instruments. They measure, they judge, they estimate. To weave a morphism entails a second step of sending, or 'passing' the message to other actants, to other points in the network. To weave means thirdly to create the net, the web, the network, and to extend it. One important variety of non-human for Latour is the 'fact', the findings of a scientific 'discovery', which for him are neither universally valid nor relative. Such facts are as universal as the networks along whose 'branch lines' the fact (findings of scientific text) is transmitted, is 'sent' or 'passed'. And the branch lines must in each case be 'paid for', in costs of lab equipment, education etc. To the extent that they are widespread and have duration, such facts are not just contingent but begin to be transcendent (NM: 129). A true theory should be true forever. But theories, we see here, are more or less true: facts and other natural artefacts more or less transcendent. The longer the period of time a theory (or a society) holds the more transcendent it is. The shorter the period, the more contingent and 'event' like the fact is. A fact or a theory can even be an 'essence' if its duration is long enough.

Human beings are then 'analogy machines'. Humans and non-humans are mediators, which transmit or 'pass'. Usually it is a combination of the two that transmits. Both humans and non-humans weave morphisms. It is not clear whether non-humans can measure analogically. It is possible that things and machines can only operate via determinate judgement and not reflective judgement. Computers thus may be not analogy machines but 'logic machines'. Pre-moderns, as Latour notes, also carry out analogical thinking, carry out also the work of mediation. But this is before the triumph of the work of purification, of determinate judgement, of cognitive reflexivity. Only then does analogical thinking lead to the proliferation of the hybrids. For Latour these hybrids are almost always *technologies*. Latour's objects are not just goods but almost always technologies. For him societies 'recruit' these technologies to enhance their stability (NM: 79–81).

Latour's objects, Latour's things, judge. They may determinately judge, but they do engage in processes of judgement, of mediation. To weave morphisms is to mediate. To mediate is to judge *and* pass, to 'interpret *and* send'. To mediate is to weave networks. But things or objects do not just mediate for Latour. They *are* mediated. Before the 'great divide' of the eighteenth century, in the laboratory of Boyle – at the time of Boyle and Hobbes – the two senses of mediation (of things and of humans) in the sense of representation, are not yet fully differentiated, have not fully become dualistic. Boyle and Hobbes thus had rather similar senses of representation. For both 'delegates' could 'represent' or 'betray'. The state was contracted from the people and represented the people, much in the same sense as scientific facts were represented. Or betrayed. Political representation and representation as knowledge were not yet so very far apart. The state as political representation was in Latour's 'third kingdom': artificial in the sense that it is constructed, yet quasi-transcendental in its durability (NM: 27–9). Scientific facts were not yet transcendent and 'objective', but still were quasi-immanent, needing to be witnessed by groups of attesting gentlemen of 'substance'. Boyle's vacuum pump became thus another one of these witnesses. Scientific facts were understood not so much as universally valid, but as transcendent and valid only so far and so long as they received the endorsement of such witnesses (NM: 22–3). Even the etymology of the thing, as *res* or *Ding*, has to do with property, with judicial proceedings, with recognition before a tribunal (Heidegger, 1971). Hence the thing is as immanent as it is transcendent. Objects thus are partly constructed as stakes in some sort of judicial procedure. They can be betrayed and falsely represented. And each sort of object would have a separate plateau from which justification would take place (Boltanski and Thevenot, 1991). Science is not a privileged plateau for such justification (NM: 44).

There is thus an extension of the theory of reflexive modernity present in Latour. First he takes us from the micro-level of the reflexively monitoring and self-monitoring subject to the macro-level of the main lines and branch lines of, not just science, but implicitly the actor-networks of today's global and post-industrial order. Second, Latour gives a vast space to the proliferation of objects generated as unanticipated consequences of reflexive monitoring. There is also an implicit critique of the theory of reflexive modernization (Beck et al., 1994). For Latour, even when we say we are engaging in such reflexive monitoring, we are instead involved in a much less determinate and implictly partly aesthetic weaving of analogies or morphisms. Here Latour is champion of reflective judgement over determinate judgement, analogy thinking over logical thinking. Here he converges with a whole French (starting at least with Durkheim and Mauss) tradition that saw non-logical classifications as the basis of logical classifications (Latour, 1996). Much more radical of course is the idea that the objects generated and set free from the reflexive subject themselves take on powers of reflective judgement: of analogy-making and morphism-weaving. Thus Latour deflates the reflexivity of the subject. At the same time he attributes an important dimension of reflexivity to the object.

Several analysts have been critical of assumptions of instrumental rationality, of rational calculation in the theory of reflexive modernization, and have noted the resemblance to rational choice theory or the assumptions of neo-classical economics. A similar criticism may be made of Latour. This is apparent in his treatment of the past, of tradition, where he notes that we are 'exchangers and brewers of time'. Here the past is seen as a resource, and not as integral memory, not as lived, not as fate (NM: 76). It is apparent in his idea of network. Relationships between individuals and between objects and subjects do not only take place in networks. They take place in worlds: in life-worlds, where individuals and things consist of much more than 'points', or nodes in networks. Individuals may be analogy-machines, but they have horizons, they have habituses. Objects too may open out onto horizons, but Latour's very machinic objects (and subjects) do not seem to. A universe of networks is a universe of 'system', in which there is no place for life-world. Latour's focus is, moreover, always on 'goods' and never on 'the good' or the good life. These goods, these technologies function to give stability to the state or society. The objects that Latour seems most often to discuss are technologies, again instruments. His theory, while attributing to the object admirable powers, remains too one-dimensional. Objects are much more than instruments. They are repositories of memory, of traces, of tradition. And memory and the trace are a lot more than a resource. Latour would seem to have a strong notion of tradition, in saying that not only are we not post-modern, but we were never modern. But his strongest argument seems to be that we were never traditional and instead that we were always indeterminate and hence perhaps always postmodern. What I am trying to argue is that objects are much more than just goods that serve to stabilize states and other actor-networks. Objects in their past-ness, it seems to me are much more than resources, but also traces, artefacts, memories.

Bad Objects

If Latour's modern and postmodern objects are goods, Paul Virilio's are, inconvertibly, *bads*. If Latour is late twentieth century thought's 'techno-romancer', Virilio is our paradigmatic technophobe, who yet takes a *schaden-freude*-like fascination with technology. Latour's objects are hybrids. His argument is that these hybrids have so proliferated at the present that we must now realize that we have never been modern. Latour's paradigmatic examples of the quasi-objects that construct today's increasingly global net-works, today's 'middle kingdom', today's economies of signs and space, are for example 'frozen embryos, digital machines, hybrid corn, data banks, sense equipped robots, radar sounding devices, gene synthesizers'. They are hybrids of the cultural and the natural, the sign and the object. And they are technologies. That is, they are part not of the mediascape, ethnoscape, nor even primarily the ideoscape (Latour is not a sociologist of ideas) or the net-worked markets through which consumer culture and consumer commodi-ties flow, but are clearly part of the *techno*scape. His objects are also not as much scientific 'facts', as he calls them, but technologies or instruments that either measure in regard to scientific facts in the laboratory, or are generated as a result of scientific facts. Latour is thus very explicitly not just a sociolo-gist of science, but a sociologist of science and *technology*.

For his part, Virilio's objects are bads. Like Latour, he is implicitly anti-Foucauldian, challenging the primacy of discourse and instead looking at knowledge as embodied in objects. Virilio is a Christian. He is a classicist. He looks back to a time in which dialogics and reasoned discourse was possible, the time of the polis, of the enclosed Greek city. Virilio looks back to an era of the political as *das Politische*, as *le politique*. He is at home with the neo-Aristotelian intersubjectivity of the polis. Latour's pre-modern objects stem from Maussian and Durkheimian primitive classifications and are para-digmatically the ancestors inscribed in totems. Here totems are pre-modern hybrids, that is, quasi-objects, inscribed with the non-differentiated social, natural (animals), religious and object properties. His pre-modernity is the 'tumult' of bands of warriors before the establishment of the *cité*. Virilio's pre-modernity is instead of a piece with the classical aesthetics of beauty of Greek sculpture, of the situated practices of communitarian thinkers like MacIntyre. But Virilio even in antiquity, even in the classical era, does not focus on embedded intersubjective ethics or aesthetics. His interest instead lies in *objects*. For Virilio (1994a), the good, or the good life, the critical space of reasoned dialogue, is protected by *things* such as walls, ramparts, blockhouses and watchtowers. These things protect the city. It is these objects that protect the good from the bads, from the catapults of those who would lay siege. Virilio, an architectural theorist, obsesses with enclosures. His earliest study was of the Atlantic Wall, the blockhouses and bunkers and other lines of French coastal defences erected during the Second World War. These objects, these walls, protected and enclosed continental space and set it off from maritime space. Thus art and the political for Virilio are modes of 'promoting an image of the world ... through the art of defending the city' (Virilio and Lotringer, 1983: 5). Virilio is indeed, if not the Levinas, than surely the Gadamer, the Hannah Arendt of things, of objects and machines, the Aristotle of the blockhouse.

For Virilio modernity is the story of time conquering space, of an ever-growing 'vectorization' that destroys the space, the architecture and (the political) of the city. The enclosure, the enclave is destroyed. But what is destroyed? The good itself is destroyed as the bads, the vectorization of the bads run rampant. The object is a casualty of this destruction. The object is emptied of truth: the 'first victim' of what Virilio sees as the age of speed and of total war is truth. The object is depleted of Aristotelian substance (Virilio, 1982: 38). In the age of the city, Virilio notes, substance was seen as necessity, contingency as accident. But in modernity's age of speed, of vectorization, of destruction of the city, substance has disappeared and accident itself becomes necessity. For Virilio technology is speed, is accident. In Heidegger and Marx, technology accumulates, it stockpiles, it is an accumulation of frames (Heidegger's *Gestell*) or of value-forms (Marx). For Latour technologies do not accumulate but constitute quasi-objects in ever extending networks. Technologies are goods which, as quasi-objects, build and stabilise networks. Virilio's technologies also are not accumulations: they are moving objects[3]. They do destroy space through their movement. They are dangers; they are accidents; they are bads. Virilio may have been the first theorist of the risk society. With the disappearance of the good, all that is left are bads. With the disappearance of the good, politics is over and all that is possible are 'strategies': strategies of the object; strategies of vectorization. The context of these strategies is, necessarily, bads. Goods in Virilio's *moderne* are only a particular variety of bads.

The idea of bads, of attack and violence structuring the good, structuring what is inside the enclosure, raise questions of theodicy and death. The streets leading from the centre of the ancient city to the walls were also the routes along which one could bear the dead for burial outside the walls of the city. And the political is for Virilio this sort of 'geo-politics' of this cult of mother earth in which the dead are buried (Virilio and Lotringer, 1983: 34, 124). This gives a frame for the continuity of time and structured religious and political life inside the city walls. This frame structured the creation of monuments, of memorials, of institutions whose duration, whose quasi-permanence is the city's answer to questions of death and theodicy. But what happens in the age of total war, in which the walls, the ramparts, the significant boundaries that confer substance and truth on the objects inside the walls are torn asunder? What happens when accident becomes necessity so that death itself becomes part of technology? The individual cannot even retreat into the private enclave of being towards death, which proves to be the most fleeting solution to the disappearing question of theodicy.

For Virilio, when death comes under the sway of technology, in our hospitals and other institutions, it invades the object as a whole. Vectorization, speed and technology are death. Pure war is death. Life went on within the walls of the city. The age of speed, in laying waste to both the religious and the political, lays waste also to life. It is like *The Invasion of the Body Snatchers*. With the destruction of the enclosure, we are taken (by the vectors) in our sleep to be transformed into benefit-maximizing automatons (Virilio, 1991). As life goes out of the subject, substance is emptied from the object. Death and contingency pervade the everyday as the graveyard outside the walls of the city is desecrated. All societies leave at least one sort of trace: in the burial of their dead. Cultures may not leave traces of births or marriages and other bondings, but they do of their dead. With cremation and the storing of bodies in hospital morgues, we erase even this trace. Compare Paris, which to Walter Benjamin was ancient, to Berlin's pure modernity (Frisby, 1985). In Paris, the Père Lachaise cemetery, on the outskirts of the city – and outside the gates of the old city – gives a space for the dead. This space structures and gives meaning to the artefacts of the city. Paris thus, as Benjamin remarked, is an 'outside' that somehow at the same time is 'inside'. But where are Berlin's dead? Berlin, and not Paris, is emblematic of modernity's speed and technology. Hausmann's boulevards were the boulevards of the bourgeois. But Berlin's are twice as wide, twice as quickly travelled and are named after generals. Where are Berlin's dead? Buried in the 'geopolitics' of the earth? Or are they not buried in the earth at all but instead floating in the maritime space, the vectors of the Landwehrkanal, whose only memorial is a tiny plaque on a remote quay, where only the specialist, only the curiosity-seeker will find words commemorating Liebknecht and Luxemburg. The old city may have been composed of live zones and dead zones. Père Lachaise may well have made possible the live zones of the *flâneur*. But today's city for Virilio has only dead zones. The boulevards have been embalmed in the concrete of the shopping mall.

Virilio reverses Macpherson on possessive individualism. For Virilio the Hobbesian war of all against all, or 'pure war', is not metaphoric of capitalist possessive individualism. On the contrary, Marx's *Das Kapital* would be a metaphor of the militaristic. Without any possibility of the good, with the destruction of the enclosure by war and death, all becomes strategy. What counts in Virilio's 'dromocratic revolution' is movement, the movement of troops, of tanks, of armaments, of artillery, of ammunition. It is the age of hard objects and vehicles. Even the body is a metabolic vehicle. With the disappearance of death and the generations, an aesthetics of remembrance and 'geo-politics' is succeeded by a 'chronopolitics' without memory (Virilio, 1984). Now all machines are 'war machines' as vectors of speed 'violently re-energise the field'. Politics has disappeared and economics is war by other means. The notion of technology in Heidegger or Marx is based on accumulation, on the stockpile, the standing reserve. But the first stockpile, the first standing reserve is of weapons, of soldiers. This is the original constant and variable capital. The reserve army of labour is preceded by the reserve army. The proletariat itself is not so much a social class as a vector of war, a vector of a new governmentality. 'War communism' *was* communism. The economy was the metaphor.

At some time in the twentieth century this 'war machine' becomes progressively replaced by what Virilio calls the 'vision machine'. This late-modern shift takes place in the context of what is still an era of pure war, pure strategy. Now the military itself begins to take on technologies of cinema, and principles of 'vision' and 'sighting' come to the fore. Now speed of movement of vehicles becomes less important than radar and other visual devices. At this point in time, speed and pure war are still hegemonic values, but now this is pure war by increasingly less militaristic means, as the principle of matter becomes displaced by the principle of light. Thus no longer is dromocracy predominantly a question of speed of moving vehicles or moving celluloid. It is instead a question of the speed of light. At the same time, and this is crucial, a logic of representation is displaced by a logic of 'presentation'. If the emblematic Virilian objects of pre-modernity are walls, ramparts and bunkers, those of (an earlier) modernity are vehicles, tanks, cars, trains, trucks, the body as metabolic vehicle (Virilio, 1989). In the late-modern age of the vision-machine the paradigmatic object is the signal: the signal moving at the speed of light. The body, for its part, is no longer a metabolic vehicle, but instead a 'point'. The body itself becomes a vision-machine. It becomes a terminal.

In the age of the vision machine, it is not the machine any more that does the moving. The machine is no longer the vehicle. The machine is instead a frame that enables the moving of light at the speed of light. The body takes on a new set of prostheses (Lury, 1997): no longer are its prosthetic limbs the material and metabolic vehicle. Now it is a terminal, a vision machine. The body and material vehicles once did the moving. Now it is light that does the moving. The age of the vision machine is the age of 'polar inertia', in the sense that the poles on a globe stand still as the globe spins. Thus bodies stand still as light is moving. Vectorization collapses in on itself as the battlefield cedes its place to the perceptual field. Or rather the field itself implodes onto the space of the terminals. The pre-modern space of the city giving way to the space of modernity's field of vectors now itself implodes into the terminal, the point, the static point. Poles are points that are interchangeable. As vision machines we become interchangeable. We become terminals. Computer terminals and the terminals of international airports are equally interchangeable (Virilio, 1999b).

The vision machine is war by another name. Here the logistics of hard objects is displaced by the 'logistics of perception' in which quasi-objects carried at the speed of light appear on our terminals. If for Virilio we once were hybrid quasi-subjects merging with things as metabolic vehicles, now we are hybrids as 'electro-optical watching machines' (Virilio, 1994b). We experience our prostheses with soft, immaterial objects. But there is a new generation of quasi-objects about as well. Thus the digitalized time-lapse video cameras in the Paris metro are also electro-optical watching machines. Reflexive judgement or analogical thinking is possible only in Virilio's pre-modernity. As moderns we are under the spell of machinic and determinate judgement. Dromology is replaced by 'dromoscopy': the moving body is replaced by the impact of speed on the senses: moving power is replaced by emotional power. The vision machine is a virtual machine. It is the exteriorization of the human sensorium (Croker, 1992). The logistics of perception take place in real time. Gone is the classical time of 'graphics', in which memory was incorporated into aesthetic objects. Gone is the 'dialectical time', the deferred time, the *temps différé* of the logistics of movement. In this until recently dominant temporality, representation was still possible. In such re-presentation, in photographs, in cinema, a thing from the past is re-presented in the present. In photography the past is represented and preserved. In relation to the enduring permanence of classicism, there is at least a relative permanence of the (earlier) modern age of movement. Now, however, with the omnipresence of the object as signal, there is no deferral. There is only real time. There is no need to re-present. There is instead television, 'tele-presence', that is, 'presence at a distance'. Even if modernity's object had lost substance some sort of representation and permanence, some materiality was possible. Now the object also loses not just substance but also materiality: without representation and the possibility of any permanence, materiality is destroyed. With the new hegemony of not deferred but real time the object becomes reduced to the status merely of information. We move from an original 'graphic' age through a 'cinemato' and 'photographic age' to a contemporary 'infographic' age (Virilio, 1987). Here real-time images are no longer representations but information. This is an age of the purest utilitarianism. And there is no use, little market value, for past information. Who wants yesterday's papers? In the real time of Virilio's polar inertia, culture is reduced to information. It is the final triumph of utility. Now it is not only we who watch the electro-optical machine: the vision-machine watches us. Governmentality through (not discourse, but) the projectile turns into machinic surveillance. The old *'prise de vues'* of the hand-held camera becomes the *'surprise de vues'* of the time-lapse video camera recording the IRA bombers coming into the petrol station.

Dead Objects

I want very briefly to introduce some ideas from Walter Benjamin as a corrective to Latour and Virilio. Benjamin adds a hermeneutic dimension, a ground to any adequate theory of the object. For Latour such a hermeneutic dimension is impossible. For Virilio the possibility of such a ground disappeared hundreds of years ago. Though nostalgic for the walls of the *cité*, Virilio like Latour is riding a rollercoaster at full flow, is moving forward on fast forward. Latour and Virilio, like Beck and Giddens, presume that we live in societies that are fully de-traditionalized. Walter Benjamin for his part, as has often been noted, is a writer who is being dragged into the future looking backwards. There is a very strong dimension of the past in the way Benjamin views artefacts or objects, whether literary or material. Benjamin is at home neither in modernity, nor postmodernity, but instead in tradition.

The young Benjamin, before the book on German tragic drama and the work on Baudelaire and Paris, wrote very much in the Romantic influenced idiom of German *Sprachphilosophie*, or the philosophy of language. Here in *Über Sprache überhaupt und über die Sprache des Menschen* (1977c) he worked from an opposition of the 'semiotic', on the one hand, and the 'magical', on the other. In this the semiotic was understood as the instrumental use of language, that is, things were accomplished and meaning generated *'durch die Sprache'*, or through language. In the magical, in contrast, meaning was accomplished *'in der Sprache'*. Here language is not an instrument, but a finality. Indeed, Benjamin would have found an instrumental and utilitarian rationality and an unacceptable positivism in Peirce and Saussure's signifier, signifieds and referents. Benjamin, as Sprachphilosopher, had little time for Nietzsche.[4] His early book on Goethe's elective affinities published by the more traditional Hugo von Hoffmansthal was an attack on Friedrich Gundolf's Nietzschean interpretation of Goethe. To attack Gundolf, a central participant in the Stefan George Circle, was also to attack contemporaneous versions of *Lebensphilosophie*. Hannah Arendt was right to liken Benjamin's early work – in its very groundedness, and implicit notion of life-world – to Heidegger's hermeneutics, though in its pronounced traditionalism it is surely closer to Gadamer and Arendt herself. Benjamin, however, was never concerned with intersubjectivity or the political or ethics, but always with language and the aesthetic. His work stood very much in the tracks of the Romantic *Sprachphilosophen*: especially of Hamann, eighteenth century predecessor of the *Stürm und Dränger*, and of Wilhelm von Humboldt's work on national languages. The young Benjamin also wrote in the lineage of the Romantics themselves – of the Schlegels, Novalis and Schelling. These thinkers influenced him in their understanding of poetry or fine art via the opposition of the semiotic or instrumental, on the one hand, and the magical or revelatory or 'cabalistic', on the other (Menninghaus, 1980). Recent books on Benjamin have understood him in terms of a characteristically Jewish tradition. But these influences (despite their use of 'the cabalistic') were Protestant with few Jewish connections.

The point for, say, Humboldt was that language could be cabalistic or revelatory to the extent that it captured the mode of expression, the essence of national languages. Poetic language, moreover, could evoke universals – of revelation – through individual national languages. Benjamin's contrast of the instrumental versus the magical owed much to Goethe's notion of elective affinities. For Goethe, human existence was coming increasingly to resemble the sort of bonding – through elective affinities – of isolated atoms in physics and chemistry. This said, Benjamin was not fully pessimistic. Like the Romantics he hoped that through poetry a certain hermeneutics of retrieval was possible. Benjamin would thus have little use for what Ricoeur called the 'hermeneutics of suspicion', and was much closer to the hermeneutics of retrieval. To say something '*durch die Sprache*', through predicative utterances, exemplified the instrumental use of language to which Benjamin contrasted 'naming' in the sense that the name captured the magical content of language (Benjamin, 1977b). The young Benjamin (and the Romantics before him) used theological notions in this eminently secular context. Unlike in theological revelation, being would lie in the essence of language, or the object, itself.

Benjamin's notion of the object undergoes a sea change in his work just before the *Origins of German Tragic Drama*. Before he spoke as if the object was alive, filled with spirit through which the magical could be retrieved. Now his object is killed: the world of objects becomes a dead world. Language can no longer be revelatory. Benjamin begins in his later work to understand modernity as a world of dead objects. In this the comparisons with Weber multiply – there is the crucial importance of the Reformation. In the *Ursprung des deutschen Trauerspiels*, it is thus the two-world cosmology of the Lutheran Reformation that holds the key to the deadening of the object and the secular world altogether. Previously Catholicism had provided for generous doses of spirit in nature, through its symbolism, ritual and doctrine of good works. With Luther's asceticism and the dismissal of the importance of good works for salvation, the secular world is denied of spirit. It becomes the barren landscape in front of which German baroque drama found its context. This dualism is reinforced by the triumph of absolutism. The world becomes a dead landscape; nature is deprived of spirit; history becomes meaningless. All aesthetics, whether of beauty or the sublime, becomes impossible (Benjamin, 1963: 36). Art can no longer be a pathway to freedom through a glass darkly in the beautiful, or through the overwhelming of the senses in the sublime. The senses in the baroque and for the nineteenth century Paris *flâneur* cannot be overwhelmed. The baroque attitude – whether in the seventeenth century or in nineteenth century *raison baroque* (Buci-Glucksmann) – is *blasé*. Spain's baroque courtier and *fin de siècle* Vienna's urban *flâneur* is neurasthenic. His nerves are shot. He cannot be overwhelmed by the sublime. With freedom fully displaced into the transcendental world, the beautiful too is impossible.

This leaves space for the mature Benjamin's aesthetics of allegory. This is his famous landscape of the melancholic, wandering among the dead objects, among the ruins, experiencing an entirely other sensibility. The younger Benjamin could logically have few complaints about the classical theory of 'symbol' and 'allegory', defined by Goethe in response to Schiller and preserved in its essentials by Schelling. Here 'symbol' is understood very much along the lines of Kant's aesthetics of the beautiful, in which a content is expressed in a form (*in der Sprache*). In contrast, allegory is didactic, like Kantian determinate judgement; like predicative utterances. Here a content is designated through language or through a form. But Benjamin in the *Trauerspiel* book noted that in the Renaissance the notion of allegory was changing. That allegory too was not necessarily didactic or determinate, that in allegory too the content was present in the form. The point was – in Renaissance and baroque allegory – there was something *dead* about the content. There was something like the masque of death in the ornamentation of the form. What kind of object is at stake here? In ancient times, paradigmatic for symbol was classical sculpture; for allegory the legends of Homer's epics and the emblems of Egyptian hieroglyphics. Renaissance/ Baroque allegory was exemplified in Albrecht Dürer's emblematic engravings. Whereas symbol operates in the register of metaphor, emblems and hieroglyphs (and *Trauerspiel*) work metonymically (Benjamin, 1977b: 167). The content of *Trauerspiel* was not myth (as in symbol) but history: dead and secular history, often set in Far Eastern or Byzantine courts. The form was heavily rule-bound (i.e. not free), and tended towards the ornamental.

In Baudelaire's nineteenth century, it was no longer Luther's Protestant ethic but the commodity that left in its wake a world of dead objects: old books, disused household objects, the rubble of deserted urban housing and the like.[5] The allegorist was to concern him (her)self not with the commodity itself, but with the detritus of the commodity, with twice dead objects, with their trace. The allegorist was to be concerned with their history, deprived of spirit, revelation and meaning. The allegorist's real object was dead nature. Thus Benjamin preferred Baudelaire to Mallarmé's symbolism. Benjamin saw himself, as Menninghaus (1980: 137) notes, as moving to a position of a *'dialectische Verschränkung'* from his previous idealism, and towards a dialectical materialism. The young Benjamin had followed in the footsteps of Goethe and the Romantics, starting from Kantian freedom, or existential meaning and looking for this through a glass darkly in the aesthetic object. The later Benjamin began as a materialist from the commodity, or from the traces of disused and discarded commodities, and from this material basis in the object looked allegorically for 'superstructures' of meaning. Thus the later Benjamin too practised a hermeneutics of retrieval: only retrieval was of the irretrievable, because already dead. The later Benjamin thus proffers a horizon, a ground, a world in which we are to think and live: but it is an enucleated horizon, a groundless ground, a desolate world.

Conclusions

The theory of reflexivity has it seems a case of cultural amnesia. The theory of reflexive modernization has forgotten the object. The theory's core concept of unintended consequences does, however, lay open space for a sociology of the object: for a sociology of the object that escapes largely the grasp of the reflexive subject. I have attempted to lay bare the bones of such a notion of the object in this chapter. We have seen with Latour that once reflexivity becomes not cognitive monitoring, but a more analogical process of judgement and interpretation that the object comes to gain substantial autonomy. We have seen, again with Latour, how the object itself can become reflexive: itself judging, weaving morphisms, interpreting and transmitting in the production of knowledge and the time–space extension of signatures of knowledge. These objects are different than 'discourse'. They are a matter not of words but things. The same is true of Virilio's objects, whether the hard projectiles of an earlier modernity or the signals, the 'phatic images', as characteristic objects of the contemporary information age. Latour versus Virilio is in an important sense a repetition of the old Habermas–Foucault debates, only displaced from the realm of language to the register of the object. Latour finds emancipation, or at least the freedom of innovation, not in discursively redeemable validity claims, but in objects. Virilio finds surveillance and governmentality, not in discourses, but again in first material and then informational things. Latour and Virilio are not structuralists, in the sense of salience of either social or linguistic structures. Thus the irrelevance in their work of the question of structure versus agency, for it is the objects that become structure, that possess agency.

The consequences of reflexivity then are quasi-objects, bad objects and dead objects. The unintended consequences of reflexive modernity are monsters, dangers and death. The theory of reflexive modernity may seem new. But, as Jonatas Ferreira (1997) has noted, it stands in an old sociological and cultural-theoretical tradition of the question of what Max Weber called theodicy: of how we account symbolically for suffering and especially for death. For my money it surely is no answer to try to subsume this under reflexive calculation and monitoring of dangers and 'bads', even when we see these as uncontrollable outcomes. The theory of reflexive modernity transforms (and reduces) the question of theodicy and death into a question of risks and dangers. These are reduced to a set of calculable or incalculable entities, of what can and cannot be accounted for through reflexive monitoring. Thus reflexivity theory can account for the accumulation of bads, the stockpiling of bads to go along with the stockpiling and accumulation of (informational) goods. And indeed the two leading post-industrial economic sectors are the 'chip sector' and a 'risk sector': the first, computers, semi-conductors, software, telecommunications, dealing with the accumulation of goods, and the second, bio-technology, health, insurance, sports and leisure, genetic technology, with the accumulation of (capital and of) bads. But can death and suffering be treated in the language of accumulation and calculative prediction of unintended consequences? *The* Enlightenment might tell us to treat death and suffering like this, but enlightenment tells us we cannot. We inhabit perhaps the dead, cold and deserted territory of Benjamin's melancholic, both desolate and dry according to the classical doctrine of the humours. We may be fated, in both Benjamin's and Freud's senses, to be the melancholics of the information age, irretrievably in search of the lost object, whether mother, nature or being. But as vulnerable and wounded bodies, as melancholics, we must try once again to cart the generations of our dead and bury them outside of the city gates.

Notes

1 See Chapter 11.

2 Latour (1993) will be designated as NM (*Never Modern*) henceforth in citations.

3 In the context of this book, I would argue with Latour and Virilio that if the axial principle of manufacturing society is accumulation, then that of the information society is *circulation*.

4 But see the fascinating *amor fati*, Nietzschean, reading of Benjamin in Howard Caygill's *Walter Benjamin: The Colour of Experience* (1998).

5 This bears comparison with Koolhaas's (2001) notion of 'junkspace'.

6

Media Theory

The Strong Programme in the sociology of science holds that for a theory to be valid it must be reflexive (Barnes et al., 1996). That is, it must be applicable to itself. In Chapter 5 we just saw how reflexive and information-rich knowledge had as its unintended consequences an out-of-control object. This poses questions about theory itself. Does it not follow that theory itself would be an unruly object? Ideal-typical for such unruly objects in the contemporary era is not industrial goods, but information and communication products. In other words, ideal-typical for such contingent circulating objects are, in a very important sense, *media*. It follows thus that social and cultural theory would increasingly take on the form of *media theory*. If critique can be no longer transcendental, but must be immanent to the information order, the critique of information becomes, increasingly, media theory. What follows, in a context in which both critique and reflection are in perhaps terminal decline, are some critical reflections on what such a media theory might be.

Media Society, Media Theory

What this chapter intends to do is explore the idea of 'media theory'. This chapter will explore not the social theory of the media, nor cultural theory of the media, but *media theory*. What I will suggest below is that media theory is the paradigmatic form of thinking in today's global information society. What I will suggest is that the media give the model, establish the paradigm for information in today's world. More specifically, we will see below that the mass media of communication, which preceded the computer age by a great number of decades, already established a paradigm for the information age: a model that only has much more recently, with its mass pervasion through explicitly information technology, achieved hegemony. I want to suggest that in this sense the information society is just as much and perhaps more accurately labelled the 'media society'.[1] What I will finally suggest is that sociocultural theory itself at the turn of the twenty-first century increasingly must take on the form of information, increasingly take on the form of media. Please note once more that I am not saying that social and cultural theory need to be increasingly about the media, or that they need to focus on the media as an object of research. But instead that theory will be increasingly in the same genre as information, as media. There are two parallel arguments in this chapter. They are that both society and theory are coming increasingly under the spell of the paradigm of media. The argument is that the cultural paradigm, through which the mass media work, is one of not narrative, nor discourse, nor representation but instead *information*. It is that both society and theory are becoming in important respects more informational. It is finally that this informational model was established not by computing but by the mass media themselves.

Mark Poster's *Second Media Age* (1995) interestingly and paradoxically makes the point that the first media age already established the basic model of the media for the 'second media age' as well. Hence there would be no need to call the contemporary era the second media age, but only the age in which the principle of information established by the mass media beginning a century ago has now become predominant. There have been mass media for a long time, but the media age only becomes established with the convergence of media, computing and telecommunications. Jean Baudrillard (1978) signalled the idea that 'the social' was becoming increasingly absorbed in the 'mediascape' in the late nineteen seventies. I began to understand this in terms of the 'machinic' nature of the media much more recently in reading Paul Virilio's work.[2] I became aware of the informational nature of the media through encounters with Walter Benjamin and especially Marshall McLuhan. Finally, empirical research into the movements of global cultural products and the multimedia sector in London has convinced me of the extent to which the media have taken on the character of objects, of technologies.[3]

Yet probably the leading international social theorist of the media has explicitly rejected 'media theory' for a social or sociological theory of the media (Thompson, 1995). By 'media theory' Thompson seems to be referring in the general direction of Marshall McLuhan. There are a number of northern European electronic journals dedicated to 'mediatheory', resolutely joining the two words as if they were one (for example, http://www.inode.at/hipe/mediatheory/). These journals' influences are most obviously the work of Virilio and McLuhan. There will be substantial discussion of McLuhanite themes in what follows, and especially his ideas on temporality. McLuhan has strongly influenced Leon Rosetta's *Wired* and Nicholas Negroponte (1995) in *Being Digital*. Negroponte and Rosetta understand the information age not at all in terms primarily of technology. They do not deal thus with the hardware and more structural and fundamental software issues that have engaged computer science and much of microelectronics. Their focus is instead on the interface, less on production than consumption, as much on communication as information, as much on content as technology. Rosetta and Negroponte have been fascinated by the marriage of content, technology and marketing. Their vision features the centrality of lifestyle, the importance of space. It is an architectural vision. The very fact that MIT chose to call their research centre The *Media* Lab speaks volumes for the understanding of the information age as a media age. What I want to call 'media theory' has a lot to do with all of the above.

Media theory is only possible in an age in which social and cultural life has been pervaded by the media. Here what was once 'society' is just as much media as it is society. And what was once 'culture' is again just as much media as culture. Hence what once was the Heritage Secretary in Britain is now the Secretary for Culture, Media and Sport. Media theory can be seen as stealthily yet surely displacing both social and cultural theory. This can only have been the case in the past decade or two. But I suppose only in the course of the new millennium will social and cultural theory predominantly become media theory. What media here means is not just the 'electronic media of communication'. It is a much wider category. Media theory would not, for instance, make a lot of sense without the spread of computing (information), the Internet (communication), the coming to a position of prominence of the culture industries, again in the broadest sense; and the proliferation of fast-moving consumer goods, of the global brands. It is all of these that make our society and culture a media society and a media culture.

What is a Medium? Instrumentality and Finality

Media theory must necessarily ask the question, what is a medium? It cannot accept however the argument that a medium is first and foremost a 'means'. This idea of medium as means is very often found in sociological and critical theories of the media. Here the media are seen often as commodified, as exchange values, and in this sense 'means' or 'instruments' that serve the interests of the accumulation of capital. On this view the media are weapons of bourgeois ideology through which the dominant classes can enforce a system of beliefs on the subordinate social classes that will reinforce the domination of the dominant classes. In this sense the media are also understood as means or instruments. *Cultural* theory, for its part – in the tradition of Continental philosophy – tends to draw either directly or indirectly on Kant's Third Critique, *The Critique of Judgement* (1952) to understand what a medium is. *The Critique of Judgement* contrasted two types of judgement: 'determinate judgement' and 'reflective judgement'. When confronted with an object, nature or a work of art, that is, when confronted with a medium, we may judge it 'determinately'. Here the judgement is *determined* in that it comes under a pre-given rule. The object or medium, however, is also 'determined', in the sense of being a means to an other, external end. The object or medium here is an instrument, an 'instrumentality'. We may, on the other hand, judge an object, nature or work of art (i.e. a medium) in a 'reflective' manner. Here the judgement is not determined by a pre-given rule, but must find its own rule. To the extent that the medium (or object or work of art) entails that judgement find its own rule, it too is undetermined. It is indeterminate. As indeterminate, it cannot be used as a means or instrument. In its very indetermination it becomes very much an end in itself. It becomes not an instrumentality, but instead what Kant called a 'finality'. It becomes a *'Zweckmäßigkeit ohne Zweck'*, a finality without an external end. Thus an object or a medium may be on the one hand an instrumentality, a means to an end or, on the other hand, a finality.[4]

Kant's dualism of instrumentality versus finality was to bequeath a considerable legacy. This legacy has dominated social theory. It is the basis of Marx's counterposition of use-value and exchange value. Exchange value – or the commodity – is an instrumentality. Use-value is an end in itself: it is a finality. It informs Max Weber's counterposition of *zweckrational* and *wertrational* social action. Here *zweckrational* action has a means–ends rationality, and *wertrational* action has a rationality governed not by means but by ultimate values. It informs the Critical Theory of the Frankfurt School. Thus Theodor Adorno contrasts the instrumental rationality of 'identity thinking', with the critique of his negative dialectic, based on an idea of finality. Thus Jürgen Habermas contrasts strategic action with communicative action. In each case a given content is either an instrument, a means to an end, or it is a finality, somehow authentic, an end in itself. This same juxtaposition is found in cultural theory. Here 'the same' (i.e. instrumentality) must be deconstructed to lay open its determinacy and hence its finality. This is central both to Jacques Derrida's idea of *différance* and to Martin Heidegger's thinking about technology. For both Derrida and Heidegger, the deconstruction or destruction of determinate reason or 'instrumentality' opens up an indeterminacy that once again can raise the question of existential meaning, of the meaning of being.

But 'media theory' disputes this Kantian juxtaposition of both social and cultural theory, of both critical theory and post-structuralism. Media theory is impossible in an age of such binaries. Critical theory and post-structuralism had the most important purchase on sociocultural life previously. But the rise of the information order, of the media society, explodes the binaries, explodes the 'difference' between instrumentality and finality. It explodes this previous transcendence into a more general immanence, an indifference of information and communication flows. Information and communication are neither instrumentalities nor finalities: information and communication build networks, they make connections. Information and communications are now – in what is no longer an industrial society, but now primarily a media society – prior to both instrumentality and finality. Information and communications are the material, the new and third nature of the global information society.

Machines

Media only reach maturity with the emergence and pervasion of *information-machines*. The information machine is a combination of content and technology: information refers to the content and machine to the technology. Television is the first information machine. In this sense television is no different than a computer. The personal computer is an interactive information machine, permitting interactivity with both content and other users. Information is one among many types of cultural content. Information is one among many types of material culture. Information is distinguished from other cultural contents through its duration, its temporality. It is thus distinguishable from other cultural entities that have different temporalities, and different spatial extensions. Information is not narrative, not discourse, not the novel, not cinema, not poetry, not architecture, not art, not artefact. Though of all of these it has most in common with architecture, and the artefact (design).

Television is of course not the first *culture*-machine. Radio precedes it. So does the phonograph, telegraph and telephone. Cinema and photography involve culture-machines, but not information machines. Cinema and the phonograph operate in the realm of representation. They present something not new but old, from the past. Hence they *re*-present it. They operate from a temporality of either narrative or stanzas, movements, codas, allegro and the like. But their particular content is not information. The telegraph is an information machine, a textual information machine. Telephones are phonic interactive information machines. But television, with the introduction of the visual alongside sound and moving images, and its chronic persistence in real time (with now 'no time out') sets the paradigm (Boden and Molotch, 1994). Television's characteristic content is information: the news, sporting events, soap operas, comedy. These, like other sorts of information, decline quickly in value after they are transmitted. They take place more or less in real time. Television broadcasts other sorts of non-informational content, especially film and drama. But to the extent that these are on television they tend to lose their characteristic narrative form and take on an informational dimension. A movie like *Lethal Weapon 4* is more informational than say a film by Kurosawa. It is viewable through not the concentrated 'gaze', but through the 'glance' under conditions of distraction. And a made-for-TV movie is even more informational than *Lethal Weapon 4*.

The mass media consist always of modes of information and modes of dissemination: of both the machines that disseminate the content of the media and that content itself. The media also are the content produced by these machines. Yet the idea of content falls a bit short. Surely it is information, or 'bits' of culture that are produced by these machines. Narrative and the picture-plane of the painting are clearly content. In contrast, information partly eludes distinctions of form and content, or technology and content. The technology–content distinction does reiterate the old form–content distinction, from both classical and modern philosophy. This comes from Aristotle's notion of final and material causes. For the ancients a material content is worked upon by form to provide a new content. This is true also today. Only now the sculptor who is forming content is not God but technology.

The media are about communication at a distance. John B. Thompson (1990) has written with insight about this. The face to face, that is, communication-in-proximity, is progressively displaced by communication-at-a-distance. This in German television is called *Fernsehen*, 'far seeing'. One literally sees far when one watches television. In this sense the TV is a bit of a 'space-machine', a machine that allows you to see far away into space. When coupled with video recorder, video-on-demand and multichannel viewing, broadcasting playing a great deal of very old content, it is a time machine. A telephone is thus too for 'far-talking'. Tele-scope, tele-vision, tele-phone. Is a newspaper for 'far-*reading*'? Tele-text literally is. The difference is that you do not need to operate a machine to obtain information content through the newspaper. You do for tele-text and information sites on the Internet. For example, the CNN site is one of the world's predominant sites with the greatest quantity of content and frequency of visits. A newspaper is a paper that carries new information. A news station is a station that broadcasts new information. A news network broadcasts new information much wider. This is also the spatial element of the media. You need machines to communicate at a distance. In this sense telephone and television are fully fledged information and communication machines. The telephone at least once carried solely sound information.

The post, i.e. 'snail mail', does carry mainly information, that is, not normally narrative or discourse or art. It carries considerable image information as well as textual information. It also carries material objects and money transfers. Yet the post, unlike the newspaper, is interactive, with the increments of interactivity being not immediate or several hours apart (like telephone, fax or email), but normally three days to a week. The newspaper is not interactive. The post carries content but produce none. It is thus not a medium. It is a means of circulation. This is not entirely true because letters are textual media and they are inseparable from the post. Like the newspaper, the post is not machinic in the sense that you do not need to operate a machine to receive it. Like other informational media, the post and newspaper come to you instead of you going to it as you do in many more 'serious' forms of culture. Post and newspaper circulate or disseminate not through information machines (like telephone, television, Internet) but through the more manufacturing era transport machines – trucks, planes, trains and vans. Machines produce newspapers but the latter are not machines. They do not somehow self-disseminate as does telephone or television or the CNN or *Guardian* website. For these you do not need vehicles. Email in this sense, and in comparison with tele-text, is an interactive narrowcast text machine. In each case the content is the message. This is an informational content. This is one fruitful way of understanding McLuhan's dictum. For McLuhan the old medium was the novel or poem and the new one the newspaper, television and radio. The media thus had changed. Previously the media's content was narrative or lyric and surely a 'deep meaning'. It surely was not a *message*. Only with the new mass media is the content the message. Only then is the content information. This is just as valid in the computer age as it was when McLuhan was writing. The message is the byte or bit of information. The question is whether this new content, that is, information or the message, can yield existential meanings, as once did epic poems or novels. If there is no transcendental level any more, then clearly it cannot. Or perhaps it can yield existential meaning only as memory for a lost object, only in a melancholic mode.[5]

The media are machine-like in another way. They are machinic in the way that they descend, so to speak, into the world. Poems, novels, cinema, paintings, like ancient ritual, have always existed in a separate world than the everyday world: in a world of, if you like, 'the sacred' in comparison to 'the profane' of everyday life. As the media descend into the world they become 'technologies'. The old 'auratic', in Walter Benjamin's sense, media – ritual, poetry, art, the novel – were encountered in the world of the 'sacred' as representations. The mass media and the new media are encountered in the everyday world of the profane no longer as representations, but as *technologies*. Representations are encountered as an audience, as a spectator, as a reader or viewer. Technologies are encountered as 'users'. They do not have to be literally machines. Fast-moving consumer goods, brands like Nike, Swatch, McDonald's, are also now 'information' and we encountered them in the world of the profane as in some sense users. We do not encounter them as representations. We encounter them not just as information but also as communications, as messages. We surely do not encounter them primarily as narratives. We consume them as we receive them in a mode not of 'contemplation' but of 'distraction'. In this sense too these new media are machine-like or machinic. We encounter branded products through machines – TV, Internet; in machines, as we drive through neon and billboard brand environments; or on the way to machines, in, for example, airport concourses.

Traditionally we had, as I mentioned, media of representation. Partly because something that was already present was somehow – more or less realistically – depicted or re-presented. The mass media and new media are instead media of not representation but of *pre*sentation. Once you went to a bookshop or library or concert or art gallery and reflected in a time specially devoted to the medium. You reflected on the medium of representation. But the newer media of presentation come to you. They turn up in your house and present themselves. They work unconsciously and preconsciously. You don't even expect them or even necessarily invite them. You may not trust the papers but you *read* the papers. They turn up in your house in real time, not in 'time out'. In time out you go to the movies or book shop. The media come to you in 'time in'. And often they will not turn off, will not stop producing and delivering messages to your house, presenting messages in very close to real time. Representation itself was a reflective process. It took time. Presentation, under time and budget constraints, is more machinic, more factory-like than representation. In that, you went to the old media; the newer media come to you, they are also machinic. They are either delivered by a transport machine or directly disseminated through an information machine. Production, dissemination and reception are either, really or metaphorically, machinic (Silverstone and Hirsch, 1992).

Duration, Information

The cultural contents produced by the media machines are characterized by their ephemeral nature, by their relentless, non-stop, real-time circulation. This is true even when the informational media is dialogic and interactive, whether this is interactive mass media, from the one to the many, or one to one communication of telephone, Internet and fax (Boden and Molotch, 1994). It is indeed the *content* of the information media that is ephemeral – whether in newspapers, on television, the Internet, telephony, or the branded products of fast-moving consumer goods. What are the units of culture that they produce? There is a literature that attempts to understand the nature of cultural objects. The sociology of science has referred to the nature of a large range of such objects as 'artefacts' (Latour and Woolgar, 1979). But are these particular cultural objects *'artefacts'*? Their duration is briefer than that of artefacts. Artefacts are the kinds of things found in *Kunstgewerbe* (Handi-crafts) museums. They are intended for immediate use but may endure a very long time. They provide a window of sorts onto an entire culture, an entire way of life. The units of culture that the media machines produce tend less to be a window on a form of life, than lifted out and abstracted from any given form of life.

Anthropologists such as Kopytoff and Appadurai have understood cultural objects in terms of on the one hand 'commodities' and the other 'singulari-ties' (Appadurai, 1986). In many ways this distinction runs parallel to the distinction of exchange value and use-value. The content of the media machines, however, does not in the first instance come under either category. The content of the media machines is neither artefact, nor art, nor singular-ity, nor commodity, nor narrative nor discourse, but *information* itself. This content must be understood in terms of the very specific nature of what con-stitutes information. Perhaps the major distinction between, in McLuhan's sense, 'old media' (painting, cinema, novels, lyric and epic poems, sym-phonies, philosophy, science, even tribal rituals) and new media (from tele-graph through newspapers, television and Internet) lies in the duration of the former in contrast to the ephemerality of the latter. Thus there are long- and short-duration cultural entities. Long-duration forms include narrative, lyric, pictorial, discursive – while the short duration entities can most of all be understood under the rubric of 'information'. That is why I would refer to such modern media, not as 'mass media of communication', because they are often not mass but one to one or they narrowcast instead of broadcast. Nor would I call them electronic media: because they are often pre-electronic – the newspaper – or micro-electronic. But they are all informational. They contain the information society in germ.

Information, as I argued above, is not primarily an instrumentality or a commodity. Exchange-value or commodities have a certain future-value, a value for a future exchange. For their part use-values have enduring value and a past. But this sort of 'information-value', which I think may make sense to call 'sign-value', has value only immediately and for a very short period of time (Baudrillard, 1981). Sign-value is not primarily concerned with social status, but with the ephemerality of the value of signs, as well as their relentless, no-time-out ubiquity. This short duration culture started of course with the newspaper. It printed *news*. Why call it 'news'? Because it was new. When it was old it lost value. Newspapers are connected with time, with instantaneity of a sort. Hence in French they are a *jour*-nal, in Germany a *Zeit*ung. It always has to do with news, with what is new. Informational content thus not only does not endure, but is constantly new. Indeed the content is *so* new that there is no time for re-presentation as in the cinema or novel or theatre. There is no time to take what Husserl called the 'reflective attitude'. The reflective attitude always needed to operate on an experience, on an event in the past. The newspaper must operate instead in the *natural* attitude. But in a natural attitude deprived of memory, deprived of history, without the 'long intersubjectivity' that Schutz, Gadamer and Ricoeur wrote about.

Whereas all of the old media operate in a time of representation, the new media work in the register of *presentation*: presenting in a brutal manner, without interpretation, without even ideology – at least in the pure form of information. There are to be sure conventions and protocols for information production, whether for the nine o'clock news, a televised sports event or broadcast political meeting. But these are protocols, methods for presentation, not representation. They do comprise a certain 'framing' of presentation. They are a selection of the signals we receive. But again, very much in the present. Hence the French *'nouvelles'* for the TV news, and the German *'Nachrichten'*. *Nachrichten* means not just the TV news it also means message. One leaves a *Nachricht* on a telephone answering machine. And the message is a unit of information – it is a unit of neither narrative nor discourse, but a unit of information. This information is valid, has value for a day. Some newspapers are *Wochenzeitungen*. They last a week. Magazines last a week or a month (*Zeitschrift*). Some, like soccer programmes, are collected. Intellectual work in comparison to journalism is not just 'higher level'. It lasts longer. It aspires to and achieves a comparative timelessness.

Journalists run on a vastly different time scale than do scientists. Academics, novelists, those working in 'culture', are about the *longue durée*. Even the 'shock of the new' type work of a Duchamp, a Bunuel lasts fifty, a hundred years.[6] A book, an academic book can last ten to fifteen years. It can take four years to write. Research grants are for two to three years. What a different time scale journalists operate on. As does the entertainment industry. What an extraordinary set of – time and budget – constraints they work under. In this sense they *are* an 'industry', a 'culture industry'. They are industrial in being machinic. Information and entertainment are different from representational culture in that they immediately lose value. They are immediately forgettable. Georg Simmel's Jew was here today and stayed tomorrow. Media event-like communications are here today, *gone* tomorrow. Along with fast-moving consumer goods, they are *communications*. Communications are event-like. Novels, films, books are not communications. Communications do not last.

Marshall McLuhan's (1997: 1–6) academic background was in literary studies: in discursive, literary studies. He was supposed to work in the medium of discourse. The object of his medium (which was discourse) was other media – the novel, theatre, poetry. McLuhan began later to write not in discursive form on the mass media of communication, but instead in the form of bytes of information, indeed in messages. Discourse does not work through messages, but through more serious speech acts, through propositions, statements, organized in frameworks of concepts supported by legitimating argument. The informational media – television, newspapers and digital media – for its part, works not through discourse. It has no time for discoursing. It must go directly to press 30 minutes after the event. It must produce that television broadcast tonight or at least this week. Newspapers and other informational media make you believe what they say not through logical argument but through the brute facticity of their messages. You read them, having just woken up, in the morning paper at the breakfast table; or hear them while attending to the baby, on the six o'clock evening news; or listen to them struggling through a traffic jam on the way to work, on the car radio. You receive them under conditions of distraction, and not under the conditions of reflection necessary for engaging with discursive argument. Discursive media, like the academic article or book, work through reflection and argument. The informational media work through the brute symbolic violence of the fact. McLuhan himself forsook discourse to write in what was effectively media theory, in which a 'mediatic' – that is, from the informational media – form takes itself as object. Nicholas Negroponte works similarly. Discursive books in sociology and cultural studies, about for instance, social change and globalization, are not *per se* communications. My discursive book also re-presents. It draws on information from archives, dead information that no one else is interested in, and re-presents it. It needs reflective readers. Communications, for their part, operate with a sort of immediacy. No reflection is called for on the part of the reader or receiver. Indeed reflection is impossible for the latter. Media theory is not about 'auratic' media, not about long-duration representations, but mainly about media whose content is information or messages, that is about short-duration presentations. It works through a form that is the same as its object. Theory *per se* must work through discourse. Media theory changes this.

The old yet still modern media – novels, (social-) scientific texts, paintings, films, concertos – were effective at a spatial distance, yet offered time for reflection on the part of producer and receiver. They compress space yet relax and extend time. The *really* old, ancient media, say the use of rhetoric in political life in the polis or the storyteller or epic poet wandering from town to town, work at spatial proximity and offer time for reflection for producer and receiver. They relax both time and space. The informational media on the other hand work at a great distance. They work through the commutation of distance. But they work in a temporal immediacy. They work over great distances in nearly no time at all. This is the great paradox of the informational media. While they mediate great spatial distances, they are so immediate, they leave no time for meaningful mediation. In this sense it is not nonsense to speak of the 'mass *im*media of communication'.

Conclusions

The reader might justifiably ask, where does all of this leave the question of power? The question of power has persistently been posed in terms of instrumental versus substantive rationality; in terms of exchange-value (the commodity) versus use-value. It has been posed in terms of strategic rationality versus communicative rationality. In terms of an audience who could be 'dominated' or 'resistant' to the output of the media. If all of these differences are exploded in the global information culture, then where does this leave power? Some, like Baudrillard, might argue that we should 'forget Foucault', we should forget the question of power. That power is also swallowed up in this implosion into a generalized informational indifference. I disagree. What is more likely is that power is elsewhere. Power is no longer so much something that takes place between elements in the system, between capitalists and proletarians, but instead has to do with *exclusion* from the system. Both from the loops of information and communication flows. And from the society itself, as both underclass are excluded and 'overclass' self-exclude with their private police, private schools, private pensions and private health insurance (Hutton, 1998). Power may be less defined by real property in the means of production. Instead, with shorter and shorter runs of an ever-wider variety of (design-intensive) material and informational products, power becomes a question of *intellectual* property – of patent, trademark and copyright (Lury, 1993: Luke, 1995). If real property power in the means of production brought workers inside to be dominated by capital in relations of production, then intellectual property uses its power to exclude, through the standard in operating system software, in, for example, digital satellite television.

In any event, in order to have 'media theory' there must first be an 'information society'. The information society is not primarily a society in which the production of information displaces the production of goods. It is also not primarily a society in which knowledge or information becomes the most important factor of production. It is instead an order in which the principle of 'society' becomes displaced by the principle of 'information'. An order in which sociality becomes displaced by a certain 'informationality'. Sociality is long-lasting and proximal. Informationality is of short duration and at a distance. Hence fast-moving consumer goods, the quick cutting and mix and match of dance music, 30-second TV ads and quickly decomposing installation art are as informational as database files, J-Pegs and attached text files and software. Social relations themselves are becoming less a question of sociality than informationality. Again, at a distance, short duration and presentational rather than representational. Erotic email exchanges are presentational in comparison to representational romantic love letters. The gift reflected over for a long time is replaced by the quick direct-delivered electronic order. Fast-moving consumer goods are not a lot different than a downloaded QuickTime video from a soft porn website. They come to you. They last but a few days. They come from a distance, lifted out from ongoing forms of life. They are produced and received in immediacy, with little time for reflection at all. When informationality replaces sociality as the dominant principle there is the information society. The great contradiction of the information society is that what is produced with the highest knowledge and rationality as factor of production, in its unintended consequences leads to the pervasion and overload of the utmost (also informational) irrationality. At issue indeed is the *desinformierte Informationsgesellschaft* (disinformed information society).

'Media theory' for its part emerges when the principle of information, which is also that – as I have argued above – of 'media', becomes so predominant as to engulf the realm of theory too. As society becomes increasingly like information, theory becomes increasingly like media. Jacques Derrida argued, closer towards the middle than towards the end of the last century, that *'il n'y a pas un dehors du texte'*, or words to that effect. He was right. The principle of the text, with its readers, even its polysemy and deferred meaning, was at that point in time a structuring principle to a very wide gamut of cultural experience. At that point even the information of the media came more or less under the textual principle, a principle of representation, reflection, production and reception. But at the turn of the twenty-first century the informational principle reigns. Now the text – and theory – become just another, though no doubt with specific difference, variety of information.[7]

The domination of the text took place in the age of representation. Media theory emerges in an age in which culture is no longer primarily experienced as representation. In the era of representation culture was a separate sphere, the media constituted a separate sphere, which could be isolated from social as well as economic life. At that point in time, social theory could explain and cultural theory could interpret the media. It is only when the media so to speak 'descend' from their separate realm into the heart of the social, when the cultural superstructure to which the media belong become part and parcel of the economic base, that we can speak of media theory. It is only now that media theory comes to displace both social and cultural theory. Media theory neither explains nor interprets the media. Media theory explodes the binary opposition between explanation and interpretation. Media theory indeed resembles the media more than it resembles either explanation or interpretation. In the new set of arrangements, media are no longer 'texts' or narratives or pictorial representations, and the receivers no longer 'readers', 'spectators', viewers or audience. They are instead primarily *users*. At the same time the media become no longer representations, but things, technologies. Theories and texts now become no longer representation, but technologies themselves. Texts and theory become objects in today's generalized global networks of flow and dispersion of the whole variety of objects. Only these texts, these theories are a bit longer lasting than the other circulating objects. Their principle is one of just another mediating object. There may not be a lot of choice. In an age in which transcendence and the text are increasingly eroded, in an age in which academics increasingly must perform on time and under budget, we must all perhaps, for better though probably for worse, be media theorists. Media theory may constitutively be a contradiction in terms. But it is perhaps at the same time our fate in the global information order.

Notes

1 See Kellner (1994).

2 See Chapter 5.

3 See Lash, Lury, Boden and Shapiro, *Global Culture Industry: The Mediation of Things* (2002).

4 I develop this argument at much greater length in Chapter 7 of my *Another Modernity, A Different Rationality* (1999).

5 See Chapter 5.

6 Marcel Duchamp is arguably the father of the information culture. His conceptual art is the original 'media theory'. Yet the objects of his work incorporated at the same time ephemerality and duration. His notion of the idea is the immanent contradiction of media theory.

7 Hence publishers now talk about books and journals in terms of information storage.

Part Two: critique

7

Critique and Sociality: Revisiting the Theory of the Sign

In Chapters 5 and 6 we focused on the nature of the information order. We looked at the emerging central and unpredictable place of the object and at the transformed position of the media and media theory in the information culture. We now change registers and begin to address the issue of critique. We do this in this chapter through considerations of the *sign*. Let us ask what sort of signifying practices can constitute critique. How do we signify differently now than we did in the past? How do forms and ways of signification change as we move from a national manufacturing society to a global informational culture? In this new world order, the principle of the nation is being superseded by the global, the multicultural and the intercultural. The manufacturing economy is being replaced by the information economy. Finally, society – or the social – is being displaced by the rise of the cultural. Power has always operated also through knowledge, also through modes of signification, but we want now to explore how power operates differently through different sorts of signification in the new world order. In this chapter we want to consider how power operates through an ethos of 'productionism' and the constitution of self-enclosed subjects.

Paul Ricoeur (1981) has suggested that we are, at one and the same time, comprised of two sorts of subjectivity: on the one hand, a subject that essentially 'produces'; on the other, one that basically 'receives'. The 'productionist' subject is the speaking subject, the receiving subject listens. The producing subject is self-enclosed, the receiving subject is open. The producing subject is transcendental, the receiving subject is immanent or in-the-world. The producing subject works in the logic of predicative statements, the receiving subject operates analogically. This critique of productionism is implicit in Jean Luc Nancy's (1991) *Inoperative Community*. The original French title of this is *La Communauté désouvrée*, literally the 'unworked community' or better, the community in which the principle of work (production) is dismantled. Here the 'worked' or productionist community is composed of self-identical and self-enclosed subjects. Nancy's example is the Communist Party. Through work the lack, the absence of individual and collective subjects is, so to speak, sutured or sealed off. The *communauté désouvrée* is no longer a work or *œuvre*; it reverses this and opens up subjectivity.

Subjectivity and community become less an *oeuvre* than open and contingent. The inoperative community is a community of subjects who are not self-identical, but self-different. There is finally a critique of productionism in Bataille (1991). Here a principle of production (and reproduction) is involved in the calculated logic of the restricted economy; while consumption, indeed consumption as agon or contest, invokes the 'excess' of the general economy.

This productionism and constitution of self-enclosed subjects arguably originates and predominates in the national manufacturing society. It is, in important respects, driven to its furthest extremes in the global information culture (Virilio, 1997). If this is true, then where do we look for a way out, a chance for escape from this predicament? I want to argue in this chapter that we cannot find it in a political semiotics of 'difference'. I think instead what is needed is a break with representational modes of signification for non-representational, dialogic modes. I think this has to do with the reconstruction of value and not its deconstruction and final disappearance. It has to do with a break in our mode of existing as subjects that are self-enclosed, monologically representing and 'productionist'. It has to do instead with the constitution of a self that is not self-enclosed, but open; a self involved less in monological *representation* than dialogical *presentation*, and whose sensibility is not primarily productionist, but receptionist. I want to argue that this would entail a certain distancing from the notion and ethos of 'difference', that has perhaps become too important a source of the contemporary self. We should replace this, I will suggest, with a political semiotics of '*sociality*'. I will argue that this is possible even at the heart of today's informational order. At stake thus is a critique of information that is rooted in not difference, but sociality. In this chapter I want first to reflect on how we signify in a transformed way in an era of the sign. At one point in time, signs (and media) pointed to referents, were means to ends and designated meaning. Now the sign or the medium is at the same time referent, end and meaning. I want to reflect on the possible 'productionism' this brings along with it. I will argue that elements of such productionism are also implicit in Derrida's idea of *différance*. I will propose sociality as an alternative mode of critique.

The Sign (Medium): Referent, End and Meaning

Marshall McLuhan was prescient and, at the same time, vague in his dictum that the 'medium is the message'. Let us explore the ramifications of this dictum as a way into considerations of power and the sign in today's global informational order. In this chapter I want to understand 'the medium is the message' in three ways. First, the medium is the referent. Here the message is understood as the object of attention, the object that we are working with. Here previously the object was the commodity or capital, now it is the medium. Second, it can mean the medium is the end. Message here can designate end or ends. So the medium which was previously only a means, only an instrument, has now become the ends, now become the finality, now become the categorical. On this second reading the medium becomes that to which ultimate value is attached. The third reading is the most common one: namely that the medium is the meaning. Let us address these three dimensions of the medium in more detail.

Medium as Referent

What happens when the medium replaces the manufactured and industrial commodity as the main object produced in today's capitalism? First, there is a major shift in ownership of the referent. McLuhan, as Umberto Eco (1990) noted, spoke of the media, the medium, rather vaguely, in a sense that encompassed without distinction the signal or object, the code, and the channels of communication. And what then is the medium? To what extent is TV the sign and to what extent is TV the space in which signs flow? It could be both. It could be both the signs and the space. Ownership and power comes with ownership both of the signs and the space. Tim Luke (1995) has referred to the ownership of mediatic space as 'hyper real estate'. We rent time in such mediatic space. We rent this hyper real estate for periods of time from the owners. Commodity sellers rent the usage of space from the owners of hyper real estate. They pay for it in line with the value of the intellectual property (itself partly a factor of the number of viewers it can attract and the spending power these viewers have) that is occupying this time. Owners of mediatic space themselves compete for the intellectual property (TV series, football broadcasting rights, exclusive rights to movies) that attracts the well-off masses, so they can get commodity sellers to pay them high rents.

Luke observes that in the modern industrial order of nation-states, in the national order, nation-states entered into struggle for legal ownership of real estate. But in the post-national global and informational order, capital is strengthened in regard to the national state, as communications capitalists (and not primarily nations) struggle for ownership and control of not real but hyper real estate. In the traditional order prior to the rise of the autonomous subject, there was no object (in the sense of separate and counterposed to the subject), there was no referent in our sense of the word. There is instead tradition, forms of life, symbolic exchange. Capitalism and the modern world system of nation-states are accompanied by the rise of the autonomous subject. Only now there is the creation of the real – as epistemological or aesthetic object, as the industrial commodity.[1] This is Luke's 'real estate' that became problematized by the modern world system of nations. In each case there are struggles over the real – epistemological, aesthetic, class struggles and struggles (wars) between nation-states. Now that the medium, and no longer the industrial product is the referent, the hyperreal becomes the object of knowledge and work. It becomes the object of aesthetics and politics. This entails battles over the channels, fibreoptics, the air waves, i.e. for ownership of hyper real estate. This has been a major determinant of power in the entertainment industry. At centre stage are ownership struggles over intellectual property (Lury, 1993). More generally, in today's age of rapid innovation what counts is not so much property, but intellectual property. Power lies not so much in the possession of the bulk or weight of assets. Now power lies importantly in the ownership of the proto-type: in owning the patent or copyright of the prototype. Owning machines that make CDs is not as important as owning exclusive rights to market the latest Spice Girls album. You need to own the prototype or 'model' that can generate five million CDs. This, which used to be central only to the entertainment industry, is now the norm in any information-rich sector, in the economies cutting-edge sectors, microelectronics and biotechnology. The more that consumption is specialized, the more competition becomes a question of the generation of new prototypes. And the more the issue of intellectual property prevails over that of property.

The question in the age of the 'information highway' is, first, who owns the information, or the signs, and second who owns the highway. In the Fordist economy, we had competition and economies of scale. Now there are primarily economies of scope. This means that competition puts the primary focus on product innovation, and on obtaining intellectual property rights (patent, copyright) to those innovated products. Intellectual property rights are very much about the future in the sense that property rights bear the heaviness of the present. This may be one reason for the central importance of market capitalization in today's new sectors. Property rights (assets) of the older Fordist sectors have a lot less to do with the value of a company (in market capitalization) than do intellectual property rights. Property is in the present. Intellectual property is in the future. To have intellectual pro-perty rights in media content (the signs) is important. But the highway itself is as importantly a question now of intellectual property rights. Operating system software, for example, is part of the highway, part of the mediatic space and not the content. The same is true of Internet routers and inter-active television platforms. The highway, for example, broadband cable con-nections or the 3G mobile phone spectrum, is importantly a matter of property, but is also a matter centrally of intellectual property.

What are the implications for technology in an era in which the medium is the referent? It is fruitful to consider this in the context of Heidegger's 'Ques-tion Concerning Technology' (1977). In 'Die Frage nach der Technik' Heidegger looks at the 'essence of technology' in regard to what he calls *Bestand*, or stand-ing reserve. A *Bestand* is not an object that we encounter, notes Heidegger, but instead objects that are held in reserve in order to do something else. Heidegger's *Bestand* has a lot in common with Marxian capital in the form of accumulated means of production (see Heidegger, 1994: 20). Indeed it makes sense perhaps to conceive of the principle of industrial capitalism in terms of such a standing reserve, of such an accumulation of means of production. In the information age, however, technology would seem rather to involve the accumulation of software,[2] of means of production of *signs*. In the information age, old and disused stockpiles of accumulated means of production are transformed into heritage museums. Whilst the new stockpiled sign-generators become the dominant form of technology.

But what was it that formed this *Bestand*, this stockpile in Heidegger's '*Frage nach der Technik*'? The unit of the *Bestand* was, as we noted in Chapter 3, the *Gestell*, or 'frame' (1994: 23). The similarity with Marx's abstract units of value is striking. Concrete objects become frames or *Gestellen* as part of the standing reserve. It makes sense to understand what I have called pro-duct*ionism* in terms of *Gestell*. Heidegger goes on to discuss *Gestell*, as we noted, in the context of its root: of (1) *bestellen* (ordering), where at the same time the *Gestell* or frame imparts a different sort of ordering; (2) *vorstellen* (representing); (3) *herstellen* (manufacturing). This makes sense not only in a manufacturing economy, but also in the informational or semiotic economy. It makes sense for the economy of signs. It makes sense in an economy in which it is intellectual property that becomes the guiding principle. If previously technology as both framing and standing reserve, as both ordering and accu-mulating, came under the sign of capital, now it comes (whilst still under the sign of capital) under the sign of the sign. Now it is a productionism of signs, an ordering of signs, ordering here as both purchasing and framing. But there is also a rapid turnover of signs. Former accumulations or stockpiles of signs quickly become junkpiles. Such junkpiles are usually forgotten. Sometimes, however, as found objects or retrieved objects they find their way into our contemporary art and heritage museums.

Medium as End

The medium is the message can mean the medium as the ends, that is, no longer the means but the ends. There is in fact a second order instrumental rationality involved in the semiotic economy, where ultimate ends can often be found in sign-accumulations. We now live in an order that is doubly instru-mentally rational. In the traditional order, the good life was the end and manu-facturing, i.e. the transformation of nature, the means. In the traditional order thus *goods* were the means to the ends of the good life. In industrial society there is a first order instrumental rationality. What previously was the means, that is, manufacturing and goods, become the ends. In the modern and indus-trial order the instrument (industrial capital) becomes the end. In the indus-trial order there were a set of new means dedicated to these ends. The new means to such accumulation of industrial capital as material means of produc-tion were, on the one hand, the informational and symbolic labour of clerks, bankers, professional engineers and the like and, on the other, ideology. That is, ideology – as a superstructure – functioned as means to the end of the accu-mulation of industrial capital. But now, as Eco observes, information itself 'becomes the merchandise'. Now the industrial manufacturing sectors function for the reproduction of the *informational* sectors of the economy. Moreover, ideology, previously a means for the accumulation of capital, now becomes itself an end. Daniel Bell's (2000) *End of Ideology* written four decades ago could not have been more prescient. We are indeed in an age of the end of ideology, which is at the same time the age of *the ends as ideology*. Thus ideo-logy as information is the end, is what is accumulated in the semiotic and global order. This is, to be sure, still, indeed more than ever, capitalism, but capital itself has taken the form of ideology, of information.

In the industrial order ultimate values – what Max Weber (1980: 12) called value-rationality or *Wertrationalität* – *are* the instruments, *are* the means, are not the good life, but the goods. In the industrial order, value detaches from the good life and re-attaches to goods. It detaches from forms of life and re-attaches to substances. Value thus inheres no longer in forms of life, but in empty substance in goods, in exchange-value. Exchange-value is empty or even procedural (that is, it contains no notion of the good, or the good life) in that its basis is in abstract subjectivity. Exchange-value has its basis in the subjectivity of rational choice and preference schedules on the market place. Karl Marx himself distinguished between the work process (*Arbeitsprozess*) and the production process.[3] The production process only took place under the sign of capital, as variable capital (labour power) was combined with constant capital to produce surplus-value. The work process is a different kettle of fish. The work process makes *use-values*. And use-value has nothing to do with utilitarianism or with marginal utility. Use-values have nothing to do with any utilitarian calculus of how we would rate, how a transcendental and aggregated subject would rate, would prefer, would rank on a preference schedule, how much a good, a substance, a being (*Seiende*), a thing was worth. Use-value should be understood in the sense of the German *Gebrauchswert*. Here we see the root – the substantive *Brauche* – which means, as Weber (1980: 14) noted, usage, the integration of a good into a set of ready-to-hand activities, a set of usages. The good is inseparable from the activities, rather than an abstract value attached through aggregated preference schedules to a thing. In *Gebrauchswert* is also the verb *brauchen*, that is, to need. And work activities as distinct from the act of production have to do with systems of needs.

There is only disembedded and – as Marx says, 'abstract' (in that it is abstracted from activities) – value when value becomes a property of the commodity. Now value is abstracted to become forms of capital. Hence he speaks of exchange-value, of surplus-value, of value itself as 'congealed homogenous labour power'. Things only have abstract value as forms of capital. If there is no capital, then there is no value for Marx in the sense of the labour theory of value. The point is that once things come under the sign of capital, value in the meaningful sense of values is destroyed. What there is instead is exchange-value, capital-value, the value of constant capital, fixed capital, money-capital, circulating capital and the like. The domination of the abstract sign of capital, the productionism of capital reduces all sorts of heterogeneity to the value-form. And the value-form, which is abstract value, destroys and negates value as inscribed in forms of life, in activities, in practices. This is only exacerbated, while still under the sign of capital, when accumulation informationalizes and comes under no longer just the sign of capital, but the sign of the sign. 'Sign-value', like exchange-value and surplus-value, has more to do with the absence of value.[4]

In the traditional order, work was connected to the system of needs (*Brauchen*), and needs – though symbolically coded according to social standing – were part and parcel of what it meant to lead the good life, both when working and not working. In the manufacturing order, interests replace these needs: either individual interests or the collective interests of class versus class. In either case, empty utilitarian calculations displace embedded processes of symbolic exchange. The lifting of value from forms of life and its re-attachment as properties of substances under the sign of capital, is at the same time the shift from system of needs to system of interests. This is paralleled outside of the economy, where again value is destroyed. Value is then relocated in the abstract subject as the empty and procedural norms of the social – in institutional, juridical and political spheres – within which we are to choose, as if from 'off the shelf', the sort of good life (now become lifestyle) we want. Consider, for example, modern versus ancient constitutions: the procedural nature of the former and the notions of the good life that inform the latter. Or modern legal positivism versus pre-modern natural law. In the social-institutional, juridical and political spheres of modernity norms are procedural, abstract and monological. Consider, for example, how the notion of society changed, in the shift from pre-national community to national 'imagined community'. Such modern and imagined communities break with the dialogism of real communities, as Benedict Anderson (1989) argues, in their inscription in abstract time, abstract space and the abstract rendering of sociality as 'the social'.

In the shift to the contemporary and even more abstract semiotic order, even the hollowed out value of the social norm is displaced by the anti-institutional kitsch innovation of contemporary lifestyles and niche marketing. In the semiotic order, the semblance of value-grounding of even these procedural norms is abandoned for the 'anything goes'. Value is once again relocated, from the commodity to the sign itself, which quickly proliferates and loses its value in the era of junk email and digital satellite television. The shift from needs to interests presumes the rise of the self-enclosed subject, who in the semiotic order de-sublimates to become the self-interest and self-identity of the narcissistic and self-enclosed *body*. The forms of life of the traditional order, already reworked under the sign of capital into the interests and struggles of proletariat and bourgeoisie, now turn into the proliferation not of forms of life, but of lifestyles, which apparently one can 'get'. 'Get a life.' 'Get a lifestyle.' Lifestyles – today's abstracted forms of life – come under the sign of the sign in the global and semiotic order.

Medium as Meaning

If at one time the message or the *meaning* inhered in the symbolic exchange of forms of life; then in the manufacturing order, capital and production(ism) itself become the message, become the meaning, become the phenomenon, relegating forms of life to the periphery or interstices of the system. In the semiotic order this essence, this meaning, under the sign of the sign, and the even more autonomous anything-goes subject, is itself dismantled. Yet this remains quite productionist either as the libidinal productions of desiring-machines or as deconstruction's detoured production of meaning via the detours of the sign and temporality. But which of Charles Sauders Peirce's three types of signification seems to be occurring in the global semiotic order? Is it symbolic? Is it iconic? Is it indexical? Perhaps at one time symbolic representation via the printed word dominated, to be replaced by the iconic (through resemblance), though already partly indexical representation of the cinema and photography to be displaced by the indexical representation of the signal. Of the three, the signal or indexical signification is to the greatest extent 'motivated' by its object. A baby's cry from the next room is a signal. So is the sound of a crack when your ankle breaks when you have just been tackled by an aggressive midfielder. Somewhat less motivated because detachable (yet still largely indexical), is the photograph in its capacity as imprint or trace, or the Egyptian death mask (Barthes, 1993).[5] This is the most immediate and highly motivated form of representation. The sports, the news on television, the sending of electronic messages, playing computer games is signification via signal, and may be more or less indexical. When you watch a football match on television, the sort of signification that is going on is neither predominantly symbolic nor iconic, but instead indexical through the signal. Indexical signification often tends quickly to lose its value. There is an immediacy to its temporality. It quickly loses value as intellectual property. Consider, for example, the value of (iconic/symbolic) popular film for TV as intellectual property. But who will pay anything for yesterday's football match (you know how it resulted)? Or yesterday's nine o'clock news? Yet there is an extended temporality to indexical signification itself. A temporality approaching real time. It is the least representational of all of these three modes of representation, in terms of having less fixity in time and partaking more in the 'becoming' of real time. For example, television's gloss on the Gulf War largely took place in real time, whereas the War in Vietnam was often reported a day later. Thus the ideological in the media's relation to the war in Vietnam becomes the hyperreal in its relation to the Gulf War.

Difference

Derrida: Difference as Delayed Reduction

The notion of difference has been central to radical identity politics today. Perhaps the canonical text inscribing the theory of difference in the notion of the sign is Derrida's *Voix et phenomène* (1976). In *Speech and Phenomenon*, Derrida speaks effectively of three types of signification – they are more or less parallel to the three Peircean types. But for Derrida they are understood as phonic, visual and tactile. Like the Peircean types, Derrida's also are in descending order of mediation. That is, 'phonic', like symbolic signification is the most highly mediated form; visual representation like iconic is less mediated; whilst tactile (like indexical) signification is the least mediated, most immediate form of representation.[6] Derrida's notion of *différance* is developed via privileging the tactile against phonic and visual. It proceeds via his critique of Husserl's phenomenological reduction. Derrida addresses the reduction as a critique of Husserl's theory of the sign. Husserl understands the sign in terms both of expression (*Ausdruck*) and indication (*Anzeichen*). Indication refers to the temporal, accidental features of the sign, to its materiality, whereas expression is how the sign functions in the phenomenological reduction to intuit the essences of ideal objects. Meaning is constituted for Husserl only when the transcendental ego abstracts from indication and the sign functions only in its capacity as expression. Derrida's (1976: 59) argument is that the element of indication in the sign is *ir*reducible. Through that element of indication the sign takes on its polyvocality; through indication (cf. index) difference is achieved. What pure expression does, argues Derrida, is to deny the materiality of the sign: it reduces the sign itself to a pure (and 'transcendental') signified. Derrida insists instead on *différance*. He insists thus that meaning is to be achieved only via the detour of both the sign and temporality.

What Derrida is ostensibly involved in here is a critique of the 'productionism' in Husserl. Such productionism is also the problematique of the self-enclosed subject, to whose demolition Derrida has consecrated a whole succession of books. The critique of Western metaphysics and the problematique of the subject – from Heidegger through Adorno to contemporary post-structuralism – has *eo ipso* been a critique of productionism and the self-enclosed subject. There is thus the anti-productionism of Horkheimer and Adorno (1997) in *Dialectic of Enlightenment*, in which the rational Western subject turns on itself in a malicious twist of the dialectic – and in its aggressive search for identity negates and destroys the world as it attempts to know it. Here the autonomous subject, set loose by the Enlightenment, destroys the alterity of inner, outer and social nature by its attempts to assimilate all of this to the identity of the subject itself. This anti-humanistic reign of the self-enclosed, self-present and self-sufficient subject once again surfaces in the work of Husserl. Husserl was arguably *the* main influence on such thinker as Heidegger, Max Scheler, Gadamer, Schutz, Derrida, Ricoeur and Levinas. He broke with the Enlightenment tradition, leading the way beyond Kant's assumptions that the only way in which we could know things was through the naturalistic categories of physics and mathematics. Husserl instead proffered the possibility that we could know things in themselves. For Husserl we could know things, not according to the categorial structures of the natural sciences, but according to their own categorial structures. We (the transcendental ego) could intuit the essences of objects, could know the categorial structures of objects.

In penetrating to noumena, or things themselves, Husserl's ego had to be transcendental to Kantian assumptions of finitude. In penetrating to the core of, not the limits of the Kantian understanding (*Verstand*), but the Ideas of Reason – of noumena, God, freedom and infinity – Husserl's ego had to take on a certain infinitude; a certain infinitude in the face of the flux of empirical experience. Only then could phenomena, could meaning be constituted. This is the context of Husserl's notion of the sign. It is productionist. It is more productionist than the subject-object naturalism of Kant. With Husserl, not just objects suitable for study by the natural sciences, but *all* sorts of ideal objects could be known through their production as essences, through their constitution as essences by transcendental subjectivity. Derrida and other post-Husserlians such as Levinas are critical of this because it assumes the *self*-presence of subjectivity. Derrida here is not so much against what he calls the 'metaphysics of presence' as against what amounts to a metaphysics of *self*-presence. The sign we recall is comprised for Husserl of 'indication' and 'expression'. Derrida is critical of Husserl for foregrounding expression at the expense of indication. This foregrounding of expression, for Derrida, entails that not just the sign, but also the world of everyday objects and events are negated. What is left more or less is the pure meaning of the transcendental subject; the pure transparent signified. Any alterity of, not just the sign, but the world, is negated; any impurities due to temporality and material accident are brushed away. The presence of the sign and the world do not matter. What matters is the self-presence of the self-enclosed subject. What counts is the reduction, carrying out the constitution of essences.

Let us look a little closer at what Derrida does. Derrida does not *per se* disagree with Husserl's intentions. He does not disagree with the intention of constituting meaning through the transcendental reduction. Derrida's theory of signification, it seems to me, is based on a certain variant of the phenomenological reduction. It is based on a sort of reduction that takes, as it were, a double detour. It takes a detour that is at the same time semiotic and temporal. In other words, Derrida's phenomenological reduction takes place through difference, through semio-temporal difference. Derrida restores the temporality that Husserl's reduction brackets. This is in the constant temporal delaying or deferral of meaning in *différance*. Second, the materiality of the sign itself is a second detour between expression and the achievement of meaning. Derrida proposes a notion of the sign as a limit that joins on the one hand expression and on the other indication. This limit, which is difference itself, is prior to – and the condition of possibility of – both expression and indication. Like Levinas (1973), Derrida agrees with Husserl's critique of Kant in which the aim now becomes knowledge of things themselves. For both Levinas and Derrida there is the necessary assumption of a meaning-constituting entity that is somehow beyond finitude as conventionally conceived. This effectively infinite subject has knowledge of things via the semio-temporal detour. In this sense Derrida fundamentally agrees with Husserl's productionist assumptions. The theory of difference, via what is clearly a detour of radical alterity, contains its own dimension of productionism.

Intersubjectivity: Against Technik and Transcendental Subjects

Derrida, in his theory of the sign, like Husserl, is sceptical of inter-subjectivity. Husserl, as has often been noted, ran into insurmountable obstacles in the Cartesian Meditations when he attempted to address intersubjectivity. Inter-subjectivity, in this context, is the problem of how one experiencing trans-cendental ego can know another such ego. How can one transcendental subject constitute the essence of another transcendentally reducing subject? Husserl (1987: 91 ff.) addresses it as 'transcendental intersubjectivity'. These are not empirical, naturally occurring individuals, but transcendental egos involved in constituting phenomena. Husserl tried to grasp such intersubjec-tivity on the basis of analogy. But it would seem that without any materiality of 'aspects' or 'impressions' to work from that it would be impossible to con-stitute pure spatio-temporally unchanging phenomena. Derrida, at least in his work on the sign, and in many other of his texts often ignores intersubjec-tivity. Heidegger at least broke with Husserlian infinity by locating Dasein as eminently finite and in the world. But even Heidegger, like Derrida, presumes with Husserl that the key relationship is between the subject and things (or Technik), and avoids largely the problem of intersubjectivity, the problem of what might be called 'sociality'. The politics of difference more generally posits the unknowability of the other. Such a politics too often leads to look-ing at the other as abstract difference. This would seem to be a problem in the ethics of Immanuel Levinas. In Levinas's intersubjectivity, it is impossible to recognize the other. The other, like the text, is to be left by us – in its unrecognizable alterity. The unknowable other would seem to share charac-teristics with the self-enclosed subject that we addressed above.

What is needed is perhaps an alternative regime of signification. What is needed perhaps is a paradigm of signification based on a rejection of infinity – a rejection of the transcendental or reflective attitude – for what Husserl called the natural attitude. This Heidegger already did in his depar-ture from Husserl, which is why Heidegger's theory of the sign through the notion of 'Zeigen' in Being and Time remains so vital. Alfred Schutz and Hans-Georg Gadamer also followed this move from transcendental pheno-menology to life-world phenomenology. They, in contrast to Heidegger, made this move with a focus on intersubjectivity – on recognition, sociality and dialogue. At stake here is not the more transcendental intersubjectivity of Habermas's ideal speech situation. Nor is it the abstract inter-subjectivity of Levinas's and Martin Buber's (1974) 'Ich und Du'. For Gadamer and for Schutz intersubjectivity is made possible only when ego comes to know or understand the background assumptions, the prejudices (in Gadamer's sense) of the other. In Habermas like in Levinas there are instead two monological subjects. Recognition is impossible. Habermas's focus on the recognition of validity to speech acts is not the same thing as recognition of the other; its focus is not on the emergent understanding of the horizon of the other. Recognition, understanding and hence intersubjectivity cannot take place in the disembedded condition of the reflective attitude. Either you move into the natural attitude, or intersubjectivity is impossible. Transcendental (and productivist) putative intersubjectivity is only the isolated and separated single subjectivities of two self-enclosed subjects. Recognition is impossible. Transcendental intersubjectivity is a contradiction in terms. Either you have transcendence, or you have intersubjectivity.[7] You can't have both.

Sociality

Presentation: Against Representation

So what sort of theory of the image, what sort of theory of signification, does this entail? First, it presumes the finitude of the subject, the shift into the natural attitude. Second, it presumes the importance of not just subject and text, but intersubjectivity, or sociality. It also presumes *presentation* and not representation. This notion of 'presentation' is taken from Gadamer's *Wahrheit und Methode* (1990: 116 ff.). In this he contrasts presentation (*Darstellung*) with representation (*Vorstellung*). Here representation involves a representing subjectivity, externalizing his or her subjectivity as representations. In presentation meaning is not created by a disembedded and individualized subject, but inheres in situated ongoing practices or activities. In presentation the aesthetic is not a property of a subject to be externalized in art but instead inseparable from the *Sittlichkeit*, and the *Sitten* (or habits) of the community. What counts in presentation is not the contingency, the *tabula rasa* of immediate experience or *Erlebnis*. It is instead *Erfahrung*, in which experiences are neither immediate nor there to be ascribed meaning via the transcendental reduction. In *Erfahrung* experiences are never immediate but ever already mediated through tradition, memory and practice.

In presentation aesthetic experience stands out from the flux of signifiers, of impressions, not because it is the expression of the interiority of a creative and self-enclosed subject: it stands out from the flux because of its relevance to the *Erfahrung*, the background assumptions, the prejudices of everyday life. Gadamer (1990: 107) likens presentation (*Vorstellung*) to play. When children play, they are acting, but they are not representing. There is none of the fixity of the signifier that is involved in representation. Representation is by definition monological; it is the fixed creation of a subject. Presentation, like play, is dialogical, in that it opens up and involves the playing off against one another of playmates. When a jazz band improvises it is like play. So is football when it's working, when a team is really knocking the ball around, creating openings, running off the ball, moving into space. For the musician and the football player both play not out of the highly reflexive aesthetic 'speech acts' of a disembedded subjectivity (representation), but instead unreflectively, from *Erfahrung*, from the habitus, from the natural attitude. Once they move into the reflective attitude, it becomes stultified, the dialogic breaks down, the play breaks down, the opposition catches you on the break; the audience walks out of the club.

Paul Gilroy (1993) in *The Black Atlantic* speaks of emancipation not via the ideal speech situation but through the aesthetic creation – through black music – of an inter-ethnic, inter-cultural, indeed 'black Atlantic' public sphere. This takes place not through any transcendental aesthetic subjectivity, not again through representation, but through presentation, which he understands as 'performance'. Here he draws on Benjamin's invocation of the storyteller. The storyteller is prior to symbolic (phonic), iconic (visual) and indexical (tactile) signification, both historically and so to speak ontologically. The storyteller partakes of oral culture, of the give and take of dialogism. Gilroy likens this dialogism to the give and take of jazz improvisation, in which each musician plays off the other, indeed tries to outdo the other as one solo succeeds the next. This open-endedness of such an agon of performance and performativity stands in contrast to the logic of fixed and monological representation. In this symbolic exchange of gift giving, each musician competes with the next by making the most lavish gifts, by making gifts that challenge the possibility of any counter-prestation or counter-gift.

Reception and the Vulnerable Body

This dialogism, this displacement of abstract and monological 'difference' by the performativity of sociality, presumes no longer the self-enclosed subject. The self-enclosed subject, as transcendental ego, yields a productionism of meaning, homologous to the productionism of the commodity. In both there is technology both as *Gestell* (or frame), and as standing reserve or accumulation. In the economy, capital imposes a frame on the variety and situatedness of work life; in knowledge, the phenomenological reduction imposes a frame in its constitution of essences. There is equally an accumulation of, on the one hand, capital and, on the other (via the intuition of essences), knowledge. But, as suggested above, a different sort of meaning may be constituted if the subject is conceived in bodily form. This has a more prominent aesthetic dimension. Its mode of production is, to a greater degree, bodily. It is not the phonic or discursive meaning of the cognizing, 'egological' subject, but instead tactile, visual, indexical meaning.[8] But even this second subject may be self-enclosed, even its tactile, its figural aesthetics is productionist and monological. An aesthetics, less of difference than of sociality would depend not on closed subjects or bodies, but the open body, on signification through not production but primarily reception.

Philosophical anthropology, especially in the work of Arnold Gehlen (1962), has noted that unlike animals, 'man' is characterized by an *Instinktarmut*, a poverty of instincts and hence an 'unfinished body'. This unfinishedness, this opening where the instincts are missing, only becomes finished or completed by institutions. Gehlen worried that in the age of technology, with the decline of these institutions, a sort of anarchy would result. This was his explanation of the Third Reich. Given the weakness of such institutions in the information age, there are two possibilities – and this has been well grasped by Jacques Lacan. The first is that the unfinished body, the lack, i 'sutured' by the imaginary or the symbolic (or even the 'indexical'). Today it is not traditional institutions, but the self that is carrying out this suturing. That is, the self-enclosed subject does the work of completion and enclosure itself. The second possibility is the refusal of self-completion. It is the consequent opening of the body, recognition of the lack, as the body descends from a subject position into the humanness and brutality of the world. This openness is also an openness to pain (Scarry, 1987). Now deprived of imaginary or symbolic suturing, the body is exposed to the real, not as disembedded referent or object, but as the threat of ready-to-hand beings in the world. This reception aesthetics of the open body has less to do with speaking than with listening. Here we encounter the meaning of objects not through their phenomenological reduction but through openness to their *Sprachmagie*, to their magical speech (Menninghaus, 1980).[9] Now there is a new kind of truth. A truth that couldn't be further from Mannheim's view of the stranger, the Jew as the *freischwebende* intellectual without roots, who could assume an unbiased subject position, whose standpoint was above all standpoints. But perhaps the yid, the nigger, the queer is less able than the full *indigène* to suture over his/her unfinished body? Perhaps their singular perspectives on truth, on the real – is due instead to a total *in*ability to achieve the free-floating subject position: is due to vulnerability to pogrom, lynching, betrayal or murder.

Notes

1 Baudrillard in *Simulacra and Simulation* (1994a), it seems to me, uses the idea of medium as referent in the sense of both industrial manufactured real product and the real object of subject-object epistemologies.

2 I am indebted to Nigel Thrift on this point.

3 The work process here makes things but is not 'productionist'. Perhaps the idea of value as inhering in the practices of a work process which is not a production process may have something to say to the practices of artists and designers.

4 But compare Boltanski and Thevenot (1991). Their *économies de la grandeur* are economies of value. Their book is itself a justification for a plurality of value-orders. See Girard and Stark (2001).

5 See discussion of this in Lury (1997).

6 Note however that both the Peircean and Derridean types work metaphorically. That is, painting, design, the novel, cinema, the pop song etc. can represent either via symbol (phonic), icon (the visual) or index (the tactile). For me, Derrida's notion of difference *is différance*. The more sophisticated literature in cultural studies understands difference as *différance*.

7 I am not being entirely fair to Derrida in this criticism. This book, *Critique of Information*, does not have a strong theory of intersubjectivity: its focus is information, communications, objects, machines, flows. Further, Derrida does develop the intersubjective dimension in his work on friendship. My book is the weaker for its absence of focus on intersubjectivity. In this chapter and the next I wanted to point to the relative weakness of the intersubjective dimension in texts pivotal to in Derrida's original development of the idea of 'difference'. I am thankful to Mark Poster for these points.

8 Levinas often uses the term 'egological'.

9 Walter Benjamin understood this not through the constructionism of symbol but instead through the 'wound' of baroque allegory.

8

Tradition and the Limits of Difference

A number of different thinkers across a spectrum of disciplines have maintained either implicitly or explicitly that we live in a more or less fully post-traditional order. Thus sociologists such as Ulrich Beck and Anthony Giddens suggest that we live in an age of 'reflexive modernity' in which the last traditional vestiges of an earlier simple modernity have reflectively been eliminated (Beck et al., 1994). Philosophers such as John Rawls and Jürgen Habermas have proposed a rational ethical order in which all talk of values, all talk of traditions is either systematically set aside for a focus on procedures and constitutionalism. Thus neo-classical, social-democratic and Marxist economics have conceived the individual as a rational-choosing, tradition-free agent possessed with preference schedules and 'interests' on the marketplace. Thus a great number of architects and planners have forsaken history, place and meaning for the sake of doctrines in which the only meaning that counts lies in the form-and-function-making practices of the architects themselves. The assumption here is very much of a piece with Max Weber's famous pronouncements on the ethics of responsibility in a culture in which rationalization had systematically, and one by one, eliminated the traces of tradition in each of the contemporary life orders.

Another group of thinkers has aspired to 'deconstruct' these notions of rationality of their predecessors. Yet in doing so they have not in any sense taken seriously or even re-problematized the issue of tradition, but have pushed the destruction of tradition even further. The rationalism of Marxist and capitalist neo-classical economics had already understood embedded economic practices of making and using things to be superseded by the fully de-traditionalized exchange-value of the commodity. But this second group proffer an even more thorough dismantling of tradition and de-territorialize even the commodity in the favour of the anarchistic practices of the libidinal economy. If the Freudian unconscious is already de-traditionalized in the eroding of symbolic exchange in favour of the abstract forces and relations of drives and the Oedipus, then its subsequent deconstruction renders even the symbolic order of the unconscious placeless, without a home, with no possible ground (Baudrillard, 1994b). Deconstruction in architecture, for its part, appears to be restoring a place for tradition in its allusions to classical, gothic, Romanesque and even Eastern sources. Yet these remain the allusions of a playful and formalist bricolage, without genuine history, meaning, value or content. In short, without *tradition*.

This deconstructive fragmentation of the self and hypostatization of the other constitute core, if unspoken, assumptions in contemporary cinema, pop music and magazines. But contemporary culture is marked by such a 'metaphysics of difference' in not just its leisure pursuits, but in its ethics, in its politics of everyday life. Thus the identity politics of feminism, anti-racism, gay politics and ecological movements, are much more at home in the language of alterity, deconstruction of the subject, the critique of logo-centrism, than they are in the language of democratic interest aggregation and construction of a rational social order. If 1968 opened up the flood-gates for such a politics of expression and fragmentation in the West, then 1989 did so in the East. But the demise of Marxism and the Berlin Wall ushered in not primarily a reassertion of the Enlightenment's as yet unrealized project, but instead the proliferation of the vastest and wildest iterations of – intellectual, subcultural and national – alterity. And in the 1990s in the South (and the South in the West) as well, discourses of modernization and uneven accumulation are progressively displaced by the deconstructive language of hybridity, diaspora and post-colonialism (Laclau, 1990, 1994).

What, however, is meant in this context by 'difference', the pivotal concept for such an ethics, a politics of deconstruction? Difference has very little to do with the value pluralism of liberalism. This is underscored by Homi K. Bhabha (1990) in his development of an analytic distinction between 'diversity' and difference. *Diversity* on this view has to do with the subject-object type thinking of the Enlightenment and liberal thought. Diversity presumes an Archimedean point (subject), outside of the 'world' (object) from which the variance of lifestyles and properties of persons and groups in the world can be categorized. Difference in contradistinction, notes Bhabha, presumes a radical alterity, one in which the other cannot be judged, cate-gorized and pigeonholed by the same. To be in the position of Archimedean point *vis-à-vis* the other is not to respect the other. Difference thus denies the existence of such an Archimedean point as well as 'our' capabilities of knowledge of the other. Difference is a politics leaving a third space, a space reducible neither to subject nor object, universal nor particular – a space open to the radical alterity of the other.

So far so good. But a contemporary radical political culture cannot have its core assumptions only in ideas and practices of difference. It must just as much have its basis in the thought and practice of *solidarity*. That is, soli-darity is as crucial in any reconstructed radical contemporary political culture as difference. At issue here is in the first instance solidarity within 'the same'. It would seem that abstract collective interests – as liberalism and Marxism presuppose – are not a sufficient basis for collective action, for soli-darity. That is, not common interests, but shared practices, shared meanings and shared traditions constitute solidarity. Solidarity is based on value, and the core values of deconstruction, as of liberalism, do not concern so much the revaluation, but instead the irrelevance of values. Thus shared under-standings, a genuine intersubjectivity, and shared – albeit often invented – traditions are a basis of solidarity within a collectivity of individuals sharing roughly similar properties. But tradition is also important for solidarity with the other. Difference is insufficient. There must also be *recognition*.

And recognition presupposes not just blind alterity but understanding, a sufficiently 'deep' intersubjectivity, and some sort of shared tradition.

What I want to suggest in this chapter is that it is no accident that the politics of difference, no more than Marxism or contemporary 'third way' politics, is weak when it comes to solidarity and tradition. I will argue that this absence of tradition is central to fundamental philosophical assumptions of the politics of difference. I want to argue that this is because the notion of difference, at its core, excludes any coherent notion of *intersubjectivity*. Although deconstruction does speak the idiom of 'same' and 'other', of the 'I' and the 'Thou', I shall claim that its fundamental assumptions are not of intersubjectivity, not of Same and Other, but the same and text, not the 'I' and the 'Thou' but the 'I' and the 'It'. I want to challenge these assumptions where they are intellectually strongest – in Derrida, Heidegger and Levinas. All three of these writers begin from a heterodox phenomenology, from a disagreement with Husserl. Husserl spoke of the counterposition of the reflective and natural attitude. His phenomenology was based on the constitution of meaning from the reflective attitude. All three of these thinkers – Heidegger, Levinas and Derrida – turn the tables on Husserl and deconstruct the reflective attitude in favour of the natural attitude. The problem is that none of their versions of deconstruction gives space for intersubjectivity within this natural attitude. Thus their notions of difference lack tradition and exclude the possibility of solidarity.

Deconstruction: Phenomenology versus Finitude

Let us consider in more depth what Jacques Derrida has meant by *'différance'*. There have in the Anglo-Saxon world in fact been two waves of reception of Derrida. The first, in spanning the late nineteen seventies and eighties, took place primarily in literary criticism and the study of modern languages. Here Derrida was understood as a post-structuralist, who deconstructed crucially the structuralism of Saussurean linguistics. Here, for Saussure, meaning was a matter not of the relation of signifier to signified, but of the difference among signifiers in a *langue*. Derrida followed Saussure's structuralism this far. He was characteristically *post*-structuralist in deconstructing the distinction between langue and parole. Difference became then not just a question of the 'spatial' relations among signifiers, but took on a temporal dimension. *Ecriture* or writing, displacing the *langue–parole* distinction, took on not the synchronic and static character of *langue*, but the diachronic and temporal character of *parole*. And in *écriture*, meaning as the differential and spatial relation among signifiers became also always temporally postponed. Because of the temporal non-contiguity of signified and signifier, meaning is constantly alluded to but never quite achieved.

Critical literary theory derived a lot of mileage from this idea of *différance*.[1] The fundamental point of reference however, as second wave

Derrideans (mainly philosophers) have understood, is not Saussure, but Husserl. Derrida was not trained as a linguist or in literary studies but as a philosopher. For some fifteen years, in his twenties and his early thirties, he was primarily a Husserl scholar. His concept of language comes from Husserl and not Saussure. It has more to do with the notions of language involved in logic, and especially in Frege, than in linguistics or literary theory. Although heavily influenced by Heidegger, Derrida, unlike Levinas (1973), does not give us a primarily 'ontological' reading of Husserl. He focuses, unlike Levinas, not on a possible notion of Being, nor on the undermining of positivism and naturalism in Husserl, but instead on Husserl's theory of the sign. Readings of Husserl can be divided into 'ontological' and 'logical'. Heidegger, for example, and the phenomenological sociologist Max Scheler as well as Levinas proffer an ontological reading of Husserl (see Srubar, 1988). Derrida, however, like other French theorists such as Ricoeur, as well as most Anglo-Saxon philosophers, give us a reading as much in the context of logic as ontology.[2]

Derrida's (1978a) initial breakthrough, in his mid-thirties, into the non-specialist literature was via his critique of structuralism in a book edited by Jean Piaget.[3] Here he criticized the notion of 'finite totality' – shared by Saussure, Levi-Strauss and, for that matter, Althusser – presumed in the idea of 'structure'. In structuralism, the relation between elements of such a finite totality, or system, determine the place of various instances of the system as well as the value of statements and meanings. For Derrida, Husserl's transcendental, and in this sense 'infinite', ego offered the possibility of breaking out of this structural and finite totality (Critchley, 1992: 64) Here we can see an implicit critique not only of structure as finitude but of the *phenomenology* of finitude of the generation of Derrida's teachers, of Merleau-Ponty and Ricoeur (1981). Both these philosophers want to reconceive Husserl in terms not of the theoretical attitude of the transcendental ego, but of the natural attitude of the body, desire and perception.

What can Derrida (1978a: 156–7) mean by this? Derrida would understand structuralism's assumptions of the finite to be very much of a piece with Kant's idea of finitude. Kant uses the word transcendental in many senses. He speaks for example of the 'transcendental aesthetic', the 'transcendental analytic', the 'transcendental dialectic' and 'transcendental argument'. But each of these terms is used not in the realm of infinitude but of finitude. Each of these entities are conditions of the possibility of not metaphysical or infinite knowledge, but empirical and finite knowledge, of synthetic a priori judgements for which experience is necessary. Kant counterposes this realm of the 'understanding', of empirical knowledge, comprised of objective truths – on the model of mathematics and physics – to the realm of 'reason'. He counterposes the 'empirical will' of such experiential knowledge (which can only know appearances and not things-in-themselves) to the 'pure practical will' of the moral imperative. The will in the realm of finitude is for Kant 'heteronomous', while the will of infinitude is autonomous, the realm of freedom. He places God in this critique of pure reason, this critique of metaphysics, firmly within the realm of reason as inaccessible to the understanding. The Kantian categories, for example, cause, substance, existence, which are mobilized in the knowledge of appearances or phenomena, are part and parcel of the finitude of the understanding. The infinitude of reason contains God, freedom, ethics and noumena or things-in-themselves. They cannot be known, as the metaphysics of Leibniz and Descartes claimed; their acceptance must be on the basis of 'rational faith' (Walsh, 1975).

Derrida, in his initial Husserlian critique of structuralism, would seem to have a notion of transcendence and critique of finitude that is quite similar to Levinas's (1973) early Husserlian phase. He would understand Husserl's transcendental ego as breaking out of the immanence and finitude in which Kant's synthetic unity of apperception is mired. This would entail a mode of thinking characteristic not of Kant's understanding, but of the realm of reason. But this would be a mode of thinking that is at the same time a departure from what Kant called metaphysics. The suggestion is that we can know noumena *without* metaphysics. Husserl implies that Kantian objective knowledge (through the categories of the understanding) is not universal but only knowledge in the mode of natural science and mathematics. For Husserl, Kant's objective knowledge of appearances through the logical categories is in fact the way that the natural sciences know things. Such knowledge (of appearances) is in fact knowledge of things in themselves to the extent that such things possess the categorial structure presumed by the natural sciences. Husserl encourages using the phenomenological method to know things, not according to the categorial structure of the natural sciences, or according to how these things are for the natural sciences, but according to their own categorial structure; their own mode of existence. Such knowledge of noumena is called the 'intuition of essences'. It is also the transcendence of the finitude and immanence of consciousness (Levinas, 1973: 42–3). For Derrida, the scientistic assumptions of structuralism, and its substantialist conception of the relations of elements, are those of Kantian finite totality.

The Sign: Difference and Natural Attitude

In *Speech and Phenomenon* Derrida first develops the notion of 'difference' through deconstructing Husserl's theory of the sign. This notion of the sign is based, as we noted in Chapter 7, on the distinction between expression (*Ausdruck*) and indication (*Anzeichen*). This is dependent on, though not derivative of, Gottlob Frege's distinction between sense (*Sinn*) and reference (*Bedeutung*). Frege had already effected a departure from the epistemological tradition, that is, from the high modernist and substantialist tradition that located meaning in the mind of the knowing subject. Frege displaces this for a logical notion of meaning. For him meaning is more closely identified with truth and validity. It is attached to statements themselves rather than to images in the minds of epistemological subjects. Meaning is defined instead in terms of certain logical truth conditions of statements. Meaning here comprises not just sense, but also reference. Frege was an influence on logical positivism, on Bertrand Russell and Wittgenstein of the *Tractatus* (Searle, 1969: 168–71; Thompson, 1981: 50–7). In this context we should note Derrida's involvement with Husserl's logic. This is with Husserl's work at its most 'transcendental': with his *Logical Investigations* and *Ideas*, rather than the *Cartesian Meditations* and *Crisis of the European Sciences*, in which the transcendental attitude begins to give way to the 'natural attitude'. Let us note that Derrida, in contrast to other post-Husserlians (e.g. Schutz, Gadamer, Levinas), not only privileges the 'I-It' relationship over the 'I-Thou' (or intersubjective) relationship; he also, unlike them, tends often to privilege the reflective attitude over the natural attitude. Both of these points are central to deconstruction's weaknesses on tradition and solidarity. We should further note that when Derrida speaks of logocentrism, he refers in particular to that break with classical epistemology effected by Frege, Husserl and other 'later' modern philosophers in quite literally the name of logic, and in the sense of meaning as the truth conditions of statements.

Where, then does *différance* come in? Frege and Husserl were agreed that in any empirical statement, or sign, there was some sort of mix of 'sense' and 'reference', of 'expression' and 'indication', but that analytically the two dimensions of meaning were distinct from one another. Derrida deconstructs this analytic distinction. He argues that expression and indication are inseparable even analytically, that they interpenetrate each other at their very core; that they are primordially joined (Derrida, 1973: 31; Critchley, 1992: 169–71). In this first deconstruction of Husserl, Derrida is also introducing the concept of *différance*. This is deconstruction not so much of the analytic distinction between 'expression' and 'indication'; it is in fact deconstruction of 'expression' and the transcendental reduction itself. The eidetic reduction is achieved by means of 'expression'. Here the elements of indication in signs must be reduced in order to obtain pure 'expression'. 'Indication' is how signs function outside of the reduction. Derrida argues that expression is primordially, at its origin, always contaminated by indication. The conclusion is that Husserl's phenomenological reduction is impossible. For Husserl, the logical condition of the possibility of meaning is the reduction. That is, only when expression is purged of indication – through the reduction – do we have meaning. Only then can a sign have meaning. But because the contamination of indication can never be reduced, argues Derrida, there is always an irreducible difference between a sign and the meaning of a thing or experience.

For Husserl, expressions have a single meaning, whilst indications have occasional meanings (Schutz, 1974: 169). Expressions meet logical truth conditions, while indications have a set of different meanings that may be trivial. For Husserl, only for the transcendental ego, only with the move out of the natural attitude into the theoretical or reflective attitude is meaning (and he means univocal and also logical meaning) achieved. If the sign is always already also indication, than the reduction is impossible and meaning must be delayed or deferred. The reduction is for Husserl how we can know things in themselves. Knowing things in themselves does not mean knowing the outer surfaces of trivial things such as a table. The sort of things whose categorial structure, whose mode of existence, is at issue are things like man, society, number, colour, consciousness, the world. The reduction entails bracketing the succession of appearances, of *Abschattungen* of things and thus grasping the categorial structure of things, thus grasping their essences; it is the 'intuition of essences'. Knowledge of the specific categorial structure of objects is knowledge of their meaning (Derrida, 1973: 92–94; Levinas, 1973: 9–10). For this the reduction and the sign as pure expression is necessary. And since the sign as pure expression is not even analytically possible, meaning in the ontological sense of knowing the categorial structure of entities must be deferred.

This original sense of *'différance'* has little to do with intersubjectivity.[4] The notion of indication in Husserl may well be multivocal, may well be uttered from the natural attitude, but it none the less has to do with the relations between people and things and not intersubjectivity. Signification through indication bears extensive similarities with Peirce's notion of indexical signs. Peirce thus, as we noted, distinguishes between symbol, icon and index in terms, effectively, of a sign's closeness to the natural attitude, its situatedness, the extent of what anthropologists call the sign's 'motivation'. Indexes like indicators are not uttered from a transcendental position. Unlike indicators, indexes are not *per se* multivocal, but instead their meaning is determined by the concrete position from which they are uttered. Pronouns, for example, are thus indexes, in that they make no sense unless the concrete antecedent is already known, whereas a generic substantive like 'capitalism' may be meaningful without any reference to its concrete context (see Habermas, 1971; Eco, 1984: 137–9).

Heidegger: Signs and the Other

The Peircean notion of index, more than Derrida's indicators, is a step towards the natural attitude. It is very much in the natural attitude that Heidegger addresses the sign in *Being and Time*. Heidegger addresses the sign specifically in the chapter on the 'Worldliness of the World'. Here, section 17 is entitled 'Reference and Signs'. Only reference is not, as in Frege, in semiotics and linguistic philosophy, rendered as *Bedeutung* but as *Verweisen* (Heidegger, 1986: 76). *Verweisen* in German is a much more concrete term than *Bedeutung*, it also means assigning. That is, *Bedeutung* can also be translated as meaning, while *Verweisen* would be 'with reference to', that is, *'Verweisung auf'* or *'Verweisung an'*, something. *Verweisung* has the sense of an 'arrow', literally an indicator (turn-signal), almost more like a signal than an index, in the sense that *Bedeutung* does not. Yet having introduced reference, Heidegger (1986: 77) says that the ontological structure of the sign is not to be understood in terms of sense and reference (of *Sinn* and

Bedeutung). That is, that formal relations are derivative of this more basic structure of *Verweisung*.

Heidegger continues to say that signs are in the first instance to be understood as 'equipment' for indicating (1986: 78). This is consistent with his understanding of the world as a ready-to-hand, spatially articulated structure of equipment (*Zeuge*). Because signs are equipment, their categorial structure or their being is determined as ready-to-handness (p. 78). Thus Heidegger's signs do have a prima facie resemblance to what Husserl and Derrida mean by indication. But Heidegger does not use the Husserlian term *Anzeichen* for indication, but instead uses *Zeigen*, which also means show or point (p. 78). Again, *Anzeichen* would be an abstract derivative of *Zeigen*. *An-zeichen* includes *zeichen* (sign) in its meaning. *Zeigen*, in contrast, is like pointing with your finger. The example Heidegger uses is the turning signal (indicator) on a car (p. 78). Thus signs, as equipment, are *Zeigzeuge* (p. 78).

Heidegger notes that signs are more than equipment. They are a particular kind of equipment that 'gives way' to something else (p. 79). This giving way is also raising to our attention the totality of equipment (p. 79). In this sense the sign is the way the ready-to-hand announces itself. This second aspect of the being of the sign is not the same as the being of equipment or the being of the world. It instead partakes of *Dasein*'s 'Being' and *Dasein*'s 'Being in the world'. This second dimension of Heidegger's sign bears similarities, though placed fully in the natural attitude, to Husserl's notion of expression. In this sense a sign is still a *Zeigzeug*, that is, equipment for indicating. But it is not a thing, as it is in its capacity purely as equipment. Husserl's expressions allow us to intuit the essences of things, that is, to know their categorial structure. Similarly Heidegger's signs, to the extent that they do not function purely as equipment, allow us to orient ourselves in the equipmental totality of the world, bringing this totality into our view.

This is heady stuff. It is crucial for Heidegger's displacement of Husserl's reduction and would seem to be of the utmost centrality in any social or culture-theoretical discussion about the situatedness of knowledge. The problem is that all this goes on outside of any context of intersubjectvity. Heidegger's *Destruktion* of the sign, like Derrida's deconstruction and Husserl's original intention, is a matter not of intersubjectivity but of *Technik*. Postwar German philosophy commonly stresses the counterposition of *Philosophie der Moral* and *Philosophie der Technik*. Most schematically, *Philosophie der Moral* addresses relations between *Menschen und Menschen* while *Technik* addresses relations between *Menschen und Dingen*. Heidegger, it is argued (by his supporters), is in this context very much a philosopher of the 'I–It' of *Technik*. Heidegger's famous belated criticisms of the Third Reich are on the basis of its being caught up in the sending of '*Being as technology*', while he steadfastly refused to criticize Nazis on the basis of *morality*.

This refusal of intersubjectivity is most apparent in the chapter on Being-In (*In-Sein*) in *Being and Time*.[5] If the chapter on the worldliness of the world concerns the categorial structure, or being of beings (*Seienden*) and the being of the world, then the chapter on Being-In primarily addresses the categorial structure, the being, the 'existential analytic' of *Dasein*. Here we see how beings are disclosed to *Dasein*; that is, we see the 'ways of existence' through which beings are disclosed to *Dasein*. Heidegger addresses this through explication of the categorial structure of 'the there'. But inasmuch as *Dasein* is not a subject that is found inside some sort of abstract space, *Dasein* 'is', as Heidegger (1986: 134) notes, 'its there'. Here Heidegger is giving us a hermeneutic explication of notions of knowledge addressed in the Kantian categories and Husserl's intentionality. Husserl, as we noted, would understand the Kantian categories as not so much categories of the understanding, but as the categorial structure of things insofar as they are conceived in the natural sciences. For phenomenology, consciousness would have a very specific categorial structure, a very specific mode of existence. The categorial structure of consciousness, the essence of consciousness lies in intentionality. Consciousness is the only kind of being that can intuit the essences of other beings. Only consciousness can assume the transcendental attitude and perform the eidetic reduction. Intentionality, Levinas (1973: 41) stresses, means rather the opposite of a relation between a 'subject' in regard to an object. Consciousness is neither a substance nor a subject. The notion of substance itself, in the categories of Aristotelian logic and the Kantian understanding is naturalistic. And the idea of subject and object entails that of two substances. This is quite similar to Heidegger's 'Being-In'. Instead of intentionality we have *Dasein* as 'the there'. We have *Dasein* as 'that Being which carries in its inmost Being the character of not being closed off ' (Heidegger, 1986: 132). *Dasein* is also the being through whose illuminated opening the being of other beings is disclosed.

Heidegger, like Husserl, looks at knowing (or in this case disclosure) via a temporality of consciousness (*Dasein*). For Heidegger this contains moments of past, present and future. The past moment he calls *Befindlichkeit*, literally 'finding oneself ', and specifically, 'finding oneself thrown' (in a Kierkegaardian sense) into existence (p. 135). We should note here that *Dasein*'s access to truth via the past has nothing to do with tradition, with, as in Gadamer, a previous historical intersubjectivity of experience. It has to do with no intersubjectivity at all, but instead the immediacy of thrownness and 'mood'. The future moment of the temporality of *Dasein*'s access to the truth of beings is called *Verstehen* or understanding. It has to do with the projection of future horizons against which the being of beings disclose themselves (p. 145). It is revealing to compare this with the notion of understanding (*Verstehen*) in other phenomenological accounts such as Alfred Schutz's sociological phenomenology. For Schutz, as for Weber and Scheler, 'understanding' is specifically differentiated from 'meaning' in that it entails intersubjectivity. It has to do with *Verstehen* of the other, not of objects or experience (Schutz, 1974: 137–8; Srubar, 1988). The other thus plays a very small role in Heidegger's existential analytic. It is the I–It relation not the I–Thou which dominates. Similarly, though Derrida (1978b: 123–4) subsequently aligns himself with what he sees as intersubjectivity in Levinas, his initial deconstruction of Husserl was not of Husserl's lack of a notion of intersubjectivity. Difference had nothing to do with the same and the other. It had to do not with an exploration of 'the limit' or 'the frame' of Husserl's I–It relation in order to find 'the trace' of the I–Thou. It was instead the displacement of Husserl's I–It relation with Derrida's own spatio-temporally deferred I–It. The other is nowhere in sight.

Temporality and Intersubjectivity

There are, of course, two senses to difference. The first, discussed at length above, is, taken graphically, spatial. The second is temporal. It is where Derrida speaks of the temporal deferral of meaning or *différance*, which is why difference is spelled with an 'a'. Let us look at this temporal deferral, which again is a deconstruction of Husserl. As in other deconstructions, what Derrida does here is to find traces that, against a thinker's will, escape from the space of the metaphysics of presence and point to its outside, to its limit conditions. In this second temporal deconstruction of phenomenology the starting point is Husserl's *Phenomenology of Internal Time-Consciousness*. Here intentionality (and the reduction) designates neither the intuition of objects' essences, nor knowledge of the categorial structure of objects. Intentionality is not even transcendental in Husserl's normal sense of the word. It is instead immanent. That is, intentionality is not exterior to consciousness in the intuition of the structure of objects, but is directed interior to consciousness at *experience* (Levinas, 1973: 37–40).

This entails a notion of meaning based on the relationship between consciousness and immediate experience. Meaning is dependent on fixing the flow of experience, through what Husserl calls the 'reflective glance'. Once fixed, units of experience become in principle discrete and repeatable. That is, experiences do not have meaning or only have trivial meaning until they are reduced through the 'ray' of the reflective glance in order to constitute the experiences as phenomena. Here at issue are two attitudes towards immediate experience, and Husserl (like Derrida) enjoins us to begin not with thought or the 'I think' but with the 'I experience'. The attitude of immediate experience is the 'natural attitude', and the attitude of the transcendental and eidetic reduction is the 'reflective' or 'theoretical attitude' (Schutz, 1974: 68). In the natural attitude as Husserl describes it, the ego undergoes a flux of experience, a sort of temporality that is very much, Derrida later noted, like Bergson's *durée*. The reflective attitude – with its fixing and 'lifting out' of units of pre-phenomenal experience in order 'polysynthetically' to constitute phenomena and achieve meaning – involves a certain spatialization of time, though not that of the substantialism of naturalism and positivism (Game, 1991: 92–8).

Given the temporality (of the natural attitude) of immediate experience, of the ebb and flow of overlapping shadows, and confused images of *durée*, then where does '*différance*' lie? It lies in the first place in that meaning for

Husserl can never be a matter of 'presence'. That is because even in the reflective attitude, the ego itself cannot be lifted out of experience. Some units of the ego's experience are in the natural attitude whilst others are in the reflective attitude. And because units of experience must temporally succeed one another the ego cannot be in the natural attitude and the reflective attitude at the same moment. Thus to create meaning in an act of eidetic reduction the ego must reflect on the immediate experience of a *past* moment. Thus meaning can never be a matter of presence, never a matter of identity but must have the character of absence and difference. There must thus always be temporal difference or deferral between experience and the constitution of meaning. Meaning is even less a matter of presence and identity for those chains of acts that Husserl calls 'actions'. These involve a goal and a project. Here meaning is always delayed into the future of any given moment of experience. So again there is deferral or temporal difference. Only, whereas with the reflective 'act' temporal difference was a matter of memory or recollection, in the project-action it is a matter of 'anticipation' (Derrida, 1973: 63–5; Schutz, 1974: 74–5).

There are two major problems with this idea of temporal difference. The first is that Derrida again does not fully break with the reflective attitude for the natural attitude. This was already apparent in his deconstruction of Husserl's sign. Whereas Heidegger, as we saw, fully departed from the reflective for the natural attitude, Derrida stays in what he sees as a largely corrupted reflective attitude. Derrida does the same in regard to temporality. Bergson's temporality of *durée*, his *Lebensphilosophie*, in part pits the uncorrupted natural attitude of 'life' against the theoretical (reflective) attitude of 'thought'. Derrida, however, still inside the reflective attitude, goes no further than noting the unavoidable deferral of meaning. My point here is that to take solidarity and tradition seriously, is not just to strongly thematize the I–Thou; it is also fundamentally to break with the reflective for the natural attitude. Thus Habermas's intersubjectivity of the ideal speech situation is placed *par excellence* in the reflective attitude. It counterposes itself to the tradition-based intersubjectivity of Gadamer. It will not speak the language of substantive values, only that of formalist procedural norms (Benhabib, 1992: 72–3). Its speech acts are lifted out from ongoing forms of life. Its idea of validity claims recalls the logical truth conditions of Fregean propositions. This is hardly surprising. This alignment with the reflective attitude is much more surprising in Derrida.

There are a number of different ways of departing from the theoretical for the natural attitude. In *Lebensphilosphie* there is Bergson's move from thought to life, or Nietszche's from slave moralities to the (natural) will to power. There is, for example, the late Wittgenstein's counterposition of (natural) forms of life with the early Wittgensteinian descriptive logical positivism. There is Heidegger's counterposition of present-at-hand and ready-to-hand, and the corresponding opposition of the categorial and the existential. The notion of existence in existentialism, for example, partakes of the natural attitude as opposed to the essences (substance) and thought of the cogito.

There is Lacan's counterposition of the unconscious to (Anna) Freudian ego-psychology. Likewise, there are different ways of conceiving of temporality in the natural attitude. Though Derrida's initial deconstruction of Husserl's notion of time retains a stance largely in the reflective attitude, his later, and most of deconstruction's, philosophy of temporality does pit natural against theoretical attitude. Here the viewpoint is largely Bergsonian, pitting time as radical contingency versus time as abstract order. Here as *durée*, the natural attitude's temporality is also the time of immediate experience (*Erlebnis*). It is disconnected, follows no logic of its own; it is contingent and disruptive; it starts and stops in fits; it erupts; its images or figures overlap. It is temporal without at all having any kind of narrative organization; it is de-territorialized. But pivotal to all these characteristics of deconstruction's temporality is *Erlebnis*, or immediate experience.

In contraposition to deconstruction, hermeneutics – still inside the natural attitude – opens up a vastly different sort of temporality. The notion of temporality in *Being and Time* is conceived in the natural attitude. Time is the horizon of *Existenz*, conceived in counterposition to the theoretical abstraction of the metaphysical tradition. But insofar as things are encountered against the background of a horizon, *Dasein* never has immediate experience or *Erlebnis*, but experience is already mediated by the horizon. Experience is then to be conceived not as *Erlebnis* but as *Erfahrung*; as always already mediated. Heidegger's temporality owes little to intersubjectivity, and *Dasein*'s horizon is that against which the being of beings (*Seienden*, not other *Daseins*) is disclosed to *Dasein*. The temporality that forms this horizon is not conceived in terms of tradition. It is conceived as defined by our finitude in regard to death. It is conceived in terms of our thrownness, our falling and our understanding as 'projection'. In *Being and Time* Heidegger gives very little space for intersubjectivity. Only in the small, weakly developed section on *Mitsein* does he address this. *Mitdasein* here is not, *pace* Bauman (1993) and Levinas, primarily a matter of *Miteinandersein* or a national and militaristic '*Miteinandermarschieren*'. *Mitsein*, as Derrida notes, is not an ontic but an existential category. Yet the point for us is not that Heidegger's notion of intersubjectivity partakes of Black Forest tribalism; it is that he has very little notion of intersubjectivity at all. It is telling further that even this short discussion of intersubjectivity in *Being and Time* is followed directly by Heidegger's ominous introduction of *Das man* (Derrida, 1978b: 319; Heidegger, 1986: 117–18). What notion Heidegger has of *Erfahrung* – in comparison say to Gadamer (1986: 352 ff.; 1989: 346–62) and Schutz (1974: 111–12) – is rather individualistic. Given the workshop model of the world in *Being and Time*, one would have expected a notion of *Erfahrung* more like the everyday German idea of an *erfahrender Geselle*, an experienced journeyman. Such experience, such *Erfahrung*, in contrast to either the immediate experience of *Erlebnis*, or the heightened individualism of being-towards-death, is mediated by the 'long intersubjectivity' of tradition (Ricoeur, 1981: 127–8). Thus Bourdieu's 'habitus' and the notion of the body in Mauss are 'practical', and practice in this sense is located in the natural attitude. But in such notions of practice, the body, habitus is not like a self or consciousness confronting immediate experience. Experience is always mediated through a body, a habitus, which itself is learnt and infused with intersubjectivity and tradition.

Time Against Being: Levinas

Perhaps a better way into an ethics of difference, of deconstruction, is via the work of Emmanuel Levinas. Levinas explicitly draws on Buber's 'I–Thou' to construct a notion of intersubjectivity that he calls 'sociality'. His work is explicitly an ethics and comprises a strong notion of temporality that is not ultimately that of the immediate *Erlebnis* of *durée*, nor *Erfahrung* as described above. Levinas, we noted above, has a strongly ontological reading of Husserl. Conversely, his reading of Heidegger is phenomenological, in that focus is on the Being of beings, that is, the existential structures of beings, rather than on the 'sending' of Being. If Derrida should be read as primarily deconstructing the logical dimension of phenomenology, Levinas's deconstruction is literally a challenge to '*ontology*'. Levinas recognizes an affinity with Derrida, but views his own work as exemplifying phenomenology. He wants to 'intuit the essence' of (Heideggerian) ontology. In the course of this reduction of Heidegger he will find instead the 'I–Thou' relation of ethics.

After his youthful apprenticeship to Husserl and Heidegger, resulting in his *Theory of Intuition in Husserl's Phenomenology*, Levinas wrote *De l'existence à l'existant*. Existents and existence is, he says, a euphonious way of talking about being and beings (*Sein* and *Seiende*, *l'être* and *étants*). *De l'existence à l'existant* is Levinas's first major attack on the idea of being. Here being is addressed through the notion of the '*il y a*'. Levinas (1990: 10–11) distinguishes the '*il y a*' from Heidegger's '*es gibt*', in which being gives in a 'plenitude' of 'generosity'. It gives by filling and fulfilling the Being of beings, as well as the being of *Dasein*, which it fills as the opening through which the being of beings is disclosed. Levinas's '*il y a*' is not generous but empty and stingy. It is also impersonal in the sense that '*il pleut*' or '*il fait nuit*' is impersonal. The '*il y a*' is empty, like a desert, it is 'obsessive', 'horrible', 'insomniac'. It is like a child who wakes up in a nightmare and sees not beings but monstrous shadows creeping about his bedroom (1990: 109–10). The '*il y a*' is also something that beings cannot escape. It follows human beings about like a shadow.[6] *Dasein* is oppressed by the Being of his being (p. 94). Indeed Levinas elaborates on the '*il y a*' through a phenomenology of laziness and fatigue (p. 41 ff.).

But Being is more than emptiness. It is a '*remue-ménage*' as Blanchot called it: a 'bustling', a household bustling, a bustling of equipment. The emptiness of being, of the '*il y a,*' its impersonal neutrality, is also that of the economy, of possession, of the war of all against all of Hobbes and of early liberalism's possessive individuals (Levinas, 1990: 26–7). In this, subjectivity is the mastery of the ego over the anonymous '*il y a*' of being. Subjectivity entails a materiality and solitude of, not infinity, but of immanence. 'Experience and solitude', Levinas (1983: 13) says, 'in the light of knowledge absorbs all other.' Beings or existents for Levinas are not the condition of possibility of being, but the bustling of Being is Being without existents, Being without beings. This is because existence denies existents by engulfing them. Being denies beings (or *Seienden*) of their alterity. Being denies beings of dimensions not captured by their essence, by their categorial structure, by their mode of existence. As *Dasein* or consciousness, Being for Levinas would force human beings to be 'transcendental reducing' or 'disclosing' animals. Those parts of us as human existents, which are exterior to our capacity as disclosing, or reducing, animals is denied by Being.

There is, however, a way out, an exit, from being, from the *il y a*, in an exteriority of 'the Good', which, as in Plato, is 'beyond Being'. Levinas (1974: 13) underscores that the movement by which an existent moves towards the good is not a move to a better existence, but an exit from Being (existence) and all its categories. Levinas invokes a movement outside of the 'representation' of beings as the same, towards a more tenuous 'desire' of beings as the other. This 'de-neutralization' of Being, now as the other becomes no longer mediated but 'proximate' (1974: 105 ff.). As proximate and unmediatable the other becomes un-representable and unknowable. The other is thus 'infinite', in the sense that the thing-in-itself, God and reason are unknowable and infinite. Ethics and the good outside of being are a question of the ego's (*le moi*) or *Dasein*'s relation to the other. This is a relation not of intentionality, nor of mutual disclosure, as in *Mitsein* (Heidegger, 1986: 121–2). Levinas proposes effectively a sort of intersubjectivity in the natural attitude. But unlike Schutz or Gadamer, this intersubjectivity is a matter of not knowing, understanding or recognizing the other. Levinas calls himself 'a metaphysician', and indeed he is one in several senses. First he is a metaphysician in that his ethics is a 'first philosophy'. Second, he mobilizes the 'infinity' of metaphysics against the finitude of ontology. Third he is a humanist. But his humanism is ranged against the universalism of previous humanism. It is defined against Early Modern (Grotian) natural law, eighteenth century liberalism and Marxian (Feuerbachian) humanism. Levinas's humanism is not universalist but instead proximal. For him, to intuit essence or disclose being is to be inhuman. Our humanity is instead in that leftover part, our own *part maudite*, that exits from Being's neutralization.

Levinas has characterized his immediate postwar work in terms of 'the good and time'. The lectures making up his *Le Temps et l'autre* were written at the same time as *De l'existence à l'existant*. Time here is no longer a question of existence's finitude of being-towards-death, but the 'desire of the infinite'. For Heidegger Being is neither finite nor infinite, whereas *Dasein* and existence are pre-eminently finite. 'Care', propounds Heidegger in Division One of *Being and Time*, is the being of *Dasein*. Division Two of the book is largely devoted to rethinking 'care' in regard to the horizon of temporality. Thus Heideggerian temporality is, for Levinas, bound up with *Dasein*'s self-consciousness, in that what Being gives to *Dasein* is a temporal structure of disclosure and self-disclosure. These notions arouse Levinas's ire and condemnation. For him time is neither the ontological horizon of the being of *Dasein*, nor the synchronic time in which *Dasein* represents itself. Levinas castigates Heideggerian time as a 'dispersion of Being' in *Dasein*. For Levinas, such temporality consists of 'moments, exclusive of each other, each which propels the preceding into the past, outside of its presence, but which still furnish the idea of this presence', suggesting 'meaning and non-meaning, death and life'. Levinas here would see a theological element. He stands in opposition to such an 'intellectualist' conception of god, whose time as 'eternity is a unity', and whose dispersion as 'multiple' in *Dasein* is a result of 'the death of God' (Levinas, 1983: 9).

For Levinas, phenomenological and ontological time, the temporality of *Erlebnis* and *Erfahrung*, are instances of 'synchronic time', whose basis is the knowledge or 'representation' of the other. In Husserl this other is either the flux of immediate experiences or the objects intuited by the ego. In either case there would effectively be two temporalities: one of the reflective ego and a second of either experiences or objects, in which the first temporality 'synchronically' would 'represent' the second. In Heideggerian time it would be the horizon of the natural attitude that permits *Dasein*, synchronically, to know and represent beings. For Levinas (1983: 8), in contrast, time is a 'diachronic relation' of 'thought to the other', in which thought 'desires' the other as 'infinite'. On this view, 'dia-chronic' – in contrast to the synchronic time of ontology – precludes the knowledge or representation of the other. It also precludes the nullification of the other in a 'relation of satisfaction' and 'enjoyment'. Levinas (1983: 8) here speaks of a relation to the other which 'signifies a surplus of sociality'. Who, then, is this other, and what sort of relationship are we talking about? The other is not a being (*Seiende*) or an experience or objects as in Heidegger and Husserl. The other is also not a consciousness, an ego or *Dasein*. The other for Levinas is either 'God' or 'the other man' (*l'autre homme*). Whether deity or human, this other is infinite in the noumenal sense that he/she cannot be known.

In this de-synchronization, thought cannot represent or cognize the other. Thought can only relate to the other through 'desire'. The relation of thought or the 'I' to either God or the human other is via desire. This is a sensible relation, through the senses, rather than through reason, law or 'rational faith'. Its locus classicus is Kierkegaard's *Fear and Trembling*. Here, as in the Old Testament, God addresses Abraham, not as if the latter were general ego, transcendental consciousness or even 'rational man'. God instead addresses Abraham in his flesh and blood singularity. Abraham cannot hide from his responsibility as *Abraham* before God. He must say 'Here I am'. Contrary to what might be understood as any sort of communion or covenant with God, contrary to any natural or codified law, contrary to reason, Abraham is asked to sacrifice his son. He is asked not even via any legitimating pretext of reason or law, but through the senses, through the sensible voice, through the 'grain', in Roland Barthes's sense, of the voice of God (Bhabha, 1994: 184). He is asked via a word whose sensibility exceeds the sentence, exceeds predicative logic. He is asked via a singular, determinate and bodily signification. Kierkegaard understands this, not as the shame, but as the glory of Abraham (Rose, 1992: 12). In this relation between God and Abraham the Infinity that is God is not a 'supreme being' as in intellectualist versions of the Judaeo-Christian tradition. It is in no sense a substantive (and neither is it a verb or adverb). God, as the Jewish *Yahweh*, not only cannot be represented, it cannot be grasped (*com-pris*). It cannot even be pointed to, as in Heidegger's *Verweisen*. Not only cannot knowledge grasp this other, but thought itself is inadequate to such an Infinite (Levinas, 1983: 10).

My relationship with the other – a relationship in which both same and other are 'singular' (that is neither universal nor particular) – is a relationship without terms; a relationship in which neither same nor other is a substance. What connects the temporality of the 'I' with that of the other is not intentionality, but 'a thread, a tenuous thread'. The 'I' here is so proximal to the other that signification cannot be mediated. It must be immediate; it must be highly motivated. It must be more akin to index than to symbol, or icon. It must be more proximal than index, more immediate even than a signal. It is a relationship with, as Levinas says, the 'face' of the other, with the 'skin' of the other's face. This neither discursive, nor figural signification deals with meanings that, Levinas says, are *'non-figuré'*, that is, that cannot separately be inscribed. This is signification between bodies that are not substances, and thus unassignable to speakers' positions in discourses.

In most instances Levinas's other remains in spite of its proximity and singularity, quite abstract in terms its particular nature. The other is God or *l'autre homme*, a face which is at the same time singular and nameless. Yet he still insists that the other is a 'surplus of sociality' beyond the concept. This surplus (1983: 8) is a 'set of figures of sociality encountering the face of the other man: eroticism, paternity'. For him, the diachronic describes the relationship of thought 'to otherness (*autrui*) – the feminine, the child, the ego's fecundity'. In these the good – 'and not the ecstasy in which the same absorbs itself into the other' – 'is articulated by the transcendence of time' (1983: 13–14). What 'opens up' time for Levinas is this transcendental alterity. Such temporal alterity does not understand difference, as does logocentrism, in terms of different attributes that similar substances have, but as different 'contents'. Thus Levinas understands femininity not as difference of quality in human beings, but as radical alterity of women from men. The ethical in 'the exceptional epiphany of the face' (1983: 14–15) depends on this sensual *'socialité à deux'*. Here the 'radiance [*rayonnement*] of the ethical in eroticism' is instantiated in the alterity of the feminine, in the 'epiphany of the face' in which alterity is 'carried' by the '"thou shall not kill"'.

Conclusions

What kind of time is Levinas referring to? It is, in the first instance, a time that is constituted in opposition not only to historicism, but to history itself.

History for Levinas is relegated to the realm of the '*il y a*'. What he calls 'illeity' is exterior to any of that. It is exterior to the public realm of history. Hence perhaps the locus of incursions of illeity in the 'private sphere', in fecundity, generations, family and the feminine. The public realm is governed by the principle of the reduction, by economy, by all against all. Temporality, as opposed to history, is 'opened up' only where there is illeity. Further, even in the private, in the sensual of the feminine, it is the also, but otherwise, sensual and revelational 'thou shalt not kill' that is 'carried' in 'the epiphany of the face'. The temporality that this invokes, is not so much the disjunctive temporality of Bergson's (and Derrida's) durée, but instead eschatology. The temporality of the good finds its determinacy in revelation and ultimate redemption. Here illeity, which is 'older', more 'primordial' than ontology, resides. What Levinas is thus saying is that ontology or tradition is just as rationalist, just as cognitivist, just as epistemological as modernity. And that history – whether in tradition or modernity – must be rejected for this primordial moment of the time of the other.

But how old indeed is Levinas's primordial sensual and singular moment of revelation, and the eschatological time it constitutes? This is not the place for involved discussion but only a few, perhaps sociological, suggestions. Is it more primordial than tradition, despite its insistence on sensible proximity versus the mediation of rational law? Or is it instead 'post-traditional' in Weber's sense? Has it got more to do with the temporality of the world religions? Is it despite its insistence on proximity and materiality of God's word, itself then 'onto-theological', or what sociologists following Weber call 'religio-metaphysical', in which the metanarrative of secular history is culturally prefigured by the 'big metanarrative' of redemption and revelation? Surely this sort of reading of Levinas would only be reinforced by his Kantian insistence on the infinitude, the unknowability of the ethical? Are we, at least in a very important sense, not back in abstract ungrounded ethics and metanarratives? Would not deconstruction in its Levinasian version be just as inadequate in conceiving of solidarity?

I have argued in this chapter for the limits of the philosophy of difference. The problem with such an ethics and politics of deconstruction has been understood very helpfully by Gillian Rose (1992: 263–4) as due to the very 'singularity' of its *problematique* in opposition to the universalism–particularism dichotomy of logocentrism. Here deconstruction is the negative dialectic, the heterodoxy of the prophetic singular. And this constitutes at the same time the richness and the limits of the theory of difference. This two-sidedness is instantiated in what is indeed one of the richest veins of deconstruction's re-thinking of contemporary political culture: post-colonial theory. Homi Bhabha (1994: 142 ff.) proposes a politics of temporality, of 'narrating the nation'. He proposes a temporality that takes place within the Derridian limit, in the 'in-between' of the historicity of totalizing 'pedagogical' narratives of the nation and the disjunctive, disseminating, 'performative' temporality of the excluded other of that narrative. As alterity, as difference, the other cannot be known by the same. This is original, provocative work, and Bhabha's notion of the limit as the in-between of Western and post-colonial peoples is an advance on Derrida's and Levinas's notions of the 'limit' in terms of abstract exteriority. Yet the pedagogical narrative resembles the atemporal yet historical '*il y a*'. The performative disjunctive incursions resemble illeity. The postcolonial other of the nationalist narratives of universalism is not the particular, but the *singular*.

Let this chapter stand as a plea for neither modernism's universal, nor the postmodern 'singular', but instead for this particular. Let post-colonial diaspora be understood not just in terms of 'routes', but also in regard to 'roots' (Clifford, 1997). Let the realm of Being, including institutions, communities, economics, space of everyday life, be understood not as the barrenness of the '*il y a*', but as the plenitude of '*es gibt*'. What militates against solidarity, against the 'we' is deconstruction's incessant constructionism. Hence not just gender but sex is constructed, science is constructed, identity is constructed, objects are constructed. But what about '*es gibt*'. What about 'the given'? Only some sort of given can account for our being born or thrown (or having thrown ourselves) into a set of already existing forms of life. Only a given can explicate our habitus; how we are our practices. Human beings are not just singular individualists, but alongside their constructions, find themselves substantially enracinated in this sort of 'given'. Without some sort of 'given', some sort of plenitude of forms of life which fill us up as subjects, no understanding, no recognition – either of same or other – is possible. Without some sort of given, values cannot be but only the norms of procedure. But who then is the giver of this given? It need not be God, Christ, the state or the family. Perhaps we are all potentially givers of this given, of *die Gabe* or 'the gift'. Perhaps the given has to do with the reciprocity of symbolic exchange. But how can this be possible in an age not of symbolic exchange, but of dead, digitized symbols; not of forms of life, but a virtualized habitus? I hope that we have taken some steps, in this chapter, at least in beginning to problematize this question. This chapter and the last – and their discussion mainly of Heidegger, Derrida and Levinas – have addressed critique. But they have been explorations not so much in information critique as in the critique of ideology. This is of course not the classical, more dialectical critique of ideology that we are familiar with in Marx, Gramsci and the German critical theorists – Adorno, Marcuse and Habermas. It is instead a Kantian critique, an aporetic critique that presumes the impossibility of resolution. The point I want to make in concluding these chapters is that the critique of ideology is at the same time the critique of the *symbolic*. This was the central theroretical contribution in Laclau and Mouffe's (1986) *Hegemony and Socialist Strategies*, which so appalled the classic left in the mid 1980s and continues to have major influence today. This book reconceived ideology and the Gramsican notion of hegemony via Lacan's symbolic.

We do not even need to start with Lacan's symbolic. There is a lineage of the symbolic from Durkheim's *Elementary Forms of Religious Life* through Levi-Strauss's symbolic structures, to the individualization of the previously social symbolic in French psychoanalysis. But it was Durkheim – and this will be instinctive to sociologists – who filled out Marx's superstructures, Marx's never very well worked out ideological superstructures – with his *Elementary Forms* and his *Primitive Classifications*. That is, once the theory of ideology becomes at all sophisticated it becomes already a theory of the symbolic. It is not just Durkheim who is at centre stage in this but Durkheim and *Mauss*, because the co-author of *Primitive Classifications* worked through the idea of a social symbolic in his notion of the gift. Here gift exchange is symbolic exchange. It is the basis of the social bond. This social bond swims in the sea of the symbolic, of ideology. Now I am not saying that the theory of hegemony – which in its developed form reworks the notion of ideology as the symbolic – is wrong. I am saying that it is better suited to manufacturing capitalism and *Ideologiekritik* than it is to today's informationcritique. I am arguing that we are living in a post-hegemonic age[7]: that we need other concepts today to understand politics and power.

In the register of ideologycritique there are two ways out. One can argue like Marx or Habermas that a particular national symbolic, or a particular set of symbolic structures attached to a given mode of production need to be criticized from the point of view of a universal, like proletarian hegemony or discursive will formation. The other way out is through the sort of aporetics of irresolvable conflict or contradiction of Laclau and Mouffe, and for that matter Levinas and Derrida. But we are still in the register of the symbolic and of *Ideologiekritik*. Now the point of *Informationskritik* is that it is neither dialectical not aporetic, not does it have anything to do with ideology or hegemony. Informationcritique takes place not in the symbolic but in the *real*. The original and strongest formulation of the real in this sense is of course Bataille in his encounter with Durkheim. Hence Bataille's wilful misreading of Mauss's *The Gift* (Le Breton 1997). For the Durkheimian, Mauss's gift-exchange constituted the social bond (*lien social*), and took place, so to speak, inside the symbolic. Gift exchange was the 'action' component that guaranteed the reproduction of structure, of symbolic structures. Bataille for his part was uninterested in the social bond. Or better his explorations were always of the place where the social bond was not. Hence his focus on gift-giving contests of waste and expenditure which made reproduction impossible and violated the symbolic in every sense. This is Bataille's excess: the original space of the real.

Informationcritique, for its part, is neither a question of symbolic and ideological struggles, nor of imagined communities. Information politics are going on not in the symbolic or the imaginary but in the real. The real is surely in excess of national and individual symbolics. But its space is not just a space of excess. The real is a space of *communication*. And this is what makes Niklas Luhmann the paradigmatic sociologist, and along with Deleuze the paradigmatic thinker of the information age. What Luhmann has understood is that the social bond itself is no longer about exchange in the symbolic but has taken on the proportions of the communication. The social bond is here compressed and stretched at the same time. And the communication is the fabric of the real. Information polities take place in conjunction with the communication. The argument of this book is that in the information age the centrality of the means of production are displaced by the means of communication: the centrality of production relations by relations of communication. Communication is here understood in its very broadest sense. The logic of flows is the logic of communications. With the domination of production there is a politics of struggles around accumulation (of capital). With the dominance of communication there is a politics of struggle around not accumulation but *circulation*. Manufacturing capitalism privileges production and accumulation, the network society privileges communication and circulation.

In the information age, the logic of flows disrupts and partly fragments the symbolic both on a national and individual level. Replacing the classic institutions of the linear social system are non-linear socio-technical assemblages. Talcott Parsons's linear social system is displaced by Luhmann's non-linear system. The linearity of reproduction of the symbolic is displaced by the non-linearity of the real. There is a move from Parsons's linear social system and Marx's linearity of technology to the merging of the social and technical in a non-linear system, a non-linear assemblage. These re-territorializations – be they operating systems, routers, post-national instances of human rights, the dispersed family, the heterarchic firm, supra-national trading blocs – are more or less non-linear in being partly self-causing, or in Luhmann's terms 'autopoetic'. They are self-causing largely though reflexivity: through observation, description and communication. Self-causation is the feedback loop of such non-linear assemblages. Through the feedback loops they regulate the flows. They accelerate, block, re-channel, solidify the flows (De Landa, 1997). The feedback loop is the locus of the critique of information. The symbolic relates to the outside as an external world, which it knows through categories and classifications. When the symbolic gives way to the predominance of communication (and the real) the logic of classification disappears. The outside is no longer the external world, but instead 'noise'. This noise is converted into information through selection by the non-linear socio-technical assemblages.

Now there is a close homology between Lacan's triptych of symbolic, imaginary and real and Peirce's symbol/icon/index. Here the real is indexical. And in terms of the critique of information the point of Chapters 7 and 8 is that Derrida, Heidegger and Levinas have got a long way there. A good portion of these chapters was devoted to explicating the important dimension of the indexical in their work. For Derrida and Levinas, the indexical is what is left, the remainder that is left, the supplement that remains after the phenomenological reduction. After the intuition of essences there is a remainder that can neither be determined nor even imagined. It can perhaps be approached like the index in a tactile manner like 'the face' in Levinas. This is that bit of accident or contingency that exceeds the reduction. It is that which resists reduction. After the description of the ontological structure of the thing-in-itself, there is that contingent aspect of the thing (and the human) that remains. This is already a move out of the symbolic and into the real indexicality of the information order. Close to four decades after his critique of Husserl, Derrida (1996) in *Archive Fever* launched a similar critique of the symbolic. The archive for him is the symbolic, but it rests on its conditions of existence in the real. The symbolic is attached to the sex drive, the real to the death drive. The symbolic replaces the phenomenological reduction. The excess of the reduction is in the index: the excess of the symbolic in the real. Heidegger, we saw, goes even further in his notion of the sign in *Being and Time*. He understands the index as signal. This signal is in a whole, so to speak machinic complex of equipment, whose elements stand in a relation of sign posting to one another. For him this is the ontological essence of the sign. For us its speaks volumes about the information age.

Yet Derrida, Levinas and more recently Slavoj Zizek (1989), give us a politics of the real as critique of the symbolic, the index as critique of symbol. The arena of politics for all of them needs to be the fold, the frontier, the third space dividing symbolic and real. In these power relations, domination is through the symbolic (or ideology): resistance is through the real. In this sense, despite all of their important contributions to our understanding of information critique they remain ensconced in a logic of the critique of ideology. In the politics of information, we shall see, both resistance and dominance take place through the real. Not just resistance, but power itself is in the flows, in the networks of communication.

Notes

1 Paradoxically the basic meaning of difference in Derrida is a lot more applicable to literary theory than it is to the human sciences (ethics, non-positivist sociology or politics and cultural studies, post-colonialism and the like). This is because it addresses the relation between statements and things or experience and thus is more applicable to texts than social relations or intersubjectivity.

2 I will argue below that some of these ontological Husserlians, in particular Gadamer (1976), are the ones who work towards a theory of intersubjectivity, also have strong notions of tradition and hence solidarity.

3 The initial draft of this paper, *'Genèse et structure et la phénoménologie'*, by Derrida, was written in 1959. It was re-drafted quite thoroughly and published in French in 1965. It was translated in English in *Writing and Difference* in 1978 (See Critchley, 1992: 63 ff.).

4 Again may I underscore that the thrust of my own theory in this book does not have a strong dimension of intersubjectivity.

5 My own theory of the information order in this book does focus on the 'I-it' relation more than intersubjectivity. The latter is broached however in Chapter 14 and elsewhere in terms of 'culture-at-a-distance', and notions of communication, flow and non-linear reterritorialization.

6 The explorations into Heidegger and Levinas in this chapter were made possible by many lengthy discussions with Mick Dillon and Alistair Black. The conclusions I draw are however rather opposite to those of Dillon and Black.

7 I am grateful to Nancy Fraser for clarifying my views on this point.

9

Critique of Representation: Henri Lefebvre's Spatial Materialism

Chapters 7 and 8 have been less about information than critique. They have been essays in critical dialectics. As such, they took the form of a challenge to the critical *aporetics* of post-structuralism, and in particular the theory of difference. Aporetics talks the language of the unbridgeable, the irreconcilable and the undecidable. Dialectics are not necessarily about the resolution of contradictions. They are, however, always about *grounding*. Dialectics are the grounding of subjectivity in history, in sociality, in tradition. They are about the grounding of ethics in everyday customs. The theory of difference has its original aporias in the opposition between signifier and signified, which is at root for Derrida (as we saw) the aporia of 'expression' and 'indication' in the phenomenological sign. Later in his encounters with ontology, Derrida will find this aporia between being and beings. If Heidegger is rather the dialectician looking for a grounding of being in the ontological structure of beings, Derrida sees far less chance of this. He sees antagonisms, tensions and the impossibility of such grounding. The same is true in considerations of the relation between 'the same' and 'the other'. Again there is an impossible, unbridgeable gap. Difference however is not the other. Difference is the gap itself. Difference is the aporia. Difference is neither the same nor the other, neither being nor beings, neither the signifier nor signified. Difference is instead the aporia each time of the first and second terms. Difference is the irresolvable tension, the undecidability. In the sense that it is always also temporal and involves a delay or detour it becomes difference. Difference is the aporia, which is for Derrida more fundamental than either of its terms. Difference is not, as it is in Hegel and classical logic, the negation of identity. It is the gap between presence (the same) and absence (the other). It is 'the fold' or 'limit condition' between presence and absence. It is the primordial condition of possibility of presence and absence. For Derrida, critique is always finding the aporia. For him critical method is the method of deconstruction: constant vigilance for the aporia. Critique is deconstruction and difference is the aporia.

The origins of critique are, of course, in Kant. His critical method also proceeded finding the aporia. The original aporia is the aporia of reason. The aporia of reason is the unbridgeable tension between, on the one hand, the 'understanding' (cognition) and on the other, reason (ethics). The understanding corresponds to the sphere of necessity and reason (ethics) to the realm of freedom. Thus Kant's First Critique (*Critique of Pure Reason*) largely addressed the understanding, and the Second Critique (*Critique of*

Practical Reason) reason and ethics. The Third Critique (*Critique of Judgement*) restated the aporia and was an attempt to find a bridge through the power of judgement. In the First Critique, reason is largely instrumental reason, or an instrumentality; in the Second, reason is finality.[1] The Third Critique was an attempt to find a bridge for the aporia. This would be accomplished through finding reason in nature, that is, addressing nature (art) as a finality (Lyotard, 1994). Yet every attempt to bridge the aporia led to a new aporia. The aporia of reason is also the unbridgeability of 'intellection', on the one hand, and intuition on the other (Gasché, 1986). Again a third term arises in the attempt to bridge this: the 'imagination'. Again new aporias are discovered. What remains is undecidability, unbridgeability.

The critique that I have preferred in these chapters is not aporetic, not deconstructive, but Hegelian. I argued for the grounding of ethics in ethical life; for the grounding of signification in history. The same and other for Kant (and the theory of difference) stand in aporetic juxtaposition. For dialectics the same and other stand in confrontation in Hegel's *Herrschaft und Knechtschaft*, master and serf. Standing in the face of one another, there is the possibility of, not only struggle, but also recognition (Honneth, 1995; Yar, 1999). Here, same and other are more than just radically unknowable to each other, as in Levinas's aporetics (Chapter 7). Recognition presumes at least possibilities of translation, for fragments of a shared horizon. Without this there is no possibility of ethical life, of sociality, especially among individuals from diverse backgrounds. There would be no possibility of genuine multiculturalism. Dialectics – and the problematique of recognition – in this context would understand the subject as characterized by lack, vulnerability and openness.[2] In comparison, the aporetic subject would seem to be closed, indeed self-enclosed.

Dialectics is, of course, the basis of the critique of ideology, as critique in the national manufacturing society. The issue is can they work as a critique of information? Both aporetic and dialectical critique presume the possibility of a transcendental place from which critique can be launched. The global information culture tends to swallow up this transcendental order into its immanence, into the indifference of general informationalization. Thus Chapter 7 advocated critique through sociality. But what happens when sociality itself becomes networked (Wittel, 2000)? What happens when sociality itself becomes swallowed up in the information order? What happens when intelligent machines mediate sociality? When it becomes a sociality of interfaces? Chapter 8 advocated critique via the 'long intersubjectivity' of tradition. But what happens when the past of this horizon is forgotten and long intersubjectivity becomes an extension into the future? What happens when the contingency of the future displaces the order of the past as our shared background assumptions? In the information age, it would seem that tradition and technology no longer stand counterposed. Instead they fuse, as in the architecture of Daniel Libeskind. Libeskind (2000) understands his Berlin Jewish Museum, not in counterposition to technology and the information order, rather, he sees the museum itself as technology. Here technology and memory stand more or less fused: even if memory is coded as a lack, as emptiness. Having addressed dialectical critique in terms of sociality and tradition, we now look at it in terms of *materiality*. The attempt to ground a dialectical critique in materiality is made *par excellence* by Henri Lefebvre. Lefebvre's materialism is a dialectics of spatial practice. As dialectics it is fully, as we shall see, a critique of representation. The ethos of materiality, of 'tactility', of what he calls the 'gestural', the 'chthonic' and the 'subterranean' in his dialectics makes his theory of space ideally suited for the critique of information.[3]

Organisms in Space

In the *Production of Space* (*Production de l'éspace*), Henri Lefebvre presents us with a fully basic model of how organisms gain their orientation in their worlds. For Lefebvre, the organismic condition is a metaphysics of space. Lefebvre's idea is truly a metaphysics of the production of space: based on the tenet that organisms orient themselves in the world by 'producing space'. This is more ambitious than Nietzsche's metaphysics, in which will to power of the human organism enables survival in the environment through use of its logical categories. It goes beyond Marxian metaphysics of the domination of agents over things, money, and means of production. For Lefebvre to thrive and survive means not so much power through slave moralities or over the means of production, but is instead a question of orientation in the world, of orientation in the life-world. It is a matter of finding our bearings in the world, and more specifically, orientation in space. For Lefebvre the way we orient ourselves in the world is through producing space; it is through the *production* of space.

In this orientation in the world, the ability to navigate is prior to the possibility of meaning. This bodily navigation is also a question of *power*. What kind of power? Lefebvre's metaphysics is far less humanist than Marx's. It is less humanist than even Nietzsche. Indeed, the model Lefebvre uses for the orientation and production of space for all organisms is *the spider*. Lefebvre begins from the spider: he begins from the way a spider orients itself in the world through the production of space. Here he differs little from his contemporaries, including the surrealist influenced Roger Caillois, who had joined Georges Bataille at the famous Collège de Sociologie (Von Grunebaum and Caillois, 1967).[4] He differs little from Jacques Lacan's early fascination with animals and mirrors (Jay, 1993). Lefebvre's paradigm case for the production of space begins from this non-human, this spider who produces space to gain its orientation, who produces space operating through a principle of mimesis. Through mimesis, through mirroring and imaging its own body, the organism – in this case the spider – extends its body through space, through a series of what he calls 'symmetries and dissymmetries'. It weaves its web through space, through producing and gaining power over space in a series of mirrors, of symmetries and dissymmetries, Lefebvre's spider is a body orienting itself in the world, through *extending* itself in the world. Through the production of space, a body extends itself in the world through copying itself, symmetrically and dissymmetrically, in its web and occupying space (Lefebvre, 1986: 75).

Lefebvre's metaphysics of space is a mimesis, in which all organisms, or at least all animals produce space. A mimesis that through these symmetries and dissymetries – through a series of movements of self-mirroring of the body – produces a web, a spatial *imaginary*. On the model of the early Lacan, animals can have imaginaries – based in the sense organs and mimesis. In weaving the web, organisms are also weaving their imaginary and extending their power over an arena of space. For all organisms there is a mimetics of space. For those very special sorts of beings that are human beings, the mimetics of space becomes also a *poetics* of space, in which orientation in the world now becomes also a question of *meaning*. In order for there to be meaning, organisms must symbolize: they must have a symbolic. In Gaston Bachelard's *Poetics of Space*, the unconscious is primordially spatial, bodily constructing its poetics in the nooks and crannies, the closets and alcoves and drawers of the house of the infantile dwelling, of childhood's memory (Game, 1995). Unconscious and spatialized memory is then the condition of adult ego activity. Childhood has woven a web of affective investment in private spaces. Childhood has indeed *produced* space, produced a spatial symbolic. What goes for individual memory is true of communities of human organisms, for tribes or cities or nations. Communities have collective memories, unconscious or unspoken. Collective or communal memory is profoundly spatial, rooted in myths of original production of space, which are origins of nations. Mythic and original communal production of space is the stuff of the tribal imaginary, the poetics of the national symbolic.

The Body

The Production of Space is a critique of structuralism. Lefebvre's anti-structuralism finds its basis in what he calls the 'habitus' and defines in contradistinction to 'intellectus'. This notion of habitus refers to a lived practice. Habitus (and *habiter*) can have two possible meanings. On the one hand it can refer to a set of meanings clustered around habit. This is the notion found in Pierre Bourdieu's (1977) early work, based on Marcel Mauss's notion of body techniques. The underlying assumptions in this are symbolic exchange and intersubjectivity. But *habiter* also means to live somewhere, and this is Lefebvre's focus. Habitus is lived space for him. It is lived spatial practices. To live in this context means much more than to reside. Lefebvre's idea of the lived is taken from the tradition of *Lebensphilosophie*, the vitalism of Nietzsche and Bergson. Lefebvre's habitus resembles Nietzsche's idea of the body.

Lefebvre's notion of the body is naturalist, a point he stresses repeatedly in *La Production de l'espace*. Like Nietzsche's will to power, it is based in a metaphysics of pre-human existence and quanta of energy. The linchpin of

Lefebvre's theory of space is the three famous types of (1) *practique spatiale* (spatial practice), (2) *représentations de l' espace* (representations of space) and (3) *espaces de représentation* (spaces of representation) (1986: 48–9). The foundational term of the three is the first, spatial practice. This is based in a naturalist conception of subjectivity. Its basis is the non-human subjectivity of the spider, who weaves his net, who weaves and creates his network, who 'secretes' his network, his lattice, in the 'appropriation of space'. He does this through the natural rhythms of life, creating paths and places as well as networks. The spider produces, secretes space from his body, working through symmetries and asymmetries already programmed into its body. Human bodies, communal bodies and social bodies also secrete paths, places, nodes, boundaries. They secrete routes and roots: they produce at the same time as appropriating space.[5] This is *'spatial practice'*.

In the beginning was, for Lefebvre, not the sign, but the body. The materiality, the tactility, the texture of space is the place from which Lefebvre can challenge representation. For Lefebvre the sign or discourse is bound up with life-destroying representations of space and not spatial practice. The sign and representation find their origins in the mirror, a material object, which gives us off as if we were someone else; which represents us at a distance. The mirror, whose precursor is our reflection in a brook or stream, bears a symmetry of image and original whose model is the bodily symmetry of the web-secreting spider. Such representations and symbols for Lefebvre are inevitable; they are not *per se* pernicious if they do not get the upper hand. The problem arises if representations separate off from and then dominate lived (spatial) practice. In this event death dominates over life, as dead labour dominates living labour in capitalism. Where the representation is an extension of, when it is contiguous and continuous with, lived practice, what is produced are 'spaces of representation'.

Lefebvre's naturalism is overlain with what might be called an 'energetics'. This derives from Bataille's Nietzschean idea of micro-energies of the brain, of quanta of information and of massive energies or excessive outlays of energies (1991: 176–80). These, measured in calories, are the energies of desiring, killing and producing. Lefebvre takes issue with functional notions of reproduction of bodies or systems, and instead underscores the excess of energy involved. It is that excess that leads to the expanded reproduction and appropriation of space. Bataille's excess is also wastage. It is unproductive energy expenditure that does not expand the system but escapes the economy – the *oikos* – of the system. Lefebvre's 'spaces of representation' are spaces of excess. Bataille was aware that in pre-capitalist formations such wastage, such useless expenditure found its way into monuments, splendour and churches. Such expenditure took the form of the games of the amphitheatre, of war as celebration. This sort of expenditure creates the initial Lefebvrian spaces of representation: in Greek sculpture, Romanesque crypt and gothic spire. Here the town or city is *imago mundi*: it is world image, deriving directly from the spatial practices of the surrounding countryside. Under capitalism, however, any such excess is reabsorbed into the reproduction of the economy. Here Lefebvre's (Bataille's) energies of dead signs of information, brought under the sign of capital, dominate. This destroys the massive quanta of energy of excess and expenditure.

The Sign

The city is for Lefebvre not something to be 'read'. Spatial practice is not a signifying practice. Indeed for Lefebvre the Peircean notion of a 'signifying practice' is a contradiction in terms. The sign for him is counterposed to practice. The sign entails 'mental space', the representation of space, and representations of space kill spatial practices. Thus the sign is intellectus as opposed to practice's habitus. The sign fixes, it is static and suffocates the becoming of lived space. What sort of signification is at stake in the production of space? In his initial discussion of the body he looks at various types of signification, focusing on the senses. He notes that the sense of smell cannot be broken into binary oppositions and so cannot constitute a signifying system. The sense of taste, however, can constitute a primitive system. He separates these 'tactile' senses – including touch and hearing – from what he calls the 'visual sense'. He talks of an architecture based on tectonics, rather than the visuality of the facade. Under the visual sense he includes both the image and the word. These are the abstract senses which in capitalism colonize the other senses. Any new spatial practice, any new representational spaces, will have to recapture the tactile against this dominance (Lefebvre, 1986: 232–3).

Semiotics includes symbolic signification, via the word. It includes iconic signification in regard to the visual. It includes finally indexical signification, defined by contiguity and often in terms of the sense of touch. But all three of these modes of signification are also regimes of representation, and in the first instance Lefebvre wants to avoid any of these. Tactility is even more basic, even more bodily, even more natural for Lefebvre than this. It relates not to the eye, but the hand, he underscores, to a materiality not of the signifier, but of material work with tools and explosions of bodily energy. This is tactility as work, and work naturally to survive. This tactility, the result of 'massive' mobilizations of bodily energy, does leave 'traces' on physical space. But these traces are not signs at all (Lefebvre, 1991: 17). They may later become symbols, these massive traces – sculptures, built huts, tools and the like. He notes that the labyrinth (that became a symbol) was in the first instance a military fortress. Lefebvre does not counterpose the more tactile signification of metonymy to the visuality of metaphor. He joins Nietzsche in opposing both metaphor and metonymy as 'lies'. He quotes from Nietzsche's early essay 'On Truth and Lies in an Extra-Moral Sense'. Nietzsche speaks of 'a mobile army of metaphors, metonyms and anthropomorphisms'. This army is 'a sum of human relations, which have been enhanced, transposed and embellished practically and rhetorically'. This army of signs 'after long use seem firm, canonical and obligatory to a people'.[6] For Lefebvre 'the point of departure of the process of metaphorization and metonymization ... is the body meta-morphosed'. Lefebvre's body 'orients' in a space, in a field. Through its orientation – up, down, left, right, through its energy and movements – its gestures – of symmetry and asymmetry – it produces space. Sense here is pre-semiotic. It is pre-human. It is more like orientation or direction.

Against semiotics, Lefebvre understands space in terms not of text but of *texture*. Thus the monument, that stands in a position of excess in comparison to the 'restricted economy', cannot – like a text – be subject to laws of signi-fication or classification. The monument is not a text but a texture 'made up of a large space covered by networks or webs', by 'strong points', the 'nexes' and 'anchors' of such webs (1991: 222).[7] Indeed the fundamental contradic-tion of contemporary space is between text and texture. The separation of text from texture initially takes place in Ancient Rome, where, unlike in Greece, purely functional buildings are devised. Unlike in the agora, purely symbolic objects begin to populate the forum. A fuller hegemony of abstract space comes only in early modernity, with Renaissance perspective. No longer was there the 'naturalness' of the aristocrat (p. 314) residing in his 'private *hôtel*', in which its 'essence' lived in its 'interior disposition' and in which there was no notion either of 'privacy' or of 'facade'. Now in the bourgeois house the private was separated from the public, the facade no longer an expression of its interior disposition. The facade now dominates, subject to the linearity of the perspectively oriented set of facades comprising the recently emerging 'street'.

Thus in the sixteenth century begins the domination of the sign over lived practice – the sign as capital, as facade. In the plan and the map, real lived space became increasingly subordinated to this 'Euclidean', 'perspectival' and visual logic. Realism of proportion and perspective in Renaissance paint-ing is also such domination of sign over texture. Mediaeval painting – clothed in darkness – contains the struggle between good and evil – between chthon-ian and telluric forces that characterized absolute and lived space. Now the empty signifier dominates. Modernist abstract painting and architecture is a further severing of sign from textures. A few modernists, however, such as Klee, embodied the late-modern contradictions of space. Such art did not show objects in space, but instead created space. The more tectonic among Bauhaus architects, such Van der Rohe, also produced not things in space, but space itself (pp. 124–5). This domination of sign over texture of lived space is exacerbated in what Lefebvre calls neo-capitalism. The domination of the sign replaces the residence by 'housing' measure in quantifications in square metres and interchangeable equipment. Simultaneously the divorce of facade and texture, of form and function sees the replacement – all within the zoned city – of the monument by the 'building'. This domination of the sign and facade is an 'externalization' of what was once as symmetry, as mirror, part of the body, part of nature. The dead externalization is effectively the projected Lacanian phallus – of the law, of heroic and military might. This externalization of the surveilling eye outside the body yields the 'violence' of 'phallic, visual and geometric space' (pp. 290 ff.). Neo-capitalism's 'flows' of micro-energy information and signs further devaluate urban texture.

Work

Work is one type of spatial practice. Gestures, Lefebvre notes, are not a signifying but a spatial practice. Lefebvre discusses work under the heading of gestures. Through gestures the body appropriates social space. Signs and other representations of space operate through the expenditure of micro-quanta of energy. They destroy the massive expenditures of spatial practice. Gestures, however, are pre-discursive. They operate through massive expenses of energy. War, sport and (with tools as extensions of the body) work are examples of such gestures. These gestures produce the space of the workshop, the barracks and the stadium. The gestures of merchants create the space of mediaeval markets. The gestures involved in spatial practices, in spatial architectonics 'appropriate space'. Lefebvre speaks of two sorts of productive relation. These are relations of, on the one hand, 'appropriation' and, on the other, 'domination'. In pre-capitalist modes of production the appropriation relationship is hegemonic. Under capitalism, domination is hegemonic. Appropriation, Lefebvre observes, is 'where nature is converted directly from an enemy, an indifferent mother, into "goods"' (p. 165). Appropriated space is a 'natural space' modified 'to fit the needs of a group'. Textured or tectonic spaces are appropriated spaces in that they 'recount the lives of those who inhabit them'. Appropriation is an expression of forms of life, while domination further reflects the 'hierarchical classifications of a group's members' (pp. 229–30). Lefebvre contrasts 'the work' and the product. The work here 'engenders' and 'fashions' a space while products circulate in space. The work is singular, while product is interchangeable and can be reproduced exactly. The work is superimposed on the use-value of nature, while the product involves exchange value. The purest and highest form of the work is the work of art. If the work of art was a spatial production of an individual body, then whole cities can be seen as works – in terms of the collective spatial practice of a social body.

Spaces of Representation: Subterranean and Absolute Space

In neo-capitalism, for Lefebvre, there is the utmost hegemony of representations of space over spatial practice. How can we redeem spatial practice in such a context? The place to look of course has to be in 'spaces of representation'. The place to look is in the sort of representations that are extensions of the 'perceiving' body. These are indeed abstract 'conceived' spaces; but at the same time they are 'lived' spaces. They are loci in which representation does not kill off practice. The original mode in which such representations take place – through the model of bodily symmetry – is in the mirror as natural and physical object. The primordial representations that Lefebvre speaks of are those of magic. Magic entails bodily orientation – of symmetries and asymmetries – of not left and right, but up and down. 'Caves, grottoes and underground places provide the starting point for representations of the world and myths of the earth mother' (p. 194). Magic comes from these chthonian depths – 'the abyss of the underworld', bespeaking fertility, 'where the seeds are sown and the dead are laid'; it is violent, it is 'cryptic' (p. 245). In magic, as Max Weber suggested, symbolic violence has real effects. This original 'space of representations' was lived by most people until well into the nineteenth century. It is not an abstract or empty space in which things happen, but an experience of space;

> by means of a representation of an interplay between good and evil forces at war throughout the world, and especially in and around those places which were of special significance for each individual: his body, his house, his land, and also his church and the graveyard in which he received his dead. (p. 79)

This underground space is 'inherited from the Etruscans' (p. 41), whose only known inscriptions are few and short and seem to refer entirely to funeral practices, and whose cult of the dead, similar to contemporaneous Egypt, produced a highly developed sepulchral art. In eighth century BC Etruria clay sarcophagi and urns were modelled with great skill, bearing the haunting smile of archaic Greek sculpture. Fresco paintings were common in the underground funerary vaults, depicting banquets, festivals and scenes of daily life. In such a setting;

> all signs are bad signs, threats – And weapons. This accounts for their cryptic nature, and explains why they are liable to be hidden in the depths of grottoes or belong to sorcerers. Signs and figures of the invisible threaten the visible world. When associated with weapons, they serve the purpose of the will to power. (p. 134)

Lefebvre thus underscores the chthonian nature of spaces of representation:

> Bearers of a clarity at once auspicious and ill-starred, symbols and signs were at first cryptic in character (but in a material sense); concealed in grottoes or caves, they sometimes caused these places to be cursed, sometimes to be holy, as sanctuaries or temples. The truth of signs and the signs of truth are contained within the same enigma: the enigma of the Roman *mundus* – the hole, the bottomless pit. The enigma too of the Christian reliquaries – those underground churches or chapels so aptly named 'crypts'. And the enigma finally, of an opaque body – or opaque bodies – whence truth emerges into stunning clarity: the body that brings light into the darkness. (p. 187)

These dark, gestural spaces of representation stand in counterposition to practice-destroying representations of space. Such cryptic and material signage predominated in tribal cultures and in the Romanesque space of Early Christianity. The latter was sepulchral, based on the holiness of tombs, based on the massiveness of Romanesque walls that enforced an inner darkness, an outer bluntness and sullen-ness. Early Christian painting was thus kept in vaults: was meant not to be seen but to be. The holiest places were tombs – of Christ and St Peter in Rome and Jerusalem. In the holiest places monks met in cloisters. They contemplated death as religion focused on church crypts, holding the remains of consecrated figures, of martyrs, 'bearing witness from the catacombs'. Here the struggle of life and death forces in absolute space took place under the sign of subterranean space, reigned over never by sculptures but by crypts and tombs, by unseen paintings containing magical forces (p. 254).

'Absolute space' is the enemy of subterranean space. Absolute space is not cryptic: it rises into the light. Absolute space can decrypt the crypt. Absolute space contains the representational volumes of the sculptural. These are omnipresent in Ancient Greece and Mediaeval Gothic. Diametrically opposed to the enclosures, the rude walls of Etruscan tombs and Romanesque crypts, stood Greek temples like the Parthenon, whose absolute space contained nothing at all, but is instead a space 'of aspects but no facades', of 'volumes, perceived, conceived and clarified by the light of the understanding'. Previous confusion of outside from inside, of form, structure and function is lifted in the clarity of the (Doric, Ionic and Corinthian) orders themselves as load-bearing structures. In absolute space facade and ornament are unified with structure: external appearance and architectural composition are one. For Hegel (1970: 33, 63), the Greek mind perceived space in order to shape it. The Greeks were a nation of sculptors, 'taking natural materials and endowing them with meaning', rendering 'concrete social abstractions such as assembly, shelter and protection'. The Greek polis, with its acropolis and agora, 'came into being upon a hilltop', 'attended by the clear light of day' (Lefebvre, 1991: 237–9, 247). Lefebvre applauds the unity of form and content in Greek space as realizing the 'concrete universal'.

The Gothic emerges with Scholasticism's enlightened Aristotelian challenge to Augustine's Romanesque blind faith. Thomism was charged with bringing potency into act, matter into form and being into essence. The Gothic was a unity of self-intoxicated vitalism and logical formalism, at once spikily linear and restlessly active. Flying buttresses had relieved the once massive Romanesque walls of load-bearing responsibility. The reduction of opaque wall surfaces led to an articulation of walls as transparent and weightless curtains, almost entirely made of stained glass. The Thomist unity of reason and faith – counterposed to Augustine's (who wanted to suppress Aristotle as the Father of heresy) idea of truth as a matter of faith alone, is reflected in the ribbed vaultings and pointed arches, giving Gothic structures an articulation of impressive clarity. No longer were there the heavily separated and clearly delineated areas of the Romanesque churches. Now there was – as in the Parthenon – airiness and a unified spatial scheme (Mâle, 1983). In Lefebvre's Gothic, the underworld had come to the surface. 'Everything formerly hidden, the secrets of the world, demonic and evil forces, even natural beings – plants and animals – and living bodies, burst up into the light and took their revenge.' The signs of the 'non-body became subordinated to the body – including (and especially) the resurrected body of the living god, of Christ' (Lefebvre,

1991: 259, translation altered). The principle of sculpture, omnipresent on facades and in the lighted recesses of the transept opened up the cryptic and cryptal space of sepulchral paintings that went before. Illuminated manuscripts embodied the clarification of thought through language of the scholastic mind, as the rise of towns and burgher democracy paralleled the increased presence of human visages on the paintings on the stained-glass windows. This tectonic space of volumes rises into the light and 'de-crypts the space that went before' (p. 260).

Thus communities, the collective human equivalent of Lefebvre's spiders, produce space, through the mimetic extension of the social body. Where the produced space ends is an edge, the edge of the city, the darkness at the edge of town, the edge of the nation, and the walls defining that edge. The destruction of the ancient and classical city by the barbarians outside laid waste the walls, and heralded the triumph of movement, of the war machine, the vehicle, of the triumph of time over space, of urbanism over architecture of the modern city. The movement of the boulevards of Haussmann's Paris, of Vienna's Ringstrasse, of Hobrecht's late nineteenth century Berlin. But the space of the modern city and of its concomitant nation-state, the production of space by vehicles, by trains and mobile troops and driving machines, produced a new space of urban and national walls. The edge at which a city's driving machines and *machines à habiter* (Corbusier) thinned out. These new edges, these new walls still constituted the imaginary and symbolic of the city.

Space of Mediation

We do not, of course, produce space from new; we don't weave the web from a *tabula rasa*. We are instead thrown into a web of already existing relations, an already created imaginary, symbolic and real, already thrown and situated in a space of objects and other subjects. Cast adrift into such space we must survive in it; we must navigate in it. Spiders and other animals unmediatedly encounter objects – plants, animals and inorganic things – through their instinct structures. Human beings encounter objects and other subjects through *mediation*, through the mediation of those cultural entities we call signs. Lefebvre's spider navigates through the world in regard to sense (*Sinn, sens*). For human beings, *Sinn, sens* become meaning, which has always been mediated. These signs at one point were narratives, images and sounds mediated between us and things. In the ancient city these signs – words, the gestures and dithyrambs of theatre, sculpture, philosophy – are said to have been integral to the fabric of urban life, were part and parcel of the practices, the situated practices of citizens. The words and the things (*les mots et les choses*) intermingled and intermixed. In the modern city these signs enter a separate order of being as our doubles, as a set of cultural entities by which we measure our lives. These signs – the novel, the poem, music, the painted image – orient us in the world instrumentally, but more so bring us in touch with existential meaning, that is, the measuring of our lives. In Walter Benjamin's novel, 'the reader warms his shivering soul with a death he reads about'. The age of the sign is not just the age of representation, but also the problematization of representation, the deconstruction of representation.

The age of the sign is an age of mediation but not yet that of the media. The media are not comprised of signs. The media – film, recorded music, radio, the mass press and television – are not signs. They are machines. The mass media of communication are made up of sign-machines, of culture-machines. The press is an information machine; cinema and recorded music, entertainment machines; radio and television, both information and entertainment machines. Media machines are presentation and dissemination machines. They transfer content over large stretches of space. All machines – including material commodity producing ones – are *means*, but only sign machines are media. A medium is more than just a means. Other machines produce things. They transform raw materials into finished product. Media machines don't produce things. They present and disseminate things. They are indeed the mass media of communication. To present and disseminate is to communicate. In media you sense the content in the machine. It is a medium.

Mediation becomes machinic in the media age. With the proliferation of digital media, the experiential density of mediatic objects becomes so significant that we can speak of a parallel space. With mass media, mediation took place through a parallel realm, but one comprised of signs that were still one-dimensional or linear narrative, or two-dimensional (painted or photographic images). With digital media and the generalized brand environment, the signs become three-dimensional. They become tactile. They constitute and inhabit a space in which we orient ourselves. Representations-of-space for Lefebvre suffocated the life from spatial practice in homogenizing the grain of their particularity under the sign of an unhappy universal. But in the information age, as these representations transform into objects, they, themselves becomes spatial.

The nature of this parallel space means that cultural entities are no longer two-dimensional representations, but must be three-dimensional objects. The implications of this for culture and perhaps cultural studies may be vast. The subject matter of cultural studies may change: it would no longer be texts or narratives, or even signs or audiences or authors. The subject matter of cultural studies would become *objects*. The problematique of cultural studies would no longer be the affirmation or deconstruction of classical narrative. It would comprise a more architectonic, object like, yet bodily notion of culture: one in which bodies navigate through a sort of object space. The encounter with such cultural objects is neither semiotic nor iconic but indexical, tactile and haptic. Thus back to Lefebvre and Caillois and insect bodies extending themselves via mimesis and alterity. Meaning for Heidegger and in German is *Sinn* ('*Der Sinn des Seins*'). *Sinn* of course also means 'sense'. And prior to logical meaning, prior to the emergence of any symbolic or imaginary, spiders, through sense (through *Sinn*), *im*mediately oriented themselves in space and produced space. The older narratives were signs that mediated between humans and material things. More specifically, narratives were our main help in navigating among these material things. But now, in the world of things, largely due to patterns of valorization of capital, the cultural things are starting to match in frequency and even start at certain points to out-number the material things. And with the increase of images, of culture machines, of information, of icons of brands and the like, narratives now just become one of many types of cultural thing. When cultural things reproduce so promiscuously, they come to be encountered directly without the aid of signs. We no longer need signs to navigate amongst the cultural things. We encounter them directly, tactilely. We encounter narratives for their part as just another cultural thing. We encounter cultural things as just one among many types of thing.

Immanent Space: Explosion and Indifference

The walls of the ancient city, as they gained in opacity, already became a sort of 'third space', a space between inside and outside, a space between death on the one hand and individual and communal identity on the inside. This is Ed Soja's (1996) *Thirdspace*, in which the boundary, the walls between inside and outside in Los Angeles, between same and other, white and black, begin themselves to take on an opacity. These boundaries, dividing the lives of the city, begin to constitute an imaginary for the city. The wall, as spatial horizon, is the border, the boundary between inside and outside, which actually imparts meaning or sense (*Sinn*) to inside (human beings) and out-side, death, infinity, angst. This third space is also quite clearly the space of difference. Derrida (1992), in his book *Given Time*, says this third space of difference is more primordial than either being, on the inside, or time, on the outside. The third space of difference is the limit, the condition of possibility of both being and time. But what happens when this third space of the wall, of difference, explodes? What happens when the symbolic, the imaginary, explodes and fragments, not implodes, but explodes? What happens when the space of difference explodes to yield instead a space of *in*difference? Now technology, death and desire, as in J.G. Ballard's and David Cronenberg's *Crash*, themselves become units of information. Now the first, real space of the global city becomes increasingly indifferentiable from the second, parallel space, as agents in the first space too, intelligent agents, pre-selected by class, gender and income category, navigate among the brands, among the icons in the international airport lounges and central business districts.

The explosion of the third space into the indifference of information, bits, chips, drives, microbes, genetic units, places, roles and terminals, brings with it a certain destabilization. This eventually finds a new order in Castells's network society, in which bit streams are managed and stabilized in the links and terminals of the networks. The network society is what comes after the risk society. It puts order into the previous disorder of disorganized capitalism. It imparts a new systematicity to the previously fragmented world system. It re-stabilizes the risks of Beck's (1992) risk society partly by calculatingly colonizing – through for example futures markets – the future. The network society creates a new order and hierarchical chain of linked global cities, of urban space and cyberspace. The network society, the parallel space of links and terminals, links and machines, brings with it new walls. There are first the new walls between the individuals and their machines comprising the terminals, what Virilio calls the polar inertia of the human-machines. The terminals of the network society are static. Each terminal isolated from the other, each in a relationship of surveillance to the others. Networks stabilize, creating another set of walls, another set of boundaries, between those with and without access to the means of information. The antidote to this production of parallel and network space is a return to Lefebvre's spider. Perhaps we might then look at two alternative modes of production of today's parallel space. These are 1) network-constructing versus 2) web-weaving. The terminals of the network society are static. The bonding, on the other hand, of web weavers with machines is nomadic. They form communities with machines, navigate in cultural worlds attached to machines. These spiders weave not networks, but webs, perhaps electronic webs, undermining and undercutting the networks. Networks need walls. Webs go round the walls, up the walls, hide in the nooks and crannies and corners of where the walls meet. Networks form linear links between objects; webs irregular and curvilinear links. Networks connect algorithmically. Webs connect analogically. Networks are in the present, looking to calculate and colonize the future. Walter Benjamin's 'storyteller' was a web weaver. Benjamin spoke of a web of stories coming from long ago and far away. Webs (for Benjamin and today) form a ladder with the past, connect the heavens with the earth, cosmology with materiality. Networks are shiny, new, flawless. Spiders' webs, in contrast, attach to abandoned rooms, to disused objects, to the ruins, the disused and discarded objects of capitalist production. Networks are cast more or less in stone, webs are weak, easily destroyed. Networks connect by a utilitarian logic, a logic of instrumental rationality. Webs are tactile, experiential rather than calculating, their reach more ontological than utilitarian.

Critique of Representation

In such a context the work of Henri Lefebvre is of the utmost significance. In Chapter 1 we worked from the opposition of, on the one hand, *Ideologiekritik* and, on the other, the critique of information. What Lefebvre gives us is a very specific type of *Ideologiekritik*, and that is the critique of representation. Lefebvre's *Production of Space* is a political challenge to capitalist production. But whereas Marx's *Capital* is a critique of political economy, Lefebvre's book is a critique of representation. It is literally, the whole book, dedicated to the critique of the 'representation of space'. But it is more than a challenge to representations of space. Lefebvre, as we argued above, lays out a philosophical anthropology in *The Production of Space*. In this philosophical anthropology all representation is the representation of space. Just as all practice – whether private or public, whether in the economy or polity or culture – is spatial practice (*practique spatiale*). Human beings are constitutively symbol-using animals: hence our spatial practice is also symbolic practice. Under capitalism, when these symbolic practices come under the aegis of capital they become representations of space. When they do not, they create 'spaces of representation'. It is unfortunate that Lefebvre uses the word representation to describe these positive spaces, because the cultural practices that he alludes to in these spaces are all anti-representational. They are 'gestural', 'material', 'chthonic' and 'subterranean', but not representational.

Lefebvrian spatial practice operates in an idiom, in an immanent world integral to what we have described as the critique of information. Yet his challenge, his spatio-political challenge, remains a critique of representation. This is not false. It was only too true at the time of writing of *The Production of Space* in the nineteen sixties and early seventies. Cultural domination then still took place largely through ideology and representation. Lefebvre's theory does not need changing for the information age. Indeed, no change of theory is necessary. This is because the representation of space is itself changing. There is something a-spatial about representations of space. There is a universalism without regard to the complexity and materiality of the particular. In the information age, however, there is a *spatialization of representation*. What were previously images and narratives take on objectual form. With the disappearance of the relatively timeless and spaceless representations of space, all that is left are spaces of representation. Spatiality triumphs in the information age. What was the ideological 'realm' or 'instance' becomes an object space, a space of technology. Political and cultural struggle now must be fought out in this immanent space.

Notes

1 This corresponds, of course, to the contradiction of instrumental reason and substantive rationality in Max Weber and the Critical Theory of the Frankfurt School: Adorno, Horkheimer, Marcuse and Habermas.

2 Lacan was fundamentally influenced by Hegel's dialectic of recognition. His subject is constituted through lack.

3 See Shields (1998) for more general and in-depth considerations of Lefebvre.

4 I am grateful to Celia Lury for introducing me to Caillois's work.

5 See Clifford (1997).

6 Nietszche here quoted in *The Production of Space* (Lefebvre, 1991), pp. 138–9.

7 All subsequent citations are from the English version of *The Production of Space* (Lefebvre, 1991).

10

Being After Time

Heidegger claims in *Being and Time* that time is the horizon upon which we are to come to encounter and understand the meaning of beings: the horizon on which beings have meaning for us. Time is the horizon on which that very specific being, *Dasein* – or our singularity as human beings – comes to have meaning for us. Heidegger was, of course, a philosopher and philosophers tend to think in terms of the transcendental. In this chapter I suggest that much can be gained in grasping Heidegger's thesis, not in terms of transcendentals, but rather in terms of sociocultural change. I suggest that we think of our identification of beings and the self on the horizon of time as something specific to modernity. I suggest that we ask on what temporal horizon did we constitute the meaning of beings and ourselves before we did so on the modern horizon of time. I want especially to consider whether we still are encountering beings and ourselves on the horizon of time. I want to think about the possibility of an epoch of temporal experience prior to that of time, which can be understood as tradition or better yet 'history'. And I want to speculate about an epoch posterior to that of time, what might be called a temporal experience, not of time, but of 'speed'. In other words, I suggest that we might think about what being may be like *after* time. I propose to interrogate how we might encounter beings and the self in this new epoch of temporal experience. I want to raise the question of where we might locate the political, or politics, in not only the temporal experience of time but also in the era before that of time and the one after the time era. I want to examine what sort of politics are possible in an era of speed, in an era of being after time. I want finally to argue that in an era of being after time there should be a politics, not of difference, but of *melancholy*.

Some words of warning before I begin. First let me underscore that I am using the locution 'time' in a very restricted sense: that is, to understand a mode of temporality that is characteristically modern. May I ask the reader to bear with me and suspend his/her propensity to think about the notion of time generically? The term that I am using to cover all the generic modes of time in this essay is 'temporality'. I want to use time only in the sense of time in modernity, because it is in modernity that the idea of time has been lifted out and abstracted from ongoing special relations in a way that it is not typically in traditional social orders. Second, when I speak about 'we' I am referring to people living in the era that is emerging subsequent to the age of 'time'. I am referring, in particular, to people who have access to the information and communication flows of contemporary technological cultures. But I am also referring to those who are more or less excluded by these flows. The experience of the excluded is also radically reconfigured in speed's temporality. And they, too, are perhaps fated to a politics of mourning, a politics of melancholy.

As a guide for these modes of temporal experience I want to use the work of Walter Benjamin in general and 'The Storyteller' in particular. This essay by Benjamin is the best I have seen in evoking crucial dimensions of temporal experience prior to the age of time, whether the latter is conceived as history, tradition or memory. If time is the horizon on which the meaning of being is constituted in modernity, then this surely was not the case for the storyteller. *Being and Time* is mostly about Time and *Dasein*, mostly about time and the self. For Heidegger (1986: 142–7) a future-oriented notion of 'becoming' is essential to the way we perceive the meaning of beings and ourselves, if there is to be authentic existence on the horizon of time. Even more important for Heidegger is that we come to know and experience ourselves in terms of the temporality of death, of our own singular death. He means that we are a death-bound subjectivity, and that we can best know just what sort of subjectivity we are through grasping our existence towards our own singular (that is, not universal and not particular) death.

Stories and Novels

Walter Benjamin's 'The Storyteller' is an essay consisting of a set of fragments which are, at the same time, a series of proverbs that juxtapose principally two types of text; the storyteller and his story on the one hand and the novel on the other. The story, or more precisely the tale (the storyteller is *'Der Erzähler'*) corresponds to a mode of temporal experience that precedes time. It is integral to a temporality not of time but of history. The novel for Benjamin – who draws heavily on Lukács's theory of the novel – is very similar to the Heideggerian temporality of the modern. The novel, 'warms the reader's shivering life with a death he reads about' (Benjamin, 1977a: 457). The novel, like *Dasein*, is concerned, indeed derives its structure, its 'inside', its meaning, from a being towards a single and singular death: the death of the protagonist, that of the novelist and that of the reader, and as importantly, the death or closure of that singular novel, that singular narrative itself (1977a: 449). The storyteller's tale for its part deals not with one singular death but instead with lots of deaths: indeed death circulated within the gift-economy of the community of storytellers and story-hearers (Benjamin, 1977a: 450). Whereas Lukács contrasted the novel with the epic poem and epic poet, Benjamin places the novel in juxtaposition to the craftsman, the artisan, the travelling journeyman of the gothic city (p. 447). Now, if the reader of the novel warms his shivering life with a death he reads about, the life of the artisan is not shivering. It is sturdy. It is embedded in a set of values, in forms of life, in collective memory that are alien to the reader of the novel.

The novel, unlike the tale, is a narrative: a single narrative with beginning, middle and end. The tale of the storyteller is not a single, disembedded narrative but is tangled up with what Benjamin calls a 'web' of tales, a web constituting a ladder that spans space and time, the profane and the sacred (p. 457). The novelist's narrative is a work of art. It is disembedded and finds its meaning as such. The storyteller's tale is, like the artisan's product, not art but artefact. It is inextricably intertwined in a set of practices (p. 448). Told slowly, the story, unlike the novel, is not written against death but has plenty of time (Foucault, 1977). The temporal experience of the tale is *Erfahrung*, of the novel *Erlebnis*. Paradigmatic for the storyteller was the experience, the '*Erfahrung*', of the '*erfahrende Geselle*', the journeyman, the master artisan who was exper*ienced*. Here experience was not separated from the grain of forms of life, from practices linked to forms of the good life. Tale telling was from the teller's to the hearer's experience. Tale telling took place at work, engrained in the experience of work, according to the rhythms of work (Benjamin, 1977a: 441). The chrono-experience of the novel and the era of time is clearly *Erlebnis*, or subjective experience, disembedded from forms of life. *Erfahrung* is grounded in a temporality where values inhere in forms of life; in *Erlebnis* we create our own subjective values. The 'novel', writes Benjamin, 'gives evidence to the profound perplexity of the living' (1977a: 455). The novelist is 'isolated'. The novelist does not speak from his experience, from his situation. The storyteller works from his experience to the listener's situated experience. The novelist and reader do not communicate experience, nor are situated in their own experience. Both reader and writer are lifted out from their experience.

If the story gives counsel through the communication of experience, the novel centres around 'the meaning of life'. The story-hearer, grounded in experience, is not concerned about the meaning of life. The story-hearer cannot get, and surely does not want, that sort of distance on life. Death, in the novel, lets the reader intuitively grasp the meaning of life, in that death is the end of temporality. In its closure (as in classic narrative) death imparts to the reader the meaning of life when the novel ends or the character dies. Thus the novel imparts meaning through death as closure, while the story imparts meaning through death as continuity. The novel imparts meaning through death as 'finis', as irreversible time (1977a: 455). The story imparts meaning through death as reversible time: indeed, through the reversible time of history (Baudrillard, 1976: 207).

The story works from a number of deaths, the novel from a single death. In the story memory is 'reminiscence' and in the novel 'remembrance'. Remembrance is 'dedicated to one hero, one odyssey', while reminiscence is to 'many diffuse occurrences' (Benjamin, 1977a: 453–4). Through reminiscence the story-hearer receives counsel in the 'moral of the story'. The single remembrance in the novel imparts to the reader not the moral of the story, but the meaning of life. This becomes available only through remembrance, that is, when, 'the subject' ... has 'insight' into the ... 'unity of his entire life ... out of the past life-stream which is compressed in memory' (1977a: 455). This unity of remembrance is the experience of death (as irreversible finality). The reader must read the novel in terms of the already known death of the protagonist. Only then can the reader grasp the meaning of life from the novel.

The novel, Lukács said, is the form 'of transcendental homelessness', and 'time' can only be 'constitutive' in this context (1977a: 454). Only in a situation of transcendental homelessness can time – in the sense of death as finality – become constitutive of the meaning of life. Heidegger's notion of time and death thus becomes no longer a philosophical transcendental, but a sociological characteristic of modernity. That is, time is the transcendental horizon of subjectivity, and of being, only in modernity. Time is integral to a quintessentially modern episteme. Time as irreversible, as abstracted from practices, as abstracted from history and tradition, would only be thinkable as a topic in modernity's aporia, in modernity's perplexity. In this sense Newton's homogenous space-time partakes of the same temporality as the novelistic time – in which death constitutes duration – of Proust and Heidegger.

Being, for the storytelling and hearing artisans, would appear not on the horizon of an 'outside' of time or death, but in the very unapocalyptic rhythms of *history*. Being would appear in tradition. The storyteller and the craftsman work to slow rhythms. The storyteller works not through the strong intentionality of the novelist, but through the habitus and habit. To listen to a story requires not the vigilant monitoring of late-modern self-identity, but 'a state of relaxation'. It requires not the alertness of the novel reader, but 'a state of boredom as the apogee of mental relaxation'. Such relaxation is only possible in 'the listener's self-forgetfulness' that arises when the 'rhythm of work has seized him'. Only then 'does the gift of retelling come to him all by itself' (1977a: 446). This is the 'web' (*Netz*), the web – 'now becoming unravelled at all its ends' – connecting listener-tellers in which 'the gift of storytelling is cradled' (p. 447). This is the slow and repetitive temporality of the story. It works only through being repeated. *Der Erzähler* works not creatively, but as a natural being imitating other things of nature. He does not create but lets things of nature achieve their own perfection. He works in an eternal time, so he has plenty of time. He does not share the novelist's worries about closure, but instead partakes in 'a patient process' in 'which a series of thin, transparent layers are placed one on top of the others' – 'a patient process of nature', a 'product of sustained, sacrificing effort' typical of an age 'when time did not matter' (p. 448).

The storyteller initiates the web, of not just the retelling (*erzählen* shares similar roots with the tale and to tell) of the one story, but of all the stories. 'One ties to the next', in an endless time, perhaps best known in the great Oriental storytellers. 'In each there is a Scheherazade who thinks of a fresh story whenever her tale comes to a stop' (p. 453). For the historian (and in historiography as distinct from history, time is already lifted out and problematized) and the novelist, the heavens and the earth 'have grown indifferent to the fates of the sons of men and no voice speaks to them from anywhere'. Now stones, for example, 'are measured and weighed and examined for their specific gravity and density, but they no longer proclaim anything to us. Their time for speaking with men is past.' But the storyteller keeps faith with the 'naive poetry' of things. His is not just a temporal web from teller to hearer, from master to journeyman to apprentice. It is also a spatial web, a vertical webbed ladder. A 'web' that is both 'the golden fabric of the religious view of the course of things' and the 'multicoloured fabric of a worldly view' (p. 452); a web that is a 'ladder extending downward to the interior of the earth and disappearing into the clouds' which is 'the image for a collective experience to which the deepest shock of every individual experience, death, constitutes no impediment' (p. 457).

Politics of Difference

The age of the storyteller was the age of what Hannah Arendt called the political: politics and the meaning of being – and human beings – were subordinated to the logic of the good life (Benhabib, 1996), to practices, internal goods, virtues and *values* woven into the fabric of forms of life. Time, in this sense, was woven into the grain of a set of embedded values. Whereas political constitutions of modern states are based on a set of procedural rules within which individuals can pursue their own value-choices, these substantive values were the ground principles of ancient political constitutions. The logic of these pre-modern values, as carried in the stories of the storytellers, centred around a substantive goal that was the good life of the political community, of the polis.

Now in the age of time, the age of the Proustian perplexity, the undecidability of the novel, the political takes on vastly different contours. The political and the meaning of beings and human beings comes to appear in the space of undecidability, the space of difference (see Grosz, 1998). Derrida thus pronounces in *Given Time*, '*es gibt Zeit*' and '*es gibt Sein*', that is, 'it gives time and it gives being' (Derrida, 1991: 201–2). Here Derrida is criticizing implicitly, and going a step beyond, Heidegger's temporal constitution of the meaning of Being. For Heidegger, time is the horizon in which the meaning of beings is unveiled. For Derrida, talking of the gift in terms of '*es gibt*' (it gives), this '*es*', this 'it' that gives, is the horizon for the understanding of both beings and time. What is this *es*, this it? It is surely the space of difference.

For Heidegger the 'same' or meaning of beings is constituted via the other, that is, death or time; the inside is constituted by the outside, presence by absence. Difference, instead, is the space *between* presence and absence, the 'third space' between the same and the other, the space of undecidability, of ambivalence of the aporia, of perplexity. The space of difference is a margin, a border, the tain of a mirror (Gasché, 1986), a fold, that is the border between the inside (beings) and the outside (time or death). It is a semipermeable fold, an 'invaginated surface' separating the restricted economy of the same and the general economy of the other. This is the place of difference, more primordial than either Being or time. The space of difference is the space of the political, it is a space of antagonisms, of perplexities, of aporias, unresolvable and unavoidable tensions between freedom and necessity, same and other, being and time. It is Bauman's (1991) space of 'ambivalence', of the unclassifiable, Bhabha's (1990) 'third space' of 'performativity'. This space is significantly referred to by Derrida as the '*es*' of the '*es gibt*'. This *es* is, of course, in contrast to the *Ich* and *Uber-ich* – is what we know in English as Freud's *id*; it is Lacan's real. It is not the papered over 'same' of the symbolic, nor the complete otherness of melancholy and schizophrenia. It is, instead, the place of political antagonisms – the unresolvable 'friend vs. foe' logic of the political.

Speed, Indifference, Apocalypse

In 'The Storyteller' there are not two but three modes of cultural inscription, each of which opens out onto its own characteristic temporality. The first is the story which connects to history (tradition). The second is the novel whose characteristic temporality is 'time'. The third type of inscription is *information*. In 'The Storyteller' Benjamin hinted vaguely towards an age of information, based on discussion of the newspapers, in which narratives of the novelistic became fragmented into the brutality of the fact. No longer either an artefact or a work of art, no longer concerned with death, these newspapers were of no use tomorrow, fully located in a temporality of 'the now'. Benjamin argued that information is facts that carry their own explanation in them (Benjamin, 1977a: 444–5). Indeed, the logic of Benjaminian history is one of the unravelling of a web. Here the ever-extending and never-ending web of stories of the storyteller, connecting cultural spaces and the generations in time, fragments into the novel's individual narratives, now are limited to the individual's subjective cultural space and to one generation of time. This is the closure of classical narrative: the web of stories fragments into a large number of short *durée* narratives. As we move to the postmodern age of information there is a further fragmenting of the web. The web fragments further into a number of events, as individuals and objects now no longer are stories or even subjectivities but only points or nodes in a network. In this age of brute information the time of events and the society of the network are part and parcel of the new post-time temporal experience of *speed*.

The chrono-experience of history, tradition and the storyteller is the embedded time of *Erfahrung*. The subjective time of the novel implies *Erlebnis*. In this context, the immediate time of information connotes a third experiential mode of '*Chokerlebnis*' (Benjamin, 1974d: 729). *Chokerlebnis* is the time of the assembly line, which is neither a tale nor a narrative but a succession of jolts as 'nows'. The *flâneur*, and more generally Benjamin's melancholic, also live in an ambience of *Chokerlebnis*, overwhelmed by the violence of the rush of images, of events, of commodities in the city. *Chokerlebnis* takes place in a temporality not of difference or perplexity of ambivalence, but, instead, in a temporality of *indifference*. This temporal experience, no longer of time, but, instead, of speed, is one which speaks volumes to the contemporary cultural sensibility – in films, pop music. If the era of time is the era of difference, as the boundary, the fold between same and other, the era of speed heralds a time of *indifference*, a time of the explosion of the boundary, of the margin, of difference, of ambivalence. The temporality of speed involves an indifference between inside and outside: it is the explosion of any limit between restricted and general economies. Now, no longer does 'technology' constitute the space of the same, of presence, and death the space of the other, or absence. Desire is no longer in the space of lack, hence undecidability. But technology, death and desire themselves become signals. Technology, death and desire themselves become bits, become units of information on the horizon of speed's electro-magnetic field. Here they take their place alongside other informational units, alongside the humans and non-humans, alongside microbes and units of genetic information caught up in the swirling vortex of speed.

Now, no longer is it a question of *es gibt* but of *es denkt*, that is, 'it thinks', in an age of the inhuman, the post-human and non-human, of biotechnology and nanotechnology. If the symbolic was collective in the age of history, and individual (psychoanalysis) in the age of time, then the age of speed and information explodes the symbolic, breaking it into fragments, the objects we track in cities (Benjamin), or track in life on the screen (Turkle, 1995). The imaginary too is fragmented, leaving only the *es*, the real, and the real no longer is a desiring, but now itself a thinking 'substance'. *Es denkt*, it thinks; the era of speed is the era of thinking, calculating, information-rich and design-intensive non-humans.

If difference is exploded, then so is the political. The space of antagonisms is not resolved but exploded, as if antagonisms no longer matter: as if antagonisms and undecidability itself are nothing more than the baroque and meaningless ruins surrounding the melancholic of *Trauerspiel* (and *Trauer* is mourning: the mourning of, among other things, difference) or the *flâneur* in Paris (Benjamin, 1974a). The age of time was also the age not of tradition, but of the human, the very end of the age of the human. Even *Dasein* is a being that, while mortal, is of fully different status than other beings: even Derrida's difference circumscribes a clearly human subjectivity. In the age of time and difference things make a difference for *subjectivity*, meaning is deferred for *subjectivity*. But when things and animals and the unconscious also think, the human, in its singularity, is no longer privileged. The perplexity, the undecidability of human subjectivity is no longer decisive. Aporias recede into relative insignificance, undecidability no longer matters. There is nothing more at stake.

The age of the novel, that is of time and difference, is also the age of the risk society. There is surely a shift of important dimensions as we move from the risk society to the network society (Castells, 1996). Risk takes place in that same space of difference, the partial determinacy, the '*riskante Freiheit*', the need to cobble together what is a partly indeterminate life history (Beck, 1986). Reflexivity, in the sense of Kant's (1952) reflective judgement, is the epistemological basis both of risk society and of difference. In each case we are talking about a judgement in which the rule is not pre-given – as it was in the age of history – but where we must find the rule and even then that rule can never cover, never finally explain, that particular case we are judging, that particular decision we are making about our lives or in politics. Hence the centrality of not just knowledge, but also non-knowledge in both notions of difference and risk. But what happens when that space of difference explodes, when that margin, that third space vanishes into air? When all the fears and dangers of the risk society become realized in apocalypse, in disaster, in catastrophe? What happens when difference turns into indifference, when risk turns into apocalypse or disaster? What happens when the greatest fears of the politics of insecurity are realized: when we are living in the vortex of disaster?

The chrono-experience of the age of speed is a temporality of the apoca-lypse, not of risk. And Benjamin's *flâneur* is, at the same time, apocalyptic and post-apocalyptic. In post-apocalyptic time, perplexity is not at issue because what really counts has already happened and there is nothing to do but stroll, or better stagger, among the ruins of dead landscapes, cityscapes and 'culture-scapes'. Apocalyptic or catastrophic time is the chronology of a series, an uncontrolled rhythm of shocks, a vortex of overstimulation. The *flâneur* is both overwhelmed by the *Rausch* of commodities, of images, and yet his attitude is not one of perplexity, but indifference, it is blasé (Benjamin, 1974b: 560 ff.). Since meaning and the possibility of the good has been removed from the world, he is at the same time underwhelmed. The temporality of speed is, at the same time, apocalyptic and post-apocalyptic. The reaction, again, is that of the neurasthenic to sensory overload. It is Simmel's (1971) blasé attitude. What was at stake in the age of difference (time) and undecidability preceded the apocalypse. Apocalyptic time thus is not at all the time of perplexity. At issue is not a sort of existential tempo-rality of *Dasein*, of difference or of risk. In the age of history, predominant in the continuity of the generations was the past, the given-ness of the past. In the age of difference and risk, predominant is the future, the undecid-ability of the future. In the age of apocalyptic and post-apocalyptic time, the age of indifference and speed, there is nothing more at stake, there is no future. Here the melancholic is already dead; or at least lives amongst death – as just another signal, yet another sensation.

The new temporality is neither reversible as in history, nor irreversible as in the novel. The reversibility–irreversibility of pre-modern and modern time only makes sense if chronological experience is of past, present and future. But whereas the storyteller operates in reversible time and the novelist in irreversible time, the allegorist, the *flâneur*, operates in a now without past or future. This is the time of hypersurveillance, in which the past, digitized and stored, is available all of the time, and the future – that is techno-capitalism's future – is omnisciently and algorithmically and more or less probabilistically predictable, as man approximates God's omniscience and begins to be stationed outside of time (Lyotard, 1991). The now time's chronology is the speed of light: the instantaneous time in which – as the increment between departure and arrival incessantly shrinks – there is the simultaneous arrival of everything without there ever being a departure (Virilio, 1990). In an experience of generalized simultaneity, the experience of simultaneity – so central to the temporality of the novel – itself vanishes. Without a temporal horizon of narrative, simultaneity loses significance.

The age of speed is, for Virilio (1986), an era in which there is no longer an opposition between culture and technology. No longer is culture a property of the 'I' and the eye of the transcendental subject, occupying a space still metaphorically of the sacred and standing counterposed to the world of objects, to the profane world of technology. In the age of speed, technology and 'the machinic' invade the space of culture and the subject. This emerges first in the First World War with the appearance of the 'war machine'. The principle of technology and the machinic displace the principle of the subject in war once the weapon is no longer an extension of the eye. Now the eye and subjectivity is disrupted by the lightning of air attacks, and the more rapid and disruptive movements of machines (tanks), of troop dispositions and *blitzkrieg*. The war machine, like recently emergent cinema, is also a 'vision machine'. In cinema, as distinct from the novel, we view the narrative through the eyes of not the protagonist, but of technology, of the camera (Poster, 1995). We no longer identify with the unified and coherent field of vision of the protagonist, but with the machine and thus a plurality of perceptual fields. In these early days only the margins of social life were affected by the encroaching logic of speed. Subsequently, however, the culture-machines have come to invade the home. Now the brown goods, information and image machines like television, video, computers, computer game consoles, satellite consoles, set-top boxes and telephone answering machines come to invade the household. With encroachment into the space of the private the age of speed also becomes the age of the most crippling and static inertia.

What happens to the meaning of Being, of both things and human beings, in the age of speed? Where do we find the political? If in the age of the storyteller the temporal horizon for the meaning of Being was history, in the age of the novel, the horizon for the meaning of Being has been time, or more recently difference. But when the tale and the narrative are de-legitimated, neither history (collective memory) nor time (individual – conscious or unconscious – memory) can function as the temporal horizon. Not even difference can be such a horizon for the (deferred) meaning of beings and the self. What is emergent here is Being after time. In Being after time, the meaning of beings and the self take place against the background of what Paul Virilio (1984) calls a 'negative horizon'. The horizon, whether as history or time, as tale or narrative, comprises an imaginary and a symbolic. In the age of history – of collective memory, of reminiscence and reversible time – the symbolic and the imaginary were collective (Durkheim and Mauss, 1963). Both symbolic and imaginary were in the habitus. The imaginary is staged on the level of perception, it works through resemblance. It is learned and it consists selectively of the images, icons, indices that are significant to a society, though not yet in any systemic way. The symbolic works through the systematization of these icons into a system so that classifications and law are possible. The imaginary works, more or less, analogically, the symbolic, more or less, logically. Now, with the shift from collective to individual memory, to Proustian remembrance, there is an individualization of the symbolic and the imaginary, as well as a repression into the unconscious. The images and symbols are still learnt, but now they are no longer merely unreflected as they were in the age of the storyteller. They are now unavailable to consciousness because repressed.

But what happens to symbolic or imaginary in the age of speed, the age of the negative horizon, in our apocalyptic and post-apocalyptic culture? Both symbolic and imaginary are exploded into fragments and disseminated outside of the subject into an indifference in which they attach to a set of human and non-humans, to objects of consumer culture, to images, to thinking machines, to machines that design. All that is left is a body without organs, a body that thinks, a machinic body that thinks, that symbolizes, that imagines. The individual, the human along with the symbolic, does not implode, but like the heads in David Cronenberg's *Scanners*, explodes, spewing microbes, non-humans, information, units of desire, death, images, symbols and semen: the sex-drive and the death-drive mix and mingle with the hard drive.

What about value? What if the embedded values and virtues and good life of the era of history, that is, where values are attached to virtue and the good life, cede to an age of time in which values are either no longer attached to the good life but to *goods* (homogenous labour *time* as capital) or to the subjective time and *Erlebnis* and the subjective do-it-yourself values of the individual? What happens in the age of speed in which the individual, the human, dissolves in the vortex of catastrophe? Perhaps the only thing possible, then, are neither traditional values, nor human values, but also non-human values. Here not only do values inhere in non-humans; but also non-humans are agents of evaluation, agents of judgement (Latour, 1993).

Politics of Melancholy

Where do we look, then, for the meaning of being, of beings and of the self when the political has been exploded? We might ask who is the subjectivity of such an age? Who is *Dasein* in a problematics of being and speed? What might political subjectivity be like? The answer may be that the existential hero of the age of time as political subject would need to be replaced by the melancholic. At stake in the age of difference is an existential politics of undecidability. At stake in the age of indifference, the age of speed, is a politics of melancholy.

This is the baroque melancholic that Benjamin discusses in *The Origins of German Tragic Drama*, an Early Modern melancholic. This is literally a melancholic in the sense of the doctrine of the humours: of the melancholic, the choleric and the phlegmatic. The melancholic is always mournful of a dying epoch. In the Reformation the melancholic is engaged in mourning the sociality of the traditional *Gemeinchaft* and the ritual of the Catholic Church as these are threatened by the transcendental God, Protestant ethic and absolutist ruler of emergent modernity. The melancholic appears again in a later modernity as mournful of the ruins of the commodity in Baudelaire's and Benjamin's Paris. This is an initial and precocious appearance of speed's melancholic, again mourning an earlier memory.

The politics of melancholy is first of all a politics of limits. *Dasein* is supposedly a finite being, a finite human being, a mortal, Heidegger insists. Yet there is something Faustian, something heroic, something activist, something of a life-world intentionality, and especially a fully different ontological status from other beings which suggests the nearly unlimited powers of *Dasein* or the existential hero. He makes his own decisions. She puts meaning into her own life. The politics of speed, of indifference, is a politics of much more radical finitude and limits. Now rights, for example, are granted to non-humans – thus Latour (1993: 144–5) speaks of a parliament of things, of non-humans including animals and nature. In these post-human politics, non-humans are recognized as having powers of judging (Latour), gazing (Benjamin), thinking (Deleuze, see Zourabichvili, 1994: 7–8), procreating (Haraway, 1992). Post-human politics is siding with the microbe, the virus, the gene, which attain an enhanced ontological status.

Unlike *Dasein*, unlike existential subjectivity or the subjectivity of difference, the melancholic is basically passive. In the age of history, in the premodern age of the polis, politics was embedded in the good life: this was largely an aristocratic politics, a noble politics, one had to be a man of substance to be a citizen. But melancholy is the basest of the humours. The melancholic, unlike Aristotle's virtuous and noble man, is a man not of the mean but of the extremes (Benjamin, 1974a: 318–19). The melancholic – the figures of the city, the prostitute, the rag picker, the opium eater and the thief – is not virtuous but vicious (Menninghaus, 1980). They are inactive. They do not use time, they – like prisoners – 'kill time'. They are the outcasts, occupying the wild zones, the dead zones of the city. The politics of speed, of melancholy, of indifference, is a politics of the outcasts, of the wild zones. The melancholic leads not the good life, but the bad life. These outcasts, for Benjamin, are most likely to be allegorists, most likely to glimpse the meaning of being and the self through the disused objects and the ruins of the city. This is not a politics of those living in the margins as undecidables or unclassifiables, but of people living on the other side of the margins, abjected or extruded into the wild zones.

It is a politics of innovation. Another group massively increasing in the age of speed, of indifference, are the legions of technoscientists and technodesigners, of techno-artists, coming to populate the advanced sectors – biotechnology, applications software, communications technology, but also for example, printing and multimedia in general (International Labor Office, 1996). These workers in the vastly expanding techno-culture sectors are producing life: they make thinking substance, they manufacture reflecting and reflective objects. They form communities with non-humans – with biotechnological and info-technological objects. They work less often in organizations or institutions than in unstable rhizomatic networks that dissolve and once again reform – operating in disorganizations. These techno-scientists and designers can run counter-current to the 'now' temporality of capital – of omniscience and surveillance of a determinate or probabilistically determinate past and future. They create indeterminacy in the future and resist its colonization. But for all the exhilarating innovation opened in the lines of flight of these technoculture workers, theirs will be an impoverished politics of irresponsibility in the absence of melancholy's memory and work of mourning.

Walter Benjamin's *angelus novus*, we remember, was dragged into the future. He was dragged into the accelerated now-time of speed, while always looking back at the past. Cast aside onto the junk heap by the utilitarian time of capital accumulation, the melancholic directs his gaze to past objects, to disused things, to the ruins of the city. The melancholic, as allegorist, has not forgotten the storyteller. Dragged into the future he looks back on not just the *Erlebnis* of individual memory, but onto and through the retrieval of collective memory, into the *Erfahrung* of the collective symbolic and imaginary. The melancholic looks back on tradition. He invents tradition. The melancholic, looking backwards, is a practitioner of a hermeneutics of not suspicion but of retrieval. Indeed, one of the archetypal memories that this politics of melancholy is straining to retrieve is the memory, the ghost, of difference itself. The politics of the melancholic reunites in another register dimensions of both time and value. For the storyteller, values (and virtues) were part and parcel of the grain of everyday temporality. Similar to the modern sociologist's separation of fact from value, the world of the novel prepares the diremption of time and value. Value in modernity may well be the condition of possibility of time. But, as between the realms of necessity and freedom, there is a gulf, an aporia, between the realms of time, on the one hand, and value, on the other. The indifference of global information culture for its part involves the explosion of the aporia: the disintegration of both time and value into the immanent and planar space of speed – a space from which it seems that there is no way out, no time out. Yet the melancholic may still inhabit the edges, the margins, of the space without margins of these global and digital forms of life. Through his work of mourning, through his chronic inability to forget, the melancholic may be our best hope of retrieval of any sort of politics of value.

Note

I would like to thank Scott Wilson for his comments on a previous draft of this chapter.

11

The Disinformed Information Society

Information

What is at stake in the information society? At issue are two types of information. Let us address the first type of information: it is inscribed in a problematic of rationality, of intelligence. It is inscribed in a problematic of knowledge: of knowledge-intensive production with increasingly intelligent machines and information-rich goods and services. This first type of information has to do with the fact that at stake is a knowledge-intensive society, not a work-intensive society. Knowledge, not material production, is the key. The information society is a knowledge society. It deals with the stuff of discursive knowledge. Discursive knowledge is analytic knowledge. It is based on abstraction, on selection, on simplification, on complexity reduction. Training in the information society is discursive: typically one-third of the labour force has completed university or tertiary education. This is an increase in what Max Weber called rationality. Such training in discursive knowledge, in highly codified knowledge stands in contrast to craft training in the manufacturing society. Discursive knowledge tends to work deductively as often as inductively. Craft knowledge is largely inductive, discursive knowledge deductive; craft training empiricist, discursive training rationalist. Discursive training teaches us to subsume cases under rules; craft training to look for what worked in the most recent similar case. Craft training has been most importantly developed in Britain and effective on a predominant scale up until a much more recent date in Germany. Work forces in France, the USA and Japan have for a much longer time undergone training in the context of more codified knowledge: in mathematical and verbal skills, and more recently computing skills (Lutz and Veltz, 1989).

Manufacturing requires learning through the habitus. Information production requires training that works less through the habitus than the ego. Information training requires distanced reflection, chronic problematization. Manufacturing training encourages more immediate and habitual, hands-on familiarity with materials and tools. Information training requires a Cartesian attitude. Craft training skills are concrete and not so easily transferable. Information training requires abstract skills that are eminently transferable. Craft training is somehow Heideggerian. In craft training the apprentice is very 'in-the-world' with the material objects: what Heidegger called a 'ready-to-hand' (*zuhanden*) relation with things. This contrasts with a distanced *vorhanden*, or 'present-at-hand', relationship more characteristic of Cartesian subject-object thinking. In the information society we are taught to be Cartesians; to chronically relate to the world in subject-object terms. We are taught to be Popperians. We are taught to be positivists – not empiricists – who are always testing out concepts, always involved in conjectures and refutations. We are taught to be rational – not just in the application of abstract rules; but also in the sense of reflexivity. We are always to be reflexively aware of other possibilities. All of this is absolutely central to the information society.

Labour-power in the information society contributes ideas. Labour-power innovates. Labour-power undergoes discursive education. Labourers-to-be produce papers justified through discursive argument, much like pure research laboratories do. These papers are structured through predicative utterances, evidence, formal cohesion and economy of formulations. Training in the information society results in the production of papers. These may be exam papers with multiple choices and correct answers. Often they are argued proofs, or theses backed up by experiential evidence. These immaterial and abstract products are proof that you have gained the knowledge to acquire the qualifications necessary to succeed in the information society. In the crafts, the apprentice became the journeyman and the journeyman a master with the production of a *maître œuvre*. This was a work in the material sense of the French *ouvrier*. The *art*isan produced an artefact: a finished *art*efact.

In the information society labour, or labour-power, has become informational. The means of production also become informational. In manufacturing capitalism, workers use practical knowledge in conjunction with material machines to process raw or semi-finished materials, in order to make material products. In information-capitalism labour power operates with not practical, but discursive knowledge; operates with not classical, but information machines; and works on not raw material, but on raw or semi-finished information in order to produce informational goods. There is thus a shift from material processing to information processing. Information processing works somehow logically. It brings particulars under universals (concepts, propositions) and produces new particulars. This is the notion of information that the vast social scientific literature – from Daniel Bell to Manuel Castells – has given us on the information society. Information processing works through a certain distance that the subject has over the object that he or she works with or consumes. In information-capitalism, Fordist accumulation is displaced by 'reflexive accumulation' (Lash and Urry, 1994: 60 ff.). In Fordist accumulation the producer is subsumed into the unreflexive mass: so is the consumer. Fordist accumulation is only, as Ulrich Beck (Beck et al., 1994) might say, halfway modern. Fully modern is reflexive accumulation. Now the subject-object thinking of modernity, the discursive consciousness, reaches full flower. The information society's reflexive accumulation witnesses a shift from economies of scale to economies of scope as reflexive consumers want to consume very different things from one another. This is because consumers too are rational, reflexive. They consume less out of habit than through reflection in terms of alternatives on the marketplace. On the production side, the design (or research and development) process starts to take over primacy from the labour process as ever more models, ever more prototypes for ever shorter production runs, comes to be the rule.

In the information society the production process begins to marginalize what Marx called the labour process. The knowledge-intensive production process displaces the work-intensive labour process. The labour process produces many or very many of roughly the same things. It produces commodities. The knowledge-intensive production process makes not commodities but 'singularities'. In many sectors – the media, digital media, advertising and a number of industrial sectors – this is design-intensive production. It involves a design process. In others it is mainly an R&D (research & development) process. Thus there is a shift from the centrality of the factory in the manufacturing society to the laboratory or the studio in the information society.[1] Note the operative term is not art or the aesthetic but design. The artist's studio produces singularities that remain singularities. The singularities that the design studio makes are *prototypes*; they are to be reproduced in great numbers. This represents a certain technologization of previously autonomous art. Note also that the operative term is not research, but research and development. This represents a certain technologization of previously autonomous science. The R&D laboratory is not exactly the sort of laboratory Latour and Woolgar (1979) wrote about in their extraordinarily prescient *Laboratory Life*. This was a pure research laboratory that produced abstract products, scientific papers as its output. The R&D laboratory doesn't prove scientific theses: its output is not scientific truths. The R&D lab makes *prototypes*. When consumption becomes specialized or reflexive, then competition becomes less a question of who can produce the greatest amount cheapest, or even of quality mass production. Competition becomes a struggle of the prototypes.

These prototypes are very often information-rich themselves. They are often intelligent machines, or software. These intelligent products of the information society come under the laws of intellectual property (Lury, 1993). They come under the laws of not real property, but intellectual property. Real property is about the present, intellectual property about the future. This is why market capitalization varies so vastly from assets and turnover in the new economy. It is true that in nineteenth century railroads there was vast investment, vast purchase of stock for decades before a profit was made. But there is a crucial difference between then and NASDAQ today. First the railroads transformed that investment very quickly into assets. In the railroads market capitalization was many times disproportional to profits and many times higher than turnover, but not much higher than assets. In the new economy market capitalization is many times higher than assets too. Market capitalization was connected to real property (assets) in the manufacturing age. Now it is connected to intellectual property. This real property (assets) is property in the means of production. Intellectual property has to do with the prototype. Real property in assets primarily accumulates, while the governing principle of intellectual property is circulation. The hegemonic principle of the manufacturing society is accumulation: that of the information society, circulation. In national accumulation, things stay largely 'under control'. In global circulation, things tend to fly out of control. This is at the heart of the contraction of the information society. It is why it is always also a *dis*information society.

In any event the principle of informationalization has invaded even the older manufacturing sectors. They too are coming under the logic of the new economy. Their workforce is increasingly trained in discursive knowledge. Their means of production are increasingly comprised of intelligent machines. Their machines and products contain an increased proportion of micro-electronic components. In automobiles it is estimated at cost that roughly one-third of components are mechanical, one-third electronic, one-third microelectronic (Urry, 2000). In the manufacturing sectors too consumption is increasingly specialized. Hence the production of prototypes and the R&D process is beginning to take precedence over the labour process.

Disinformation

Let us turn now to the second type of information. Its basis is not so much social-scientific as literary. If the first type of information is somehow post-industrial, then the second notion is somehow 'postmodern'. If the first type of information has to do with the (global) information society the second has to do with (global) information *culture*. If the first type of information has to do with the sociology of the media or even media studies, then the second type has to do with 'media theory' (see Chapter 6). The second type of information has to do with the consequences, the unintended consequences, of the first type of information. It has to do with information overload. The second type of information becomes ubiquitous, spins out of control. Now informationalization leads to an overload of communications.

We need to go no further than the newspapers to understand the nature of the second type of information. Marshall McLuhan (1997: 61–71) was struck, as was Walter Benjamin, by the attitude of the poets Lamartine, Baudelaire and Mallarmé. They were fascinated by the newspaper and considered it to be the literature of the future: written immediately, without reflection, for that day, under pressure of a deadline; of no use tomorrow; of value for 24 hours and no longer. Such information loses meaning, loses significance very quickly. This might also be a clue to the way that value might be understood in the information society. This sort of information-value and its temporality is different from both use-value and exchange-value. Use-value and exchange-value comprise a past and a future. Information-value is ephemeral. It is immediate. Information-value has no past, no future: no space for reflection and reasoned argument. Unlike discourse or discursive analysis, it does not subsume particulars under universals. It is instead a mass of particulars without a universal. Baudelaire and Lamartine were fascinated by news items, *les fait divers*. Newspapers as a whole may be understood to consist of such *faits divers*. Here *faits divers* means not just news but literally 'diverse facts'.

This sort of information in its pure facticity, in its pure particularity, may be understood in terms of two contrasts. First it must be understood as having little connection with the universal. Discursive knowledge is universal. It is valid over large stretches of time and space. It works through concepts (cf. Popper, 1972) of greater and ever-increasing universality. This is the logic of scientific discovery. Information type-2 is indeed *produced* by discursive knowledge but in its own characteristic particularity it has none of the universalism of the latter. It does not pretend to the temporal universality of the Popperian concept. It is ephemeral. It works through a sequence of particulars, a collage of particulars. *Fait divers* are indeed news items, news in brief. They have no particular order: like an unconnected set of newspaper headlines or telegraph messages (McLuhan, 1997: 62–3). There is no logical or analytic ordering. The newspaper headlines are ordered perhaps only by what sells papers: telegraph and newspaper ordered by urgency. Universal knowledge needs a separate realm of discursive justification. Newsprint, as Benjamin noted, does not. Its force – which is great – is through its own facticity. Newsprint's power comes not through argument, but through a violently forceful facticity. Operating under the most restrictive of constraints – time deadlines, space considerations – its force and temporality is similar to the violence of the event.

Newsprint is also shot through with the facticity of the particular, not just in relation to any universals, but also to any transcendental. It is the pure empirical with the disappearance of the transcendental. Poetry, art, the novel, music, opens a window out onto not the *universal*, which *à la* natural science and instrumental reason occupies the realm of the same, but the *transcendental*, which opens out onto the realm of the other, of the ungraspable. Science and the universal are a question of logical meaning. The novel, the painting and the concerto open out onto the space of existential meaning. Newsprint, or information, has neither logical nor existential meaning. It is often not subsumed under universals. Its meaning is accidental, ephemeral and very often trivial. And surely gone tomorrow. The existential time of the transcendental lasts even longer than does the logical time of the universal. For their part, newspapers and other forms of information have neither logical nor existential temporality, but only immediate temporality. They have no meaning at all outside of real time. Outside the immediacy of real time, news and information are, literally, garbage. You throw out the newspaper with the disused food and the baby's disposable nappies. You shine your shoes on it. You wrap up glass in it. Sometimes there is so much of it you cannot even fit it in the garbage cans along with the rest of your rubbish. Media theory is also necessarily 'garbage theory' (M. Thompson, 1979).

Not just newsprint, not just digital messages, but the whole of the con-sumer capitalist city may be understood as information. In the heavily branded environment of the informational city, goods, lifestyles and design are ephemeral (Lury, 1999). Duration is short. Turnover is fast. Muzak is infor-mation; adverts in the cinema, TV, the Internet are information, even when fully non-didactic and image-based. Indeed the older early twentieth century adverts, that instructed you in what something was worth and how you would use it, were utilitarian rather than informational (Leiss et al., 1990). FMCG, fast-moving consumer goods, are information. It is indeed branded products that are closest to being information. Other products, such as turbines, we know nothing about. They are for what Giddens (1990) calls the 'expert-systems'. Fast-moving consumer goods, the branded products, we know lots about. We are all experts.

The point is that information type-2 is the unintended consequence of information type-1. The information society has for its unintended consequences the information culture. The rational control of reflexive accumulation has as its consequences the out-of-control anarchy of information diffusion. Information type-1 works through a logic of binaries: without it the hybrid chaos of information type-2 would be impossible. Modernity is ordered: modernity's consequences disordered. The consequences of order are disorder. The consequences of an initial and ordered aesthetics of beauty are an informational aesthetics of the monstrous. The consequences of simplicity, of the complexity reduction, the classificatory simplicity of information society, are the vast and uncontrollable complexity of the information culture. The consequences of accumulation are circulation. The consequences of the stockpile are the junkpile. Of real jobs, junk jobs or McJobs.

Accumulation and Enframing

We have already addressed the 'frame' (*Gestell*) and the 'standing reserve' (*Bestand*) in Heidegger. The standing reserve was understood as an accumulation that was kept in reserve for some other use. It was a reserve of instruments for other use. The unit of the standing reserve here is the 'frame'. The frame is in principle empty and abstract and intended for something else. The frame is content-less and procedural. Marx's accumulation of capital, we noted, is such a standing reserve. The frames that it is composed of are commodities. Spatial formations in the manufacturing society can be seen also in terms of accumulations. Here the frame is the 'function'. The function is also abstract. Like the commodity, it is an 'in-order-to'. In the city before Haussmann, before Vienna's *Ringstrasse*, before New York was definitively gridded, before Hobrecht's Berlin – the artefacts of urban space were not primarily a question of the 'in order to'. In these cities the street becomes an in-order-to. It becomes a space not to live in but a route from A to B. It becomes a standing reserve. The elements of urban space accumulate. This increases its scope later with Corbusier and the housing unit.

Informational space, whether parallel space or real urban space, is today's lived space. It is not *functional* space. It is not functional space in the sense that it cannot be valorized. It does not produce something else and hence add value. It is often a space inhabited by valueless objects, by valueless information. It is not an instrumental space. Information-space is the space of the event. It is atopic in the sense of site-less. It is also atopic temporally, that is, it is neither utopic nor dystopic. Utopias value the future. Dystopias value the past. Atopic information time and space is without past or future. Its temporality is atemporality. The function as frame in spatial formations meets its economic parallel in exchange-value. Exchange-value is future-oriented. What is valoriz*able* has value in a future exchange. Use-value comprises a past. Its value is also because of its past content. Use-values are singularities, momentos. They comprise memories. Use-values are irreplaceable. Exchange-values have value for the future. Their value is judged in terms of the homogenous stuff (money) they can be exchanged for. Money has value in the future. As distinct from both use- and exchange-value, what might be called *information-value* has worth in neither the past nor the future, but only in real time.[2] Information space is a bit like information-value. It is ephemeral. It has extension into neither past nor future. Information architecture does not last long enough to accumulate. It does not so much accumulate, as proliferate. It disappears before the future. Rem Koolhaas's (1997) 'generic city' is about information space. Paris is a classical city comprising memory. Chicago and Berlin, in crucial respects, are zoned and functional. Tokyo, Saõ Paulo and Shanghai are neither classical nor functional, but generic. The generic city is the most modern city, yet rarely (an exception is Las Vegas) is the Western city. Built structure in the generic city does not last long enough to be functional. It does not last long enough to accumulate. Generic cities are informational in their unplanned, unzoned mosaics of imbalance. They are cities, less of accumulation than circulation. They are cities 'on the move'.[3]

Not just value, but *meaning* is found in a certain futurity. In classical architecture meaning and value are inscribed in memory, tradition and an idealized past. In modern architecture meaning is inscribed in the future. Modern architecture and built space are functional for the future. Their value lies in what they are functional for. What they are functional for is what they are meant for. Indeed, in everyday language meaning refers not only to deeper meanings, but to what something is 'meant for' in a utilitarian sense. Modern built space can reduce meaning to utility. The commodity and function are frames that impart a certain meaning and ordering onto real things. But narrative and discourse are also such frames. The narrative structure of the novel – as distinct from the folk tale – is a frame that finds meaning in futurity (see Chapter 10). It imparts order to, not things, but events. So does the discursive logic of science, which is another mode of such framing. Here we see how there are two ways in which the journalistic, the principle of information, can be surmounted. Science organizes the events discursively according to a propositional logic. The discursive logic en*frames* the particular with the universal.

In the information age, we frame not primarily through commodity or function, nor through narrative or discourse. How indeed do we frame information? McLuhan's (1997: 61–71) above cited essay on 'Joyce, Mallarmé and the Press' can give us some clues here. The essay is about literature and newsprint: about the relationship between literature and newsprint. It begins with a quote from Lamartine, written in 1831, in which the poet attacks contemporaneous high culture's denigration of journalism. Lamartine marvels at the time–space spread of the press, of its instantaneity, and speculates that all literature will one day come under its spell. McLuhan's point is that literature will need to move away from a mode in which it is the self-expression of a single subjectivity. His point is that literature will have to move out of this subjectivist internalization into a sort of externalization, on the model of picturesque art. He considers Stéphane Mallarmé's observations on the press as 'a traffic, an epitomization of enormous and elementary interests … the recital of diverse facts'. In the face of this 'hubbub of appetites and protests', this 'confusion of tongues', what is the role of the poet? Mallarmé used an orchestral analogy. The role of the poet (or novelist or artist) is 'the orchestration of the qualities of ordinary speech'. It is to place, as it were, a poetic or novelistic frame on the *faits divers*, on the hubbub of voices, and raise them to a level of existential intelligibility. The poet's role is not that of an expressive subjectivity. Mallarmé speaks of: a 'book which does not admit of any signature' (p. 67). 'The job of the artist', McLuhan continues, 'is not to sign but to read signatures.' It is, to quote Mallarmé, 'to recapture significance from the least sonorities'. It is, 'not self-expression but the release of the life in things' (p. 64). Thus Joyce breaks with the principle of the novelistic. Here the novel is the self-expression of the author's subjectivity. Its narrative is the life narrative, the being-onto-death, of the protagonist. Joyce's *Ulysses* is emphatically not about such a being unto death. It takes place not along a protagonist's life narrative, but in a single day. It has value for as long as a newspaper. Joyce's epiphanies, his existential meaning, happens in a decidedly anti-epiphanic time-space. McLuhan (p. 68) notes,

> In *Ulysses* in episode seven, we find ourselves in a newspaper office in 'the heart of the Hibernian metropolis'. For Joyce indeed the press was 'a microchasm of the world of man, its columns unchanging monuments to the age-old passions and interests of all men, and its production and distribution a drama involving the hands and organs of the entire "body politic".' With its dateline June 16, 1904, *Ulysses* is newspaperwise an abridgement of all space in a brief segment of time.

On this view the novel is clearly a question of the orchestration of ordinary voices. It is, in fact, an orchestration of *the information*. In the information society the frame carries out the orchestration of information. This orchestration will work spatially, architecturally. It is orchestrating a tactile space of information, a space that Lefebvre saw in terms of the gesture, and McLuhan the 'gesture as phatic communication' (p. 62). We no longer live in a culture of subjectivist distance. Culture has left its stead as representational and narrative to become – as Benjamin suspected – architectural. We live in the world with immaterial and material cultural objects. An increasing proportion of all the objects we live with, use and interact with are cultural. As culture has lost its temporality, losing first its past and then its future in the immediacy of the event, in the immediacy of real time, it has become spatial, it has become architectural. So what happens with the chaos of information type-2 is a reworking through 'planes of immanence' by architecture (Patton, 1996). What happens is the reworking of the junk, of the ubiquity of the information through the planes of an architectonic. Now culture is all amongst us rather than somehow inside us and above us. Now culture is no longer in representations but in the objects, the brands and the technologies of the information society. It lends itself much more to framing by an architectonic. No longer narrative, even primarily musical, having little to do with either Renaissance perspective or the flatness of Picasso's picture plane. Culture is now three-dimensional, spatial, as much tactile as visual or textual, all around us and inhabited, lived in rather than encountered in a separate realm as a representation. In Deleuze and Guattari's (1980) *Mille plateaux*, plateaus are themselves sorts of frames. They are 'planes of immanence', planes of thinking. The information chaos of contemporary urban space needs reworking through such a plane of immanence, through the 'plateau' of the architectonic, through architecture.

Thus the rationality and order of information type-1 leads to the irrationality and disorder of information type-2, or of disinformation. Or shall we say that information is at the same time necessarily disinformation. And the question then is how do we impose some sort of order on the chaos. Capital accumulates. It already has some sort of order inherent to it. Information on the other hand circulates, it swirls, it bombards. Capital as assets, as accumulated means of production is found in specific 'zones'. It may be exported for production in the third world. It may internationalize. Capital is becoming more like information in a greater and global ubiquity. Capital, however, is not everywhere. You are not bombarded by it from billboards and in your own home. Information is in its nature much more anarchic than capital. Capital is regulated by the hidden hand of markets, or by other modes of governance. Information escapes very often the logic of markets. It is everywhere at the same time for free. Your desktop monitor and WAP mobile phone may open up possibilities for markets. But they are much more than a market. All sorts of information come to them that do not follow the laws of supply and demand. Information may be ungovernable.

We need to put various sorts of order on the new anarchic complexity. Thus we need frames to order the information, to make it as Mallarmé said, intelligible. Frames also make the information *marketable*. One such type of frame is the law of intellectual property. Frames keep other people out and let the public know that the information inside the frame is *your* information. Another such frame is the brand. The old manufacturing capitalism, so to speak, enframed itself: its accumulation already had a certain order. In the information society, frames must be imposed from the outside. Exchange-value is empty. Yet modern law of property and contract circumscribed it. The means of production as abstract capital were owned by the capitalist, and property law meant he could keep others out, and be also *de facto* owner of labour power, of variable capital. But this was in industrial capitalism. In information capitalism the frame is the brand. The brand has its basis in intellectual property, typically in trademark (Lury, 1993, 1999). In trademark a logo, a design that is already recognized in the public domain, marks the space which keeps others out. The brand imparts a certain order to the chaos of information and communication flows. It helps what otherwise is a chaotic diffusion to be ordered *into* flows. This often leads to the greatest inequalities: the repetitive labour process takes place in the 'South', and the design process in the USA, Western Europe or Japan. A certain amount of design-intensive work in information capitalism goes into the production of specialized products, of prototypes. The people doing this sort of design-intensive work will tend to be information engineers, software engineers and the like. Some of the labour is done by individuals who are professional designers, like Terence Conran, who give the product a certain look. A final portion of design-intensive work will be on brand identity: on maintaining and increasing brand value. Channel 4 in Britain for example has been known for delivering innovative and irreverent television to a younger generation: to youth who are dissatisfied with ITV and the BBC. The channel has recently employed a brand management team to ensure the maintenance of street credibility. They must ensure that shows on gardening and national heritage for example are not broadcast.

Garbage

We are living in an age in which flows of goods are paralleled by flows of *bads* (Beck, 1992). How are we to govern these flows of bads. These flows have negative value. Pollutants emitted from cars and factories are bads that are the side effects of goods (petrol, the service of getting from A to B). Goods are converted into bads. In the risk society, dangers come from goods that are converted into bads. Tertiary sector establishments are concerned with the circulation of informational goods. Zoning separates the flows and gives them a bit of order. Industrial zones have different circulations and conversions of goods into bads than do zones for offices or housing. Piles and piles of PCs are becoming an increasingly common form of junk and sometimes garbage, with their three-year obsolescence cycles making them almost the dominating figures that automobiles have, iconically, been in our junkyards. Garbage is such a flow of bads: the refuse that we dispose of in our everyday lives. Garbage happens when the flow of goods comes to us. We use, consume these goods. As already consumed, they turn into bads that must be disposed of. The disposal of these bads is part of the general circulation. The circulation of garbage becomes a problem that must come under some kind of governance. Brazil, for example, is quite advanced in the circulation of information and culture, in broadcasting, advertising, the art circuit, music, the Internet. Brazil is quite backward in the circulation of garbage. Garbage is more than just refuse, just the disused stuff we throw in bins or flush down the plumbing. Garbage is a metaphor for the whole of the information society. It has to do with information surplus. Garbage is disposable. It needs to be disposed of. Information (and fast-moving consumer goods are information) is also disposable. It needs to be disposed of. The question is how do we regulate it? How do we govern it? How do we *frame* it? We somehow frame the garbage in art, in architecture, in urbanism. We frame it through brands, which package the garbage. Garbage dis-accumulates. It falls to bits, into disrepair. It rots. The frames can stop or delay the rot.

The side effects of the industrial society were material bads, physical pollutants. The side effects of the information society are symbolic bads, mental pollutants. We are polluted with the waste products of the information society: the sort of things that 'cultured' people do not want in their living rooms. In their front rooms are found weighty volumes, poetry, paintings or sculpture that will endure the ages, and long-duration furniture. You can add long-duration vinyl LPs. The television, the Walkman, videocassettes, audiotapes, CDs, computer games and net-connected computer are banished to other rooms further back. *Longue durée* is front of house, *courte durée* backstage. Information as garbage is worse than value-less, These symbolic bads, this symbolic garbage leaves you no psychological space. Hence junk fax and junk email. Information comes to you. You don't go to the information. You need to go out and buy a book, or take it out of the library; to go to the cinema or the video shop. In this sense TV movies are like information. Information comes to you sometimes when it is summoned, sometimes not. De-valued information is garbage. You throw it – either virtually or really – in the trash; you flush it down the toilet. Two low status jobs, jobs that men do that connect to defilement and ritual defilement, are plumber and dustman. Garbage is a special type of bad. It consists of bads that were once goods. Feces is not exactly garbage. It is lower than garbage. It decomposes far faster than garbage. Piles of shit are very ephemeral accumulations. Plumbers do not collect shit. They enable its flows. The longer something lasts, the more value it has. The least valuable goods – that decompose the quickest – are the closest already to garbage. Even less worthy is shit. To say 'what a load of shit' is an even more devaluating statement than to say 'what a load of rubbish'. In contrast, we do eat 'junk food', while we would never eat food that people labelled as garbage or devalued as crap. What was nourishing food (a good) leaves the house in the form of two bads – two items of negative value: garbage and excrement. The digestive system and cooking utensils are involved in the transformation of goods into bads. They are among other things instruments or means for the transformation of goods into bads. There is nothing that makes the transition from very high status to very low status faster than the human body. Alive, it keeps itself fit; it follows the order and togetherness of its life-narratives. Alive it is *Dasein*. It is a carrier of existential meaning: indeed of the meaning of being. Dead, it decomposes. It lets off an unbearable odour – at an amazing rate. Hence partly the modern trend to cremation.

Chris Ofili, winner of the Turner Prize in 1999, takes elephant shit and lacquers it in his paintings. This excrement serves as a base for his paintings, just underneath the frame. It is sometimes stuck on them. This shit, however, does not decompose. It becomes durable and can last a hundred years. Lacquered excrement is less like information and more like art in its duration. The work of art, whether lacquered excrement or combinations of oil paint, is a good whose value is to last for centuries, or at least for a very long duration. The designer for her part works closer to the idiom of information. Designers design goods to last for a few months, until the fashion changes. Until the goods lose enormously in value, either through obsolescence, that is, decomposition, or through going out of fashion. Designers work under time pressures that allow for a lot less reflection than artists. Chris Ofili works in the re-conversion of bads into goods, or at least the reworking of bads, with their negative values, so at least to neutralize this value. Hence the success of the anti-pollutant industry in the Ruhrgebiet in Germany. Converters, catalytic converters, minimize the abuse-value of bads. Heritage museums convert what have become economic bads into cultural goods.

Junk, Ruins

Junk is of a different order than garbage. In its way junk preserves value. Junk piles and rubbish piles are of a different order. Junk, more than garbage, concerns potentially useful cast-offs. Lots of people scout out junkyards; only gypsies are to be found around garbage dumps. Junk takes a lot longer to decompose than garbage. It is more likely to be made of metal, or have electronic and micro-electronic components. Junkyards are different than garbage dumps. Scrap metal is the sort of thing one keeps in junkyards. The late Jack Walker, one of the biggest sport multimillionaires in Britain, made his fortune with scrap metal. It is harder to be a garbage dump multimillionaire. Junk is kept in 'yards'. Garbage is kept in dumps. Garbage flows in a way that junk does not. In this sense information is more like garbage. Junk is frequently used in art. Duchamp's urinal has lasted some 85 years.[4] Tomoko Takahashi, Turner Prize winner in 2000, uses junked technology in her installation in the New Neurotic Realism show at the Saatchi Gallery. She hooks the stuff up so the mechanisms are in action and yet useless. This junked technology still 'works'.

Walter Benjamin had an entire theory of junk. If capital accumulates in stockpiles, disused commodities accumulate in junkpiles. Junkpiles consist of obsolescent, devalorized commodities. Their accumulation is a side effect of original capital accumulation. For Benjamin (1997) and the surrealists, disused objects from such 'junkpiles' could in their juxtaposition lead to a 'profane illumination'. This is not unconnected with the framing through orchestration of Mallarmé and Joyce. Only Joyce and Mallarmé accomplished this through the *materiality* of language. Benjamin and the surrealists use not so much everyday language, but follow Duchamp, in using not primarily language but objects, though readymade objects, for their orchestration. Further, these objects are not reworked at all through – as in Mallarmé, Joyce and Picasso – language or any other medium, but remain readymades. The importance is in not the material, but the idea. At stake is not the materiality of the signifier, but the *im*materiality of the signi*fied*. This signified is not transcendental, not even universal, but instead particular (Maharaj, 2000). These are common, everyday bad and good ideas. These ideas are information is *in*forme.

It is without form. It is the signified *sans* signifier. It is the signified not as lofty concept, not as symbolic or imaginary, but as commonplace, as vulgar, as real. Duchamp is the original information-artist, and Benjamin the original information-theorist. They are the orchestrators, imparting the (dis-)intelligibility to the information society.

For their part, *ruins* have a curious temporality. Benjamin was even more curious about ruins than about junk. He was a 'collector' at ruins. Ruins are different from rubble. The mess that any building makes – say after slum clearance in the Bronx or Liverpool – is rubble. Ruins have to do with the obsolescence of buildings, the disappearance of use-value of buildings that have enormous symbolic value. They have this partly due to their duration, and the fact that they – for example the Pyramids, Cologne Cathedral – were intended to endure. Rubble may signify the end of a culture. Ruins signify the end of a culture that is imputed universal value: for example, the Etruscan ruins in Rome. Archaeological sites excavate ruins, not rubble. These are recycled into museums. The relationship of ruins and the museum is an interesting question. The British Museum converted ruins from archaeological digs, from bads to goods, well before the days of the readymade and heritage museum. The classical and modern art museum preserves goods. Contemporary art galleries are largely spaces for the re-orchestration of material bads to create a symbolic good.

Walter Benjamin spoke of 'profane illumination' as coming through the disused objects of capitalism. Yesterday's dresses, cast off things, ruins, are not so different from yesterday's information. The ephemerality of yesterday's goods and information is similar to the experience of the prostitute, the *flâneur* and other figures of Benjamin's cityscape. This is ephemeral, throwaway experience. It is experience as neither *Erfahrung* (experience as traditional practice) nor *Erlebnis* (subjective experience) but *Chokerlebnis*. It is shock experience. In the manufacturing society, rational production resulted in the rational accumulation of frames. In the information society much more rational and reflexive production would seem to result in an accumulation of frames. But the frames shatter into fragments of indifference, into not an accumulation of frames but a vortex, diffusion, dispersion, a circulation of fragments (information). Benjamin's reaction to this may be less one of critique than of affirmation, of what Nietzsche called *amor fati* (Caygill, 1998). Given this destruction of transcendence, he is still able to redeem a certain measure of existential meaning. He embraces our informational fate, while at the same time looking backwards through the fragments. The frames are destroyed leaving only the informational fragments. Yet we are to look backwards through their prism: through the garbage, the disused information in all its forms. Here we see the ruins of the ancient through the prism of the hypermodern. The fragmented identity of Benjamin's melancholic is better than no identity. This is achieved through looking backwards while being dragged into the future's generalized indifference. Here the frame is destroyed through the event. Epiphany is reached through the anti-epiphanic.

Conclusions

The first part of this chapter was about information, the second about disinformation. Disinformation, we have argued, is partly the side effect, the unwanted *Nebenfalle*, of informationalization. The first part of the chapter was about reflexivity, the second about the impossibility of reflection. The first part addressed rationality and rationalization, the second irrationalization. The first part of the chapter was about intelligence, the second about unintelligence: and surely the standard neo-conservative argument is that informationalization gives us 'dumbing down'; the first part of the chapter about the goods of the information order; the second about the bads. The chapter, and the book, would be greatly misunderstood if readers took the information society to be fundamentally and basically disinformed. Indeed, a phenomenological reduction would yield the essence of information to be not disinformation, but the contradictory pair, the undecidable of *information-and-disinformation*. Here disinformation converts just as readily back into information as the reverse. The *Vergesellschaftung* of information (that is, the working of the information principle through the entirety of the society) is, at the same time, the *Vergesellschaftung* of disinformation. But this makes it no less a principle of information.

If one were to find one notion that lay at the core, that was the essence, the phenomenological essence of this ongoing contradiction of information–disinformation it would be *the idea*. The idea is at the core of all this. Here the very materiality of capitalism has led to the domination of its opposite, the idea. Here the process of accumulation led to its opposite: the impossibility of accumulation and the predominance of circulation (and networks) and dispersion of all accumulations. Thus in the new economy circulation and the moment of finance capital are de-coupled from the accumulation (assets) process. Things don't accumulate in networks. They accumulate in reserves, in heaps. Things circulate in networks. But the core is the idea. The contradictory essence of the idea – yet a further contradiction, because in the (immanent) information order there are no essences – may best have been grasped by Marcel Duchamp (Mink, 1995). Duchamp, of course, is the father of conceptual art. The idea of the concept in conceptual art is not the concept as universal that subsumes the particular. It is also not the concept as transcendental *à la* Hegel. It is more the concept or idea as immanent. Indeed conceptual art with a capital C and capital A at the end of the 1960s was explicitly informational, explicitly McLuhanite in inspiration.[5] In conceptual art, in the Duchampian sense the idea has become the particular in a world without universals and without transcendentals. The Duchampian idea is not about any sort of dumbing down or information overload *per se*. It is about intelligence (Craig-Martin, 1999). It is about the artist no longer working through the (aesthetic) materials – colour or facet planes etc. – it is instead about the artist working aesthetically through an assemblage of *im*materials, that is, ideas. Duchamp was the champion of intelligence. He hated the idea of '*bête comme un artiste*'. He worked through treatises in mathematics and engineering in his 'day job' at Bibliothèque St. Genviève. The disinformation society is shot through with intelligence.

Notes

1 See Chapter 13.

2 I would be happy to call this 'sign-value' following Baudrillard. Sign-value has little to do with Veblenian status or symbolic capital. It is a truly innovative concept and has a lot in common with what I am describing here. I do not want to call it this in order to stress its informational content. What is at stake here may be less semiotic than what Baudrillard proposes. Further, the sign is the unity of signifier and signified. And I shall argue below that information-value is based on the signified or idea in the absence of a signifier. Only the signified in this is not a universal, not a transcendental, but instead a particular.

3 This was the title of an exhibition at London's Hayward Gallery on Asian cities, curated by Koolhaas and Hans Ulrich Obrist in 1999.

4 Not the original, which was lost by the artist's patron, Walter Arensberg. But the idea. And this is the important thing in conceptual art. Also Duchamp bought his readymades from catalogues and shops. They were not cast-offs. See below.

5 I am grateful for this to discussions with Michael Craig-Martin and Sarat Maharaj.

12

Technological Phenomenology

What kind of culture is the information culture? More specifically, in what sense is the information order a *technological* culture? This chapter will address this problem through an attempt to outline what amounts to a shift from a culture of representation or a representational culture to a techno-logical culture. Chapter 1 introduced the idea of informationcritique, and suggested that the representational culture presumes an effective dualism, a distance between subject and object. In the representational culture the subject is in a different world than things. In the technological culture the subject is in the world with things. Previously existing transcendence and dualism is displaced by the immanence, monism. There are two dualisms at stake here. One between the subject, whether reader, audience or viewer, and the cultural entity s/he encounters. The other is between this cultural entity and the reality it more or less fully represents. Relationships between all three of these elements – subject, cultural object and real object – are distanciated in the representational culture. In the technological culture, all three are in the same world, in the same immanent world.

In this chapter I want to explore the dimensions of such an immanent culture through the consideration of 'play'. Here, following Huizinga, I want to contrast the play of the technological culture with the utilitarianism of the representational culture. Utilitarianism, the close cousin of instrumental rationality, deals with things from the perspective of distance: things are basically entities for calculation. Play, for its part, is disinterested. Playing, you are immediately in the world with things and people: you use neither as instrument, neither for benefit maximizing.

I shall then turn towards the problem of social knowledge. In the represen-tational culture, social knowledge was the mirror of social nature. Knowledge stood apart from society as culture did from nature. At issue is classical posi-tivism. I draw on phenomenology, and in particular on the work of Harold Garfinkel, to give an account of how knowledge in the technological culture is no longer above or transcendent to but immanent in, so to speak, social nature. I draw on Garfinkel to give an account of how reflexivity is transformed in the technological culture. Reflexivity is no longer about distanciated decision-making or life-narrative organizing (Beck et al., 1994). Instead it is about the reflexive tying of knowledge to action, so that there is no distance at all between knowledge and action. Now action is knowledge and knowledge is action. Social knowledge becomes immanent in the technological culture. I want to follow Garfinkel's phenomenology as a critique of the assumptions of transcen-dental phenomenology. Garfinkel breaks with the effective humanism and the ontological assumptions of previously existing thinkers (of Husserl and Heidegger but also Levinas and Derrida) for a radical and 'externalist' phenomenology of communications. In this the intelligible and material are compressed into a single communicational unit. This is the phenomenology of the information age. Classical phenomenology already broke with the logic of representation by presuming that the subject no longer stood above the world of objects and social relations. Classical phenomenology presumed that the subject was not above the world but in the world with objects and others. It presumed that the subject was not neutral but had an *intentionality*, an *attitude* towards the world. In this sense play already is phenomenological. What Garfinkel does, and human–machine interfaces complete, is to make this phenomenology *technological*.

Play: Agonistics Versus Representation

Agon, not Utility

In contrast to *homo sapiens*, whose differentia specifica is reason, and *homo faber*, whose specific difference is work, Johan Huizinga gives us *homo ludens*. For Huizinga (1971: 8) reason and work are inscribed in a negative dualism of spirit and matter. For him play is originary and a condition of existence of both reason and work. Play is not a compulsory but a voluntary activity. 'It is a stepping out of real life into a temporary sphere of activity.' Thus play, unlike work, takes place in another time and a different space. The time may be the festival, the feast, it may be Sunday or Saturday night. The specially marked out space may be a 'playground', card table, football pitch, a stage, a temple. Still play takes place in a real space, unlike the novel or painting. We play in clubs, in associations, sometimes with elements of secrecy. We play in disguise, in for example the replica kit of Arsenal or Real Madrid.

For Huizinga play – which is a culture not of representation, but the real – is prior to, and the basis of, cultures of representation. Play operates in the register of magic, prior to the spirit of the world religions. Play is not modern, not classical, not ancient but archaic. The world religions – Christianity, Judaism, Taoism, Hinduism and Confucianism – presume separate spheres of sacred and profane. They presume a separate symbolic sphere, and hence already the dualist logic of representational culture. Their temporality is characteristically linear. They may promise any number of afterlives, and salvation, but what they preclude is magic in this life (Weber, 1963). Play, in tournaments and contests and games accompanying festivals and seasonal fetes, operates in the register of magic. It works in immanentist cultures, immanentist religions prior to the rise of the transcendental religions (Parsons, 1968). Play and games compel the gods to effectuate an event in this-worldly reality.[1] Games and contests functioned originally to promote fertility, inscribed in archaic and cyclical time. Linear time presupposes a two-world cosmology with a utopian realm that is the motor of linear time. Linear time is presupposed in notions of free will versus determinism. Cyclical time, for its part, presumes that 'the order of nature is imprinted on human consciousness' (Huizinga, 1971: 15). Cyclical time presumes neither free will nor determinism, but fate. Determinism involves the cause and effect of the natural sciences. Free will presumes their transcendence. Fate has nothing to do with cause and effect: it has a density unknown to either.

Representational culture speaks the language of correspondence. Without representation, metaphor has no sense. Play's magical language is metonymic, not metaphoric. There is no symbolic correspondence between the man and the kangaroo. Instead the man becomes the kangaroo, hence the significance of the metonymic mask in play. Metaphor works through representation, metonymy through substitution. Play, contends Huizinga, is the first, the original translation of nature into culture. Play comes not from necessity, but is a voluntary activity. In play man is not the hunter, not reduced to barbarism or pure economic gain. Play emerges in, indeed constitutes, the general economy of excess. For philosophical anthropology, man is the 'incomplete animal'. Humans suffer from an *Instinktarmut*, an underdetermination by instincts. We compensate for this instinctual poverty by completing ourselves as animals through institutions, through culture. Hence Peter Berger (1967) speaks of religion as a 'sacred canopy'. Play, however, prior to religion, is a sort of 'profane canopy'. For Gadamer (1990: 107–15) the defining characteristic of institutions (and culture) is their relative permanence, their duration. Play sets up rules that are freely accepted yet binding. For children and for societies these rules have duration. They outlast the brutish, short life of man the hunter. Play may ritually cause fertility and a good harvest, but it is not working in the harvest, is not planting or sowing. Play, as excess, is not part of economic reproduction, whether capitalist or pre-modern. It is Marx's department II of consumer commodities that are not necessities but luxuries. Play is in excess of necessity, but also in excess of the now and here of everyday. Play is literally somewhere else. Not in the farmer's fields but on the playing field, the football ground, the playground. In taking place in a real, though other, space, it escapes the logic of the culture of representation. The symbols in the separated (dualist) symbolic sphere of representation are situated in no place at all.

Gadamer sees play as the basis for art and culture. His model is child's play. Huizinga's model is the *agon*, the contest. The agon was present in China millennia before Christ, but of crucial significance may be the sixth century BC Greeks and their contests of strength, wisdom and wealth. The agon is disinterested. It is '*zwecklos*' but '*sinnvoll*', without end but full of meaning. On the face of it, the agon as play seems to be intensely interest-bound. Play, more than work, is accompanied by tension and joy. It is much more intense and in this sense much more interested. There is an immediacy to games, a tension. When you win a stake, a trophy, a medal you are 'over the moon'. You boast. When you lose you are miserable. This is more intense than at work. You are less likely to boast when you've completed a business deal. The point in regard to interest, and this is consistent with Kant's idea of interest, is that play is not utilitarian. It has little to do with economic interests. Play (in French, *jeu*) is about a stake (*enjeu*). This can be a trophy, medals, a stake in gambling. But play is not, and gambling is not, utilitarian. Calculation may be involved in gambling. But it does not follow the logic of exchange-value. Its logic is that of fate, of luck. Play is about 'prizes' not 'prices', the latter being the utilitarian corruption of the former; the former the basis of the latter (Huizinga, 1971: 49).

Aristotle's virtues are embedded in a plurality of practices. These practices are more or less agonistic. And in each of these practices the prize for virtue is honour. At stake is honour. These agonistic practices are prior and before the right, the true and the beautiful. The agon follows a logic not of right/wrong or true/false or beautiful/ugly (or even sublime), but of win and lose. Players who win gain honour whether in agons of wisdom or of gift-giving. Aristotle's practices presume 'internal goods', goods internal to the practices. These stand in contrast to the external goods, the utilitarian goods of prestige, power and money which Pierre Bourdieu has tellingly rendered into the utilitarian categories of 'symbolic', 'cultural' and 'social capital'. Utilitarian goods 'accumulate'; internal goods do not. Symbolic capital accumulates and in doing so records the spread of the 'restricted economy', the rationalization of the former space of excess. To partake of excess through the agon is to partake of honour. Honour surely does not accumulate. Play and the agon take place in the register of honour (Bourdieu, 1984; Huizinga, 1971: 64; MacIntyre, 1981). Huizinga understands Marcel Mauss's gift in terms of agon. Contests of gift-giving were, as Mauss and Davy noted, *'un jeu et une preuve'* (Huizinga, 1971: 61). The original potlatch, the original contests of gift-giving, were between phratrai (brotherhoods), between lineages of the same tribe. This is before the existence of a 'superior instance' – an instance of representation – a state instance that could translate the idiom of win/lose into right/wrong. The gambler plays for a stake. He wins and loses with honour. The risks a gambler or adventurer runs are not the risks of the 'risk society'. The risk society is based on an insurance principle of utilitarian calculation. It is based on calculated decision-making. The gambler may think of probabilities but more central is bluffing, luck, betting more than you can afford. Gambling pays its respects less to utilitarian calculation than to *fortuna*.

Utilitarianism belongs to representational culture. It presumes representation. Goods are represented in exchange value, in price. Play is where utility is abandoned. There is a distancing in utilitarian practices, unlike the intensity and immediacy of play. In utilitarian practice you treat things as 'present at hand'. This Heidegger contrasts with 'ready to hand (*zuhandend*), in which you are immediately involved with things, such as your football club, your tennis racket, your football club's ground. Play and the agon are *Lebensphilosophie*'s 'life'. For Nietzsche the agon is life and the will to power, before rationalization through 'slave moralities'. Play is what Georg Simmel's adventurer is up to (Jung, 1990: 119 ff.). Simmel's notion of 'sociality' is a less adversarial notion of play. Sociality is at the base of Simmel's *Lebensphilosophie*, again as life, is smothered in the utilitarian institutions of what he calls 'the social'. Play is nature before the rationalization of nature via the Enlightenment's scientific attitude. It is gift-exchange before rationalization into utility, into exchange-value.

From Agon to Representation

To play is to be *so* interested, *so* involved immediately as to rule out the possibility of judgement. Judgement involves always a separate and neutral instance. It presupposes a culture of representation. Play as agon or as social-ity does not involve this. Judgement in German is *Urteil*. In law, ordeal is at the origin etymologically of *Urteil* (Huizinga, 1971: ch. 4; Weber, 1980: 441 ff.). Trial by ordeal historically preceded the judge and the neutral rules of the law. To play is to *suspend* judgement. It is to be so immediately involved that there is no space for the wise reflection of judgement. Play and cultural activities more generally in the information society presume a suspension of judgement. Kids play; the young play. Referees and judges are older. Judgement is a mature not a playful quality. Trial, philologically, was not just a question of ordeal, of competing groups, but of verbal battles, of rhetorical contests in courts. This agon then is rationalized in the neutral instance of judgement. In philosophy, the pre-Socratics, the Sophists, Protagoras for example, supported an agonistic (playful) mode of knowl-edge. Philosophy was about tricks and riddles. It addressed less the nature of things than the call and response of dialogue. Socrates and Plato then diverted the game to questions of truth; the dialogics for a while remain, to be replaced by the monologic truth of the Stoics and the Christian confessional (Nietzsche, 1966: 7–134; Huizinga, 1971: 77–81; Weber, 1980: 314 ff.).

The *rationalization* of play, of the agon, brings to the fore the question of judgement: whether legal judgement, cognitive judgement, moral or aes-thetic judgement. Pivotal here is the application of a universal to a particu-lar. For Kant, cognitive judgement takes place in the sphere of necessity, moral judgement in the sphere of freedom. Aesthetic judgement concerns more the nature of the thing being judged. Cognitive judgement is determi-nate judgement. Here the thing is judged from the scientific attitude. And nature is seen as a set of objects in linear cause–effect type relations. Nature becomes an instrument for the judging subject. This is what Horkheimer and Adorno and later Habermas meant by 'instrumental rationality'. Aesthetic judgements are not determinate judgements, they are instead 'reflective judgements'. Now the thing, that is, the object of judgement – whether nature or the work of art – is a *finality*. It is not an instrument or a means to another end, but has no external end; it is apart from interests. Poster (1995) has observed that the model for Marxian exchange-value lies in the thing as instrumentality (determinate judgement) and use-value in the thing as final-ity (reflective judgement). This refers equally to the freedom vs. necessity dualism. The thing as finality brings us into the sphere of freedom, the thing as instrumentality into the sphere of necessity. Now play is, at the same time, older and much more recent than this dualism. The thing is not a finality in play. A baseball bat is not a work of art. Playing on a mountain is vastly different than looking at a mountain from a distance.[2] Play gives us the empirical without the transcendental. Play involves use. But what is used is not an instrument; it is not used in a distanciated, calculating way.

The work of art or contemplated nature must be in another space from the viewer in order to be judged. The football match, the agon, is not in a separate space but in the space of what Heidegger called 'the there'. It is there with the players and with fans, the team's supporters, who are not spectators. It is not to be viewed or painted, but 'played', and followed. The supporters are 'in the world' with their team. Play already was in this sense part of a technological culture. Play in the information society takes place in a generic space (Koolhaas and Mau, 1997). Generic spaces are disembedded spaces that could be anyplace. Play involves face-to-face relations; but these are generic, that is, disembedded, lifted-out face-to-face relations (Boden and Molotch, 1994). They are 'lifted out', so to speak, from any particular context and could take place in any context. This intersubjectivity, become generic, this intersubjectivity-at-a-distance, is what is at stake in interactivity. The space of such technological play is not a transcendental space in any sense. It is an empirical space of 'the there'. There is something transcendental, at least dualist to the relationship between the judging viewer and the work of art. Judgement (and Kant's *sensus communis*) is in no empirical time or space: but is somehow timeless and spaceless. Exchange-value presumes distance. So does instrumental rationality. Play undercuts this. The generic play of the global information society undercuts this too. The viewer of the work of art does not experience. He judges. The trial judge is not 'in the world' with the criminals or even with the lawyers. The player in the global information culture is in the world with Nike. What he uses and plays with is in 'the there'. But this is not the routed 'there' of Heidegger's *Holzwege*. It is a disembedded, a generic, a lifted out 'there', that can be nowhere or anywhere (Lury, 1999).

Art practice itself has its roots in the agon, and stays more or less in the sphere of play. Poetry, dance and especially music, Huizinga (1971: 166) observes, are more play-like than architecture, painting and sculpture. Indeed you *play* music. Play entails movement; art – as aesthetics – stillness. Music is the most *mouvementée* of the arts, along with dance. The more an activity is empirically temporal in its nature, the more it is rhythmic, the more it is play-like. The more it needs to be performed, the more play-like. The more a cultural genre entails call-and-response, the more dialogic, the more it is like play. The epic – and once, history – was recited at times of rejoicing. Play takes place in a time of rejoicing, while architecture, sculpture, painting took place not in times of rejoicing, but normal time: they were made through work, in guilds often, as 'masterpieces'. They were monologic, involved separate institutions. Play in its nature rubs against institutions. In poetry – of lyric, dramatic and epic – lyric is the most play-like, the least logical, the least linear, the least like prose, or cause and effect. Archaic poetry in the context of cults – like the cult of Dionysius – is far removed from 'literature'. It is far removed from literature's everyday monologism, and fixedness on the page. Archaic poetry is closer instead to musical recitation. It was integral to ritual, with its incantation, its mythic repetition. Archaic poetry was not properly aesthetic, but vital, liturgical. It was antiphonal, competitive peroration. This is exemplified in the thrust and counter-thrust of the Dionysian rites. Such poetry was metrical, strophic, like archaic society itself. Dionysian ecstasy, dithyrambic rapture and masks marked a withdrawal from the everyday into a separate more symbolically loaded space and time. This 'charisma' of this agon, routinized, is at the root of 'literature' (1971: 120 f., 145).

In each case, what took place was an exhaustion of the 'life' in play and the agon and its rationalization in a form of representational culture. For Huizinga (pp. 176, 185–7, 205) this is not evolutionary but cyclical. The dialectic of play is central to the cyclical rise and fall of civilizations. There is an exhaustion of the organic play element in Graeco-Roman Antiquity as the feast comes to take on the guise of 'religious insurance'. Rome still of course boasted major donors, gift-givers of halls, baths and theatres. The ritual form persisted, but the religious spirit was gone, migrating to Christianity. Even the games with their 200,000 spectators lost the unity of play and ritual. In mediaeval times, play was predominant in chivalry. Knights, the tournament and heraldry reached beyond the Classical to the archaic past. Exhaustion set in when mediaeval culture came to draw too strongly on the Graeco-Roman spirit. The same is true in Western Civilization with the rise of utilitarianism and rational individualism, in sport, for example, in the rise of the 'rational recreation' movement in Britain (Holt, 1989). The rise of civilizations here features play and agon as a 'culture creating function'. Its rules and ritual create solidarities; it is public- and outward-oriented, an outward structuring of instincts. The decline of civilizations witnesses the rise of individualism and egotism and the 'inward structuring of instincts'. In this sense the adventurer and gambler would accompany the rise of Western civilization whereas the risk society's inward structured individuals accompany its decline. War too, during the rise of Western civilization, took on the character of agon. Rules respected the dignity of the enemy; there was 'ritual, style and dignity in unison'. This stemmed from the archaic agon of phratries and informed Grotius's International Law of the Early Modern Period. Its decline can be seen, notes Huizinga, in the friend/foe logic of Carl Schmitt, its egotism, self-gratification, denying any validity to, or recognition of the humanity of, the enemy – the 'total war' of extermination. Here critique itself would be the sign of decline and an inward structuring of instincts (Bell, 1976).

The idea of civilizations could be important. What are the implications in terms of civilizations for the 'technological culture', for the global information order? In *The Cultural Contradictions of Capitalism*, Daniel Bell understands Western Civilization as pre-eminently capitalist. The rise of Western Civilization is, for him, culturally connected to the Protestant Ethic; its decline to the culture of consumerism, of 'anything goes'. This rise is at the same time attributed to the rise of modern*ity*, its decline to the perva- sion of modern*ism*, that is, to the critical attitude associated with the rise of modernism in the arts and the spread of its ethos to forms of life in general. This for Bell is the cultural contradiction of capitalism. In an earlier modernity, culture reinforced capitalist activities. In a later modernity it undermines them. Jonathan Friedman (1994) has extended this argument, and embed- ded it in a world-system perspective. Western Civilization here is at the same time Immanuel Wallerstein's capitalist world system of nation-states. Now what is being undermined is not so much capitalism, but national identity, primarily by global movements of people and culture. National identity is undermined by global culture, by multiculturalism. In this sort of context the argument against multiculturalism has been taken up by a number of major thinkers – including Bourdieu, Richard Rorty and Claus Offe. This argument needs to be taken seriously. These authors are anti-racist, yet are worried about the fragmentation of national identity.

Opposed to this sort of assessment of civilizations would be the work of Arjun Appadurai (1996) and Stuart Hall (1999). Appadurai argues for multi- culturalism. His multiculturalism differs from that of say Homi Bhabha, which looks at 'third spaces' of 'difference'. Appadurai supports a multi- culturalism of flows. The implications are that we are not only witnessing the decline of Western Civilization, but at the same time the rise of another civilization. It is surely a bit early to think of a name for this new civilization, but (1) it is likely to be Eastern as much as Western, with especially China but also India taking on a substantial global weight: (2) The European nation- state will no longer assume centrality as motor and paradigm. It will not be primarily a system of nation-states, but also of linked global cities, of flows. (3) It will not be as 'systemic' as the Modern World System and its accom- panying civilization, partly because the previously relatively closed systemic units of nation-states will now be relatively open. (4) Its reterritorializations, its plateaux, will be non-linear. The very idea of global culture presupposes a progressive dissolution of this modern world system. This view is less worried about the dissolution of national identity. The defence of Western Civilization and national-identity culture tend to presume a 'canon' in literature, for Anglo-Saxons a sort of Shakespeare culture advocated by, for example, Harold Bloom. Scholars who defend the canon tend also to defend the boundaries of academic disciplines. In the academy such a defence is often also an attack on the emergent field of cultural studies, which is not institu- tionalized, nor easily institutionalizable, as a discipline. Here cultural studies is identified with an attack on the canon: it is identified with 'low culture' and multiculturalism.

Western Civilization, with its integral nation-state, has been above all home to the *representational culture*, to a culture of representation. In its up- side such representational culture (realism) was conducive to civilizational expansion, in its down-side, characterized by the critique of representation (and critique in general), it accompanies civilizational contraction. The modernist critique of (modernity's) representation is, however, still inscribed in a culture of representation. The global information society, and the non-linear civilizational order accompanying it, connects to not a representational culture but the *technological culture* at issue in this chapter. The paradigm of play is central to this technological culture. So is phenomenology. Edmund Husserl, founder of phenomenology wrote of 'judgement' on the one hand and 'experience' on the other. Judgement, from the representational culture, presumes a 'judger' in a separate world from the 'judged'. It presumes the judger has no interest, has no intentionality with respect to the judged. In phenomenology experience replaces judgement. The 'experiencer' is endowed with intentionality and is very much in the same world with the 'experienced'. The technological culture and global information order are profoundly phenomenological. It is to this that we will now turn.

An Empiricist Phenomenology of Communications

Intentionality: From Immanence to Ontology

Harold Garfinkel (1984: 35) ominously wrote, 'for Kant the moral order "within" was an awesome mystery; for sociologists the moral order "without" is a technical mystery.' By sociology here Garfinkel meant ethnomethodology, or phenomenology more generally.[3] If Kant and 'within-morality', and more importantly judgement are paradigmatic of the representational culture, then phenomenology, 'without-morality' and the suspension of judgement are integral to the emerging technological culture. At the heart of the phenomenological revolution against the subject-object thinking, against the positivism of the representational culture, is the notion of *intentionality*. 'Intentionality' means that the subject is already in the world with the object. It means that there is no disembodied subject, that there is no objective observer. Intentionality means that the subject has what Husserl called an '*attitude*' towards objects. There could be no more radical break with Cartesian doubt and Kantian judgement, as well as with the whole tradition of positivistic social science. All of these presume that the knowing subject has no intentionality towards the objects in the world. They presume he or she has a neutral, scientific, objective stance. They presume a knowing subject that has no attitude.

For Husserl the *Wissenschaften* must be re-thought in substantial opposition to the naturalistic assumptions of the Enlightenment. The Enlightenment's objective observer does not have intentionality. Once we are in the world with objects, events and social processes, we have an 'interest' in them. Intentionality presumes an interest in this sense, while the idea of judgement assumes away interest (Kant, 1952). Weberian 'value-freedom' also presumes the absence of an attitude. To have an 'attitude' towards objects, including those objects that are the social subjects we study, is for Husserl to 'attend' to them. To be in the world with objects and social processes, to be intentional towards them, is to *experience* them. To be in a separate world is to observe, and not to experience. In observation you do not attend sufficiently to things, they don't affect you sufficiently so as to constitute experience. Indeed you avoid experiencing them. So judgement and experience, as Husserl (1975) implied in *Experience and Judgement*, stand in contrast to one another. In two-world models of knowledge you observe or judge. In one-world models you experience. Phenomenology, in contradistinction to realism, holds that there are no objects except for an 'experiencer'. There are no objects, no meaning, no truth and no knowledge in the absence of such an experiencer in the world with objects.

The observer produces knowledge of the object through judgements, through doubt. The observer has knowledge in terms of causes and effects, in terms of 'the why'.[4] Knowledge for the observer involves explanation. The experiencer, in contrast, has knowledge of the object from his/her attitude, from the particular perspective of his intentionality. This knowledge is not through judgement, but takes place in a mode in which judgement is suspended: it is instead knowledge through belief. Such knowledge is less causal than descriptive: involves less explanation than *explication*. Explanation in German is *'Erklärung'*, which Weber famously wrote about. Explication is *'Auslegung'*, which does bear similarities to Weber's *verstehen*, but is literally 'laying out' (Heidegger, 1986: 34–8). Phenomenological knowledge is through opening up and laying out phenomena. Phenomenological description from any attitude is explication. There are infinite possibilities of attitudes – different kinds of aesthetic attitudes, scientific attitudes, attitudes of social classes, of ethnic groups, attitudes from a multiplicity of forms of life. Consider, for example, the attitude of the building surveyor, who sees immediately all the detailed cracks and faults in a house. Knowledge from an attitude is true. Phenomenology is not relativistic. Knowledge is true in regard to a specific attitude, a specific intentionality, a specific suspension of judgement. Different attitudes entail different ways of suspending judgement. For example, a Christian attitude will suspend doubt in specific ways.

Of this infinite variety of attitudes, three interest us for present purposes. These are (1) the 'natural attitude', (2) the 'scientific attitude' and (3) the 'reflective attitude'. There are an infinite number of empirically occurring natural attitudes. The scientific attitude is one empirically occurring attitude. The scientific attitude as well is a mode of experience. It is one very particular and highly influential mode of experience. It is a mode of experience that gives itself off as not being a mode of experience. It is a mode of being-in-the-world that gives itself off as observing from another world. But indeed it is just one way of experiencing from the same world. Even non-attending to an object becomes one of many ways of attending to it. To experience an object, event, phenomenon from any given attitude is to 'bracket'. What phenomenologists call 'bracketing' is the suspension of judgement. It is where you suspend doubt and describe. The scientific attitude for its part suspends doubt about suspending doubt.

Husserl's 'transcendental reduction' itself takes place from a particular intentionality: from an attitude that he calls the 'reflective attitude'. This is not at all the scientific attitude. The scientific attitude itself is bracketed in the reflective attitude. Description from the point of view of the phenomenological reduction does not yield knowledge in the sense of Kant's a priori of the logical categories of the understanding (that is, cause, effect, syllogism, identity, difference and the like) but will yield apodictic knowledge. Kant's categories privileged 'intellection'. They presumed the dualism of intellection, on the one hand, and intuition, on the other (Gasché, 1986). For Kant, intuition, our everyday vulgar living in the world with objects, yielded no meaningful knowledge at all. Meaningful knowledge was the sort gained in mathematics and physics. Husserl's transcendental reduction was instead a matter of the '*intuition* of essences' (my italics). From other attitudes, things were known trivially in regard to their appearances (though not the sort of systematic appearance-knowledge involved in maths and physics). There was thus intuition of appearances from other attitudes. Only the reflective attitude will yield the intuition of essences (Levinas, 1973). The reflective attitude gives knowledge of what Kant deemed as unknowable, that is, things-in-themselves. The scientific attitude gives itself off as timeless and spaceless. The reflective attitude for its part is an attitude, a mode of experience that works over and through the time and space of experienced consciousness. Such time comprises importantly 'protention' and 'retention'. Husserl's temporality breaks – as did Bergson, James and Joyce – with Newtonian temporality, for the temporality of experiencing consciousness. Hence Husserl's (1991) concentration on the 'phenomenology of inner time consciousness'.

Thus the fascination of a generation of students with Husserl – including Hans-Georg Gadamer, Max Scheler, Martin Heidegger, Paul Ricoeur, Maurice Merleau-Ponty, Alfred Schutz, Emmanuel Levinas. Starting from intentionality and then describing the structures of consciousness that enable the reduction, gives not epistemological, but *ontological* knowledge: knowledge of the ontological structures of things and of consciousness itself. The reflective attitude is the attitude, the mode of intentionality that never occurs empirically – hence Husserl's attacks on psychologism – but it is the condition of possibility of apodictic knowledge, of the knowledge of things in themselves. Heidegger shifts this ego into the world and calls it *Dasein*, and looks for structures of *Dasein*. Yet *Dasein* too is transcendental in that it is no empirically occurring human being. Indeed, the entirety of *Being and Time* is in 'condition-of-possibility' language. If we can just describe the structures of *Dasein*, we will have knowledge of things-in-themselves. We will authentically relate to Being through the ontological structures of beings.

Against Ontology: Towards a Radical Empiricism

Now this is where phenomenology comes unstuck. This is where classical phenomenology – whether life-world or transcendental – comes unstuck, at least in terms of its suitability for the global information society. The information society's technological culture works through the erasing of transcendentals. The global information society has an immanentist culture, fully a one and flat world culture. As such, its regime of culture is radically empiricist. For its part, phenomenology starts with a theory of immanence – of our intentionality in the world with objects – and winds up giving us a new two-world theory of ontological structures. It gives us a theory of structures of what is not an empirically occurring consciousness. Two particular phenomenologists – Alfred Schutz and Harold Garfinkel – differ here. They give us a thoroughly empirical (that is, not transcendental) phenomenology. They dispense with the reflective attitude and the transcendental reduction. For them any reduction will have to be an empirical one, an actually occurring one. Second, they dispense with any ontological structures of objects. They dispense with both epistemology and ontology for a thoroughgoing empiricism: an empiricism that is central to the critique of information suggested in this book. Such a radical empiricism is at the same time a categorical rejection of positivism. Positivism is a two-world doctrine. Positivism is neither an ontology nor a 'technology' (ethnomethodology is such a technology), but an *epistemology* of the objective observer. Among philosophers of ontology, Heidegger's phenomenology was transcendental, as clearly was Husserl's. Levinas and Derrida are also philosophers of ontology who give us a (deconstructed) phenomenology.[5] Garfinkel gives us an immanentist phenomenology.

Now the key to Garfinkel's 'ethnomethodology' is to stay with Husserlian phenomenology and think it through without the transcendental. Garfinkel's phenomenology should still thus be understood as primarily addressing not 'doing', but instead 'thinking'. It addresses knowledge. Thus the 'ethno-methods' of ethnomethodology are not methods, not the 'how' of carrying out the social practices of everyday forms of life. They are, instead, as was the transcendental reduction, methods of knowledge, of knowing. Knowledge takes place for phenomenology through *operations*. The reduction and bracketing are performed through such 'operations'. Positivism is concerned with the 'why' of explanation or what Weber called *erklären*. Phenomenology is concerned with the 'what' and the 'how'. The 'what' is the explication: it is the phenomenological description of things and events derived from bracketing in a given attitude. The 'how' is the way that knowledge is achieved. The how is the 'operation' through which knowledge is achieved. In looking at the operational structures of consciousness, at the transcendental ego, Husserl is just as concerned with the 'how', the operations of this ego, as with the 'what', the resulting descriptions or explication.

It is this 'how' of knowledge that is the *method* in ethnomethodology. There are methods for doing things and methods for knowing. Garfinkel (and

Husserl) are, to repeat, interested in the latter. Garfinkel refers to operations, but further to an 'operational structure' of 'organized settings': an operational structure of 'organized activities'. It is these organized settings, these 'forms of life', that have an operational structure. It is not consciousness, but organized settings that have an 'attitude', an attitude whose operation yields practical knowledge. 'Members' of such settings draw on these operational structures in their encounters with things and other members. Indeed, a given organized setting could not persist without such operational structures. The attitude at issue is what Garfinkel, following Schutz and Husserl, call the 'natural attitude', or the attitude of 'daily life', in contradistinction to both the scientific and reflective attitudes. But there is not one but an infinite number of natural attitudes, of empirical intentionalities of everyday life: it is these that ethnomethodologists study. What these operational structures carry out is effectively an 'empirical reduction'. Ethnomethodologists are concerned not primarily with the sort of descriptions and 'accounts' made through the operational structures' empirical reduction. They are concerned primarily with how these operational structures work. We will return to this below. For the moment let us just note that the object of ethnomethodology is this socially organized and practical knowledge; this knowledge that is itself the result of a continuing and chronic process of empirical reduction.

Garfinkel refers to these phenomenological descriptions as 'accounts'. He also calls them 'reports', 'stories' and 'glosses'. It is important to consider what they are 'accounts' of. They are surely not accounts of the operational structures themselves, the description of whose 'formal properties' is the task of the ethnomethodologists. For the practitioners of everyday life they are instead accounts of activities and expressions, what Garfinkel calls 'indexical activities' and 'indexical expressions'. By 'indexical' he means not graspable objectively in terms of a relation between universal and particular. In comparison, Husserl will speak of the description of essences (and of the structure of consciousness); Schutz mostly of 'interpretation' and 'understanding' (*verstehen*); Gadamer of interpretation; Derrida of never fully graspable 'writing'; Levinas of an ethics of alterity. But Garfinkel insists, for us significantly, on '*accounts*'. Let us go back to Garfinkel's PhD thesis to try to throw some light on what is meant by this. Remember though that our objective here is not so much members' knowledge of ethnomethodology, but instead to grasp a thoroughly immanentist and empiricist phenomenology. We are looking to develop a sort of 'phenomenology of sensation' for the global information order: a phenomenology that is at the same time immediate and takes place at a distance.

An Empirical Phenomenology of Communications

Garfinkel in his PhD thesis was preoccupied with the problem of social order. Indeed the first substantive chapter of the thesis is entitled 'The Question of Social Order'. Here his influence clearly was Talcott Parsons. Garfinkel (1952: 43), like Parsons, fully disagrees with Hobbes that 'uncommunicating monads' could be any sort of basis for social order. Hobbes,

Garfinkel notes, takes part in the assumptions of the scientific attitude, in which the scientist as observer is an 'uncommunicating monad'. These properties of the scientist are then transferred to the practices of everyday life. Here we see the centrality of 'communication' to Garfinkel's idea of knowledge. Interpretation and description are insufficient. 'Accounts', 'reports' and 'glosses' are as much *communications* as they are entities of knowledge. Garfinkel's theory of knowledge is one of communicated knowledge. Though Garfinkel takes up Parsons's problem of social order, he does not think that Parsons provides the solution to this problem. Parsons does not provide the solution because he, like Hobbes – and for that matter, Garfinkel observes, Kant and Weber – takes up a, this time more sophisticated, version of the scientific attitude. For Garfinkel, Parsons and Weber subscribe to the 'correspondence theory of reality' of the scientific attitude, rather than the 'congruence theory of reality' of the attitude of daily life. Thus Parsons spoke of an 'objective world' which is approached through the 'logico-empirical method' of what Garfinkel saw as the mainstream 'sociological attitude'. The correspondence is from a 'matching operation' of 'schema' and object. Here an 'empirical construct' abstracts features from the concrete object as an ideal type. This is at best an approximation of the concrete object, and is in the end a merely empirically possible object. It is but a 'nominalistic designation' that 'stands outside of fluctuations of circumstances and perspectival appearances' (pp. 99, 104).[6] In the 'congruence theory of reality' that Garfinkel draws from Husserl and Schutz, 'the way in which something is of interest to a witness is all of the way in which that thing is real'. In other words, the attitude associated with a form of life is inseparable from the object. Indeed, fitting is not a matching but a 'constitutive operation' (p. 96). What Garfinkel is saying here is that 'the how' and 'the what' are inseparable. Knowledge does not so much tell you about the object as is built right into the object. The empirical construct does not abstract from the real object, but 'the empirical construct stands to the object that it designates as constitutive of the unified character of these specifications' which 'in their unity as a schema of specifications means all of what is meant by "concrete object"' (p. 104). The object is thus very real as a schema of interest-relevant specifications. Objects have 'organizational properties' in a sort of 'relevance structure of objects'. What Garfinkel is alluding to is not a simple constructivism in which a subject constructs an object. There must instead be the presence of an object in order for an attitude to be possible.

At issue is a very specific type of reflexivity, one which is I think characteristic of the global information society. What is reflexive is 'the accounting practices'. And they are reflexive in so far as they are 'incarnate' (Garfinkel, 1984: 1). The reflexive character of accounting practices *is* the incarnate nature of such practices. So to be reflexive is to be incarnate. This is more like a reflex than reflection. Reflexivity does not mean 'rationality' in this context, though the accounts are 'reflexively tied for their rational features to the socially organized occasions of their use'. The accounts then are also features of their use (1984: 4). The accounts are of practical actions. The accounts are not made in a separate world – of the neutral observer – from the actions. They are instead a quality of these practical actions. The reflexivity of accounts is 'essentially uninteresting'. Accounts have rational features but don't have reflexive features. What is reflexive is that these rational features of accounts are tied or incarnate in the activities. What is accountable is observable and repeatable. You look and tell. Communications are central in this. This stands in contrast to the reflexivity involved in 'reflexive modernization' (Beck et al., 1994). As the accounts are 'features' of the occasions, activities or settings, they are reflexive (Garfinkel, 1984: 9–10). As the accounts make the settings and occasions observable to other members they do so in *not* making them topical or 'interesting'. Reflexive modernization makes events topical. It operates in a sea of doubt, whereas phenomenological reflexivity involves the suspension of doubt. In reflexive modernization, the reflection is separate from and 'above' the facts, the events. In ethnomethodology it is part and parcel of them. In reflexive modernization we come to make more and more life decisions. In ethnomethodology the reflexivity of practices – and the observability and 'tellability' of events and settings – makes decisions only rarely necessary. In reflexive modernization the individual is a judge: in phenomenological reflexivity, the individual is witness.

Weber's and Habermas's idea of legitimation of action in which the reason is separate from the action is of a piece with reflexive modernization. In ethnomethodology the reason, the defence, is part and parcel of the action. It is a feature of the activity. Reflexive modernization is in a strong sense the generalization of the scientific attitude to the community of practical 'reasoners'. In this it resembles neo-classical economics, with its disembedded actors and preference schedules.[7] Finally, reflexive modernization like the rational choice assumptions of neo-classical economics, is essentially individualistic. Empirical phenomenology's focus is on the collectivity: hence the centrality of communications, of 'telling'. Hence reasons must at the same time be accounts. This is not the case in reflexive modernization, in which reasons justify decisions. For empirical phenomenology, crucial, more than making things intelligible to oneself, is making them intelligible to others. Making activities intelligible to others is simultaneously co-ordinating the corresponding activities with others. This, then, is rationality with a purpose – that purpose being its consequences. What we have here is a resolutely anti-Kantian doctrine. Kant's pure reason, practical reason and aesthetic judgement presume that the subject is not in the world with the object, whether that object is a thing or a social process. In Kant you have interiority, in empirical phenomenology, exteriority. In the former, judgement, in the latter, the suspension of judgement.

Space, Time, Communications

Let us look at the implications for space and time. In terms of space, most important is that you, the subject, are given in the world. The world is not an object for contemplation. In the attitude of daily life (i.e. the phenomenological attitude) one is given in the world. This attitude 'maximizes presence in the world, it maximizes the perspectival character of one's attitudes towards things, activities, expressions, and social processes in the world. In the scientific attitude there is the minimization of perspectival character with the suspension indeed of subjectivity (in the sense that you have a subjective personal point of view on something)'. In phenomenology the world takes on a density, an opacity, a tectonic feeling, unlike the transparent and empty space, the light space of the scientific attitude. The world in the natural attitude is opaque and complex, with perspectivally located subjects, whose bodies take on a density. The world 'is depicted as a set of "there" positions fixed according to the actor's (bodily) "here"'' (Garfinkel, 1952: 62). For the scientific attitude objects do not have density. They are points or variables ordered in causes and effects. Neither does the observer, who is a point.[8] 'For me in the attitude of daily life these objects in their "there" positions I attend with degrees of familiarity and strangeness' (pp. 49–50). For the observer in the scientific attitude, the objects are in another world, alienated from the observer. In the attitude of daily life, the subject is an 'actor'. In the scientific attitude he is an 'observer', atomized and isolated from the fray. Thus neo-classical economics and Hobbes attribute almost observer-like positions to individuals. The actor by definition is social. He is in a play.[9] Observers, like the 'readers' and 'writers' of texts, are very much on their own.[10] Finally, spatial, at least in metaphor, is the idea of meaning. For the scientific attitude (and the reflective attitude) what counts is the 'essence' only, the 'kernel of meaning' of full rational clarity, while for the attitude of daily life also important are the 'fringes of meaning', of indexical expressions (p. 51).

More important is temporality. In fact, it is temporal ordering that is Garfinkel's preoccupation. In *Studies in Ethnomethodology*, written in 1967, the problem of social order is a question of the '*ongoing*' nature of activities. The idea of activity as distinct from the act assumes an ongoing temporality. As does of course reproduction, a term not used by Garfinkel. Yet it is the success, the successful accomplishment of 'contingent' (that is, somehow not essential) accounting practices that ensures the reproduction of the ethnomethodological setting of organized activities. In this later work, written some fifteen years after the PhD, it is no longer the problems of Hobbes or the social system that concern Garfinkel, but instead localized settings, like a suicide prevention centre; juries; an outpatient psychiatric clinic; managing of a sex change over time. What holds together such enterprises over time, he asks. The answer is the accounting practices members carry out in regard to one another; the accounting practices that are incarnate, that are reflexively tied to activities in a given setting. Thus Garfinkel focuses on conversations. He focuses on the 'how' of conversation, on, for example, turn-taking. His interest is in how every expression in a conversation is tied to an implicit giving of an account, that is analytically separate from (yet reflexively tied to) that expression. What makes a conversation possible? This is a temporal problem. Account-giving lets a conversation become a temporally extended activity. The duration of a conversation is just one instance of the duration of social order in general. This Simmelian question of 'how is society possible?' is an eminently temporal question.

Thus a set of Garfinkel's reflections on Alfred Schutz is preoccupied with temporal ordering: with how 'the rational properties of common sense activities' work in regard to 'the ordering of events' (Garfinkel, 1984: ch. 8). In this Garfinkel speaks of the scientific theorist versus practical 'theorists', stressing that the knowledge involved in accounting practices in everyday life is not just methodological, but also theoretical. The everyday theorist has an *interest* in the temporal ordering of events. The setting itself has an interest in the 'scheduling and co-ordinating of events'. Hence 'the importance of the retrospective and the prospective in conversation'; that the meaning, that is, the 'sense of conversation', is realized not through the unit expression, the unit indexical expression, but 'realized through a succession of realized meanings' (1984: 274).

Consider objects in the context of time. Objects are not just 'there': they also are 'now', just as I am 'here' and 'now'. The 'now' indicates contingency. It does not presume the infinite duration and out-of-time-ness of the observer in the scientific attitude. It points also to ephemerality of the 'now', of the series of 'nows'. The now is a specific time. Moreover, to 'treat objects in the there takes time' (1952: 50). We *attend* to objects in 'the there', in the attitude of daily life. We immediately attend to them; we are in a relationship more or less of 'care' with them (Heidegger, 1986: 191–5). The scientific observer does not attend to objects. He doesn't care. For him they are concrete things that do not have meanings in any existentially important sense, but only in the sense that he abstracts schema from them. The observer then causally orders these abstractions as mere points in time, as 'variables'. When you are given in the world with objects or with social practices, they affect you, you affect them. You are not above all of this, ordering these entities as causes and effects, unaffected, with no investment of affect. In the attitude of daily life your activities are contingent, your expressions are contingent. The scientific observer's expressions and activities are not contingent. They are universal, or have pretensions to universality. The philosopher's expressions and activities avoid contingency in being a priori, in being the unconditioned condition of possibility of. The actor in daily life is clearly not universal, and does not pretend to be. Her actions and words are not primordial, a priori nor unconditioned. She is contingent and empirical. Hence there is a vastly different attitude towards problem-solving. For the scientific, the solution of a problem is for the sake of its solution. As uninterested, there is little concern for pragmatic consequences. The phenomenological actor solves problems for the sake of pragmatic consequences. For the sake of some kind of continuity of social order (Garfinkel, 1984: 46). Hence 'blueprint Marxism' has been disastrous in terms of unintended consequences, as Weber (1946) argued in his essay on the 'ethics of responsibility'. Here Weber discards his positivist hat and ideal-typical abstractions. Politics, he implies, must be done in the natural attitude. In politics the scientific attitude is a recipe for disaster. So is the presumption, dominant perhaps more than ever today, of political scientists (of whatever political stripe) to presume the scientific attitude among the 'rationally-choosing' subjects they study.

The phenomenological actor seeks to accomplish a pragmatic project in the world. The disembedded observer, whose disembedded 'ought' might give rise to meta-narratives from the 'is', is not engaged in pragmatic projects. He wants instead cognitively to order the world. Meaning ascribed to the acts of the actor must then take into account not just the now but the past and the future; must take into account 'protention' and 'retention'. This is in stark contrast to the observer, whose chronicity is of an internal time. The scientific attitude is thus unconcerned with the interruption of such a (pragmatic) project; it has little respect for 'traditions of fact', and is always ready to discard them. The 'span of a project for the scientific attitude is only maintained if each successive step turns out according to the requirements of verification'. The phenomenological actor for his part 'maintains the temporal span of the project even in the face of experiential frustration'. In order that the project may be maintained there must be certain closedness of possibilities in the world. This is again fully opposite to the systematic doubt of the scientific attitude, whose guiding principle is openness to all possibilities. Finally, in the natural attitude we act with respect to some sort of standardized and 'outer' time scheme, while the scientific observer is external to all temporal schemes, with no intersection of his 'inner time' and standardized time. (This would hold for artists as well as scientists.) Standardized time only provides data for the scientific attitude. He orders the data of the conduct of others. The attitude of daily life is instead dependent on similarities between his stream of experience and that of other actors in his world. 'Time of occurrence' is not important for scientific data, yet is of the utmost importance in coordination of the actions and memories of two or more persons (Garfinkel, 1952: 47–8). Think, for example, of the problems of train schedules, of coordinating vehicle traffic or air traffic control. The attitude of daily life presumes that settings or states of affairs must be 'managed' over time. A sex change operation must be managed across a whole series of activities. Growing older must be managed. Appearances must be managed in one way or another with regard to temporal consequences.

Conclusions

This chapter has tried to come to grips with the shift from representational to technological culture in the information society, first, through considerations of the notion of play. Technological culture is, as has been stressed throughout this book, not a dualist, but an immanentist order. It presumes a certain hands-on-ness, a tactility, in contrast to the distanciation, to the principle of vision of representational culture (Jay, 1993). Play stands in contrast to the 'work' of the representational culture. The worker uses implements, tools, instruments; the player uses equipment, 'gear', 'kit' (Heidegger, 1986: 102–3). The player is also different than the spectator and the worker in that he plays *games*. Games, which are paradigmatic for the technological culture, are spatialized in the sense that the representational-culture relationships between viewer and painting, between reader and text are not. The latter are relations of two points outside of concrete space – a subject and an object. The representational culture speaks the idiom of the symbolic and the imaginary. You play games in neither the symbolic, nor the imaginary, but the 'real'. This 'real', however, is unlike the embedded and localized real of work in the manufacturing society. The real of games and of the global information order is disembedded and generic – whether in the digital space of electronic form of life or the 'non-place' of international airports, or brand environments (Augé, 1995). To be in the real is not to relate to other subjects and objects in a distanciated and monological way, as do the reader/viewer: it is to engage with both subjects and objects dialogically and interactively (Lury, 1999). The player operates less from her conscious mind than her habitus. She is oriented to her environment less through *mémoire voluntaire* than *mémoire involuntaire*. You play football through your habitus, there is no time or space to get the distance, the conscious distance of reflective thought.

We often play in 'fields', a concept that phenomenology uses to understand experiencing subjectivity. This chapter has understood technological culture as integrally phenomenological. The judging subject of the representational culture was timeless and spaceless and separate from any field. In the distancing of the representational culture, the judging subject worked through 'intellection'; phenomenology's experiencing subject operates instead through 'intuition'. This idea of knowledge through intuition makes phenomenology in its germ already part of the technological culture. Garfinkel completes Husserl's task in this by taking the transcendental phenomenology of apodictic knowledge and transforming it into an empiricist phenomenology of communications. Replacing Husserl's intuition of essences is now the intuition of appearances. There is no essence in Garfinkel: there is no thing-in-itself to know or not to know. There are only things, as they appear to interested actors. The result of such intuition is no longer universal statements of apodictic knowledge, but *communications*. These communications are imparted not universally, but particularly to members of the group to which the experiencing subject belongs. These communications are not descriptions of the essences of things. They are glosses or accounts of activities and expressions.[11] They concern less Husserl's relation of subject and object, than relations of intersubjectivity. It is not Husserl's subject, but such extended relations of intersubjectivity, that is, social orderings, that are Garfinkel's concern and unit of analysis. In Garfinkel's radically empiricist phenomenology thought or knowledge (theory, method) is not 'reflective' but reflexive'. In being so, it has not the distance of reflection, but is 'incarnate' in activities and expressions. It is an ongoing account giving practice of activities, expressions and events to other members of that given ordering. 'Reflection' happens in time-out from ongoing activities. In Garfinkel's phenomenology and in the technological culture there is no time-out (Boden, 1994). It is now but a few steps to a fully developed model. In the global information order such communications are increasingly at-a-distance and hence take the shape less of a local (or even national) community than a network. The communications-at-a-distance character of the technological culture also brings in the issue of machine mediation. Such machine-mediated communication is the subject of the next chapter. So is the information order's new paradigm of power.

Notes

1 This is usefully compared with art in tribal societies. See Alfred Gell, *Art and Agency*.

2 Kant used the overpowering experience of viewing a mountain as an example of the sublime. The mountain here is nature as a finality.

3 I am grateful to the late and sadly lamented Deirdre Boden for convincing me of Garfinkel's importance. And for many dicussions of 'indexicality' and reflexivity in Garfinkel. On reflexivity in an ethnomethodological vein, see Boden (1998).

4 Note that judgement presumes linear, external sensation and a two-world notion of observation. In the information order causation is internal and through feedback loops, observation becomes one-world: the selection of information from the 'noise' of the environment (Luhmann, 1997).

5 See the more detailed discussions in Chapters 7 and 8. Such a deconstructed ontology and phenomenology are still working within the assumptions of ontology, of a transcendental phenomenology. For Schutz and Garfinkel the question of ontology in the sense of deep ontology – does not exist. When I use the word 'ontology' in this book, I mean 'deep ontology', that is, with a transcendental. The radically empiricist matter-image ontology of Bergson is well suited to the information order. It is not addressed in this book.

6 I am grateful to Wes Sharrock for the introduction to Garfinkel's PhD thesis.

7 To be fair, Beck's notion of 'reflexive modernization' has also a very strong dimension of non-linearity. See my introduction to Beck and Beck (2001).

8 This 'point' is similar to the 'vanishing point' of Renaissance perspective.

9 In this sense performance artists are not actors.

10 In this sense too Derrida partakes of Kantian aporetics. Why do we want such atomized heuristics of 'reading' and 'writing', rational choosing, observing and judging? Why not instead acting, playing, conversing that presuppose sociality and not atomization?

11 The different varieties of accounts that Garfinkel mentions depends on the sort of intentionality involved. He mentions 'stories' but also 'marking, labelling, symbolizing, emblemizing, cryptograms, analogies, anagrams, indicating (models, drawings), mock-ups, miniaturizing, animating, imitating, simulating' (1984: 31). One wonders if there is a shift today towards accounts as 'marks', towards those 'emblems' that are brands. Do such accounts give stability over time? We are getting closer here to a phenomenology of flows.

13

Non-Linear Power: McLuhan and Haraway

Once media become the 'extensions of man', as Marshall McLuhan intones, they no longer are primarily the *representers* of man. Media, as extensions, become technologies. Thus McLuhan is a theorist of the technological culture. McLuhan's 'sociology of technology' is of a special kind. It is different from Marx's. The technologies at stake are not the means of production, but the means of communication. McLuhan's technologies are always technologies of communication. This includes the movement of symbols along with people that we understand as transport. Thus transport and migration are also forms of communication. You need technologies of communication only when communication takes place at a distance. What McLuhan gives us is the elements for theory of communication at a distance, or more generally culture-at-a-distance.[1] This chapter will address McLuhan at length in this context. The technological culture is, we shall argue, not just an age of generalized information, but also one of generalized communication. This is important. That is, it is important to think of global and post-industrial capitalism as a shift perhaps not from mode of production to mode of information, but as one from mode of production to mode of *communication*. This puts at centre stage not the production of symbols, but the *movement* of symbols. It puts at centre stage the question of *flows*. If the information society foregrounded the production of symbols, then the *global* information culture foregrounds the *movement* of symbols, with or without the people that move them. Hence the older social structures of the manufacturing society and its representational culture are displaced not just by information structures but increasingly by *communication* structures.

In an earlier age, when the media were primarily representational, we connected to media in relations of either domination or resistance. In the present age, when media become technological, we engage with media, we work with them. Technology becomes something that enters integrally into our forms of life. Communication at a distance, and culture at a distance involve the pervasion of technological forms of life. This would seem to entail that relations of *power* are transmogrified. Not just the media but also science become 'technologized' in the information order. This chapter will thus interrogate Donna Haraway's work. With Haraway we will see how not just machines and goods, not just culture and the media have become informationalized, but nature and life itself. This informationalized nature may then be patented as intellectual property and become integral to accumulation strategies of global capital. The critique of information, this book has argued, must take place from inside of the information order. It must include a theory of power. If power relations in the critique of ideology had a basis in real property, then power in the critique of information has a basis in intellectual property. This involves trademark law, underwriting capital accumulation in highly branded fast-moving consumer goods. It includes copyright law, concerning say operating system and applications software. It concerns patent law, in especially biotechnology, in which forms of life themselves accumulate as global capital.

Against Linearity: McLuhan

Extensions: From Nervous System to Communications Network

Today's culture is characterized by a collapse of the representational culture into the immanent plane of technology. This entails, we saw in the previous chapter, a certain reflexivity. Such reflexivity takes place, we saw, not internal to the subject, but radically external. We saw how Garfinkel took the reflexivity that was internal to the subject in Kant and Husserl and externalized it. In Garfinkel's radically empiricist phenomenology, knowledge is not internal to the subject but tied to, incarnate in actions, events and expressions. Knowledge is communicative thought incarnate in activities: it is accounts of those activities to members, to co-practitioners of a given form of life. Thus knowledge pertains not internally to the subject but externally to forms of life. The break with the dualism of the representational culture for the immanent plane of technological culture entails an externalization of subjectivity. No longer is there the dualist, depth model of an internalized subjectivity. In positivism as in all aspects of the representational culture, there is the assumption of a neutralization of the subject. The scientific observer in positivism is neutral, and knowledge is internalized in this subject. When the subject is de-neutralized in the technological culture, when the subject takes on attitude and intentionality, knowledge and reflexivity must necessarily be externalized.

In McLuhan the media are the 'extensions of man'. This means much more than the media are tools that extend man's power, range, etc. It means that the media are indeed the externalization of the human sensorium. McLuhan (1993) understands man, not in terms of the conscious or the unconscious mind, nor even in terms of the body, but instead in terms of the human 'sensorium'. The human sensorium is externalized as the media, as the electronic media. He can thus write: 'We are the television screen ... We wear all mankind as our skin' (*Understanding Media* (henceforth UM), p. x).[2] McLuhan takes Garfinkel's externalization of knowledge thesis a step further. For McLuhan the subject is not only in the world with technology. In McLuhan's mechanical anthropology the subject is *fused* with technology. In phenomenology the intentional subject has a different status than the object. Hence in Heidegger, *Dasein*'s ontological structure is vastly different than the ontological structure of other beings. In the immanentist technological culture subjects and objects converge in ontological status: the subject is so to speak downwardly mobile and the object upwardly mobile. For McLuhan, subjects and objects fuse. The media are the 'extensions of man'. More generally, technology is the extension of man. To say 'the medium is the message' is to say that the technology is the content. But this is not technological determinism because McLuhan disputes linear causation and hence any sort of determinism. Linear causation belongs to the Gutenberg age and the phonetic alphabet. When technology, when the media, are extensions of the central nervous system, linear causation is deserted for a flattened, immanent world.

In Aristotle man was *zoon politikon*. For a number of the *Lumières* the human differentia specificae was as the rational animal. From the nineteenth century we have *homo faber* (Marx) and in the early twentieth century man as symbol-using animal (Cassirer, 1995). With Cassirer, McLuhan wants to think of man as primarily symbol-using. Yet man is symbol-using not primarily through language but, with Marx, through *technology*. Both Marx and McLuhan have strongly technological arguments. For McLuhan, not just the media, but technologies more generally are the extensions of man. But technology (including transport) is the extension of man only in so far as it helps man *communicate*. Man for McLuhan is not primarily *homo technologicus*, but *homo communicans*. Thus his theory is that technology is the extension of man in so far as man communicates. Marx's presumption is that man needs technology to make things in order for his survival or reproduction. McLuhan is more about excess, less about simple reproduction.

The question becomes, how are technologies extensions of man insofar as man communicates? Here McLuhan (UM: 89) addresses two main subsets of technologies: first, those that are extensions of the human sense organs, and, second, those that are extensions of other organs. For example, he sees clothes as the 'extensions of the skin' and the wheel as the extension of the foot. Roads (including railroads) are also the extensions of the foot. The automobile, interestingly is seen as both the extension of the foot and the extension of the skin. In this sense the automobile is like a dwelling: a dwelling that separate us from others. This points to the individualistic nature of what John Urry (2000) calls 'automobility'. McLuhan stresses that at one point in time communications meant the same thing as transportation. In contemporary French, the term *'communications'* can be used to include transportation. Indeed, in English one can speak of the 'communications' from an island to the mainland in regard to mode of transport, distance and frequency of journeys. The journey in transportation thus has a lot in common with the message in communication.

In most cases McLuhan deals with the extensions of not other organs, but of the sense organs. He gives us a three-stage chronology in which oral culture is followed by the Gutenberg age, which itself is followed by the age of electronic media. In each case cultural artefacts are understood as *media* for McLuhan. For McLuhan, all extensions of the sense organs, of the sensorium, are 'media'. Here the media are the 'message' not just in the electronic age, but also in the Gutenberg and oral ages. In each age the media is an extension of a particular sense. In the Gutenberg age this is the sense of vision. In the oral and electronic ages there are much more balanced sense-extensions. In both of the latter, McLuhan emphasizes audile and tactile or 'haptic' extension, where the entire sensorium is extended, not just the visual. One mode of extension is externalization: what McLuhan calls 'outering'. Now an entity must be at one point 'inner' in order to be 'outered'. The foot, hand and skin are not inner so cannot be outered but only extended. The sensorium, the senses, are inner and can be outered. They are not, however, naturally inner. In the oral age there is a publicness of sense in embedded practices that stands very much in contrast to the inner. In the Gutenberg age – which begins long before Gutenberg with Roman roads (indeed with the roads of the ancient empires) and the phonetic alphabet – there is a growing abstraction. With this abstraction comes a progressive 'innering' of the senses. This privileges the visual; it privileges representation. Prior to the phonetic alphabet, signification was primarily concrete, with signs denoting things. The sign becomes arbitrary, abstract with the phonetic alphabet: this involves a subject that is distanced from the world, distanced from social practices. At stake in this is a differentiation of culture from social life. This vision-privileging innering of the senses is reversed only in the electronic age, the age of information and communication. The 'global village' is not just a return to the tribal village on a global scale. It is the 'outering' of the collective 'central nervous system'. 'Electronic technology' 'extends our senses and nerves in a global embrace' (UM: 80, 247). Here our sensory network becomes effectively the global actor network.

Communications – whether through the movement of messages or the movement of human bodies – entail lines or links of communication. There are two types of connection in any movement of messages (and people): 'lineal' and continuous, or non-lineal and discontinuous. Oral cultures had few connections between villages and towns; these were discontinuous, through markets, storytellers, journeymen. The two main underpinnings of the Gutenberg age are the phonetic alphabet and the straight Roman road. The phonetic alphabet underpins the 'lineality' of syntax in Western languages, which McLuhan contrasts with the 'hieroglyphic' character of other languages. The abstraction of the alphabet yields the lineality of communication. The opposite of lineality is discontinuity for McLuhan but also 'mosaic'. Languages can be primarily syntactical or mosaic. Straight Roman roads, like Renaissance perspective, are based on the privileging of the extension of vision. 'Roads' thus are continuous, lineal. Sheep tracks are non-lineal. The paths of the mediaeval villages are non-lineal. Here both roads and phonetic alphabet (and the introduction of the lighter papyrus) make possible the extension of commands and control from a central and hierarchical point. The airport and aeroplane, by contrast, signal a return to discontinuous, non-lineal connections. The extensions of the wing and the fin, in boats and planes, are not wheels, conducive to continuity and linearity, but non-linear (fins) and discontinuous (wings). Here communications take place through not roads but 'ports'. Boats and planes come into ports through, respectively, non-linear and discontinuous space; trains, cars and trucks through a continuous (road) space (UM: 179 ff.).

There are implications for power in this. There is a bureaucratic and national centralization of power with the phonetic alphabet and road of the Gutenberg age. This is broken up into a plurality of horizontally connecting yet global villages, with the newer discontinuity of airports, information ports and tele-ports.[3] McLuhan understands lineality in contrast to 'additivity'. In this context, A can stand to B in either a lineal or an additive relation. Knowledge in the Gutenberg age is a matter of causation and classification. That is, A stands to B in a relation of either causation or classification. Both causation and classification are lineal.[4] McLuhan like Hume is empiricist in his scepticism towards causal relations. Causal relations in social science and the causality in classical narrative privilege the monologic and centralized power of the Gutenberg age. This is the power of the cause over the effect, the classifier over the classified. Linear relations thus speak in terms of B because of A, and A over B. Additive relations speak of A *and* B. Of A and B discontinuously: of A *connecting to* B discontinuously. These are the connections of a network. Networks unlike roads are discontinuous. They are 'topological', as Latour (1993) stresses, not 'topographical'. McLuhan, like Deleuze, privileges the additive, the conjunction. The electronic age is the 'society of the "and"' (Van Toorn, 1998). The electronic age signals a shift from causation to additivity. It signals also a move from representation to additivity. In representation, A stands to B as in different worlds. A is the mirror of B. Philosophy is the mirror of nature, culture the mirror of technology. This again is a monological privileging of the universal, A over the particular, B: the subject over the object. The paradigmatic media of the electronic age – television, the comic, the advert, 'the world of games and models' – are not representations of situations. They are not 'mirrors' of situations, they are instead *'extensions* of situations elsewhere' (UM: 4). They are not representational but additive. As extensions of situations elsewhere they are *supplements*.

The supplement, not the representation is at issue as we move from mechanical-age linearity to information-age discontinuity. At issue – as in play and the game (Chapter 12) – is the elsewhere-extension of the situation. In the media we see this change in the declining proportion of classic narratives and the increasing centrality of football and sport (and indeed game shows) in the media. TV news is becoming less a representation of politics than a continuation of politics elsewhere. Culture takes place less in a representational 'text' than in a phenomenological field. The field is a practice elsewhere, not, like the text, a (more or less accurate) mirror of a practice. Text is to representation as elsewhere-extension is to field. We see this in the change from epistemology to phenomenology in the human sciences. In epistemology there is representation, and philosophy and sociology are a 'mirror of nature' – in Descartes, Locke, Kant, but also the early Durkheim and Parsons. In phenomenology, there is not representation but instead the field. We see this in Merleau-Ponty, Ricoeur and Pierre Bourdieu's early work. Here the previously neutral, detached and two-world observer is relocated into a force field.

Theory itself, as say sport and the other mediated practices, in the electronic age may be not much more than a supplement, a field added on, a continuation elsewhere. Theory can be no longer the representation, occupying another ontological level of critique.[5] Theory can only be supplementary. As supplement, it is only an additive to the immanent assemblage global networks. Such an additive can however contribute to reconfiguring the entire assemblage.

The Compression of Narrative: From Citizen to Communicant

The additive, the 'and', the supplement is for McLuhan the order of things when the senses and technology link up with one another in a fitting and balanced way – as they do in both tribal and information cultures. It is only in the Gutenberg culture of road, phonetic alphabet and print media that they do not. This particular technological framework 'massages' the sensorium in a way privileging the visual sense. With the privileged extension of this particular sense, the supplement, the 'and' appears instead as a representation. The hegemony of eye-extension forces the additive, forces the situation elsewhere to take the form of mirror, cause and lineal space. McLuhan does not dispense with all notions of cause, however. In place of linear causation in the electronic age appears a sort of depth structuring, a sort of semiotic and structural 'causation'. Comics, television, adverts in what he calls our 'iconic age' are a question not so much of linearity but of 'depth involvement'. Thus 'Johnny doesn't think in terms of linearity' he 'won't read' and 'can't visualize distant goals', but is 'an expert in code and linguistic analysis' (UM: 163). Thus print culture's knowledge via classification is displaced by the electronic culture's knowledge via 'pattern recognition'. Classification presumes a two-world paradigm of subsumption and logic. Pattern recognition takes place in a field of immanence in which subsumption is impossible. Pattern recognition is less logical than analogical (Caygill, 1989). This 'depth notion' of 'cause and effect', replacing sequential cause and effect, foregrounds the magical dimension in both oral cultures and electronic age. In the structuralism, the linguistic structuralism of the information age there is such a depth model of causation. McLuhan (1997: 136) notes the continued prominence of oral culture in contemporaneous Russia. 'Russians approach situations structurally', he mentions.

McLuhan notes at the same time film-maker Sergei Eisenstein's surrealist and 'mosaic' juxtapositions. Let us pause for a while and discuss this idea of *mosaic* that is so important to McLuhan: that is so central to his understanding of both oral and electronic cultures in contrast to the syntax and linearity of print culture. 'Syntax' is born with seventeenth century grammar. It refers to the grammatical construction of sentences. Its focus is the order of words. It is the rules that preside over the order of words in the construction of sentences. Later, in structural linguistics, the 'syntagmatic' is a question of the order, the grouping of words, whereas the 'paradigmatic' has to do with rapports, the associations of words, apart from linear order. The 'mosaic', similarly, has to do with 'not sequence, but simultaneity'. Hence the television mosaic is 'a total field of simultaneous impulses'. Newspapers too have moved in the age of instant news from a linear to a mosaic principle. If simultaneity is displacing sequence then linear causation or linear interrelations are no longer predominant. Instead, to understand the mosaic (which is to understand media), we must look to 'interrelations in depth', as in magic and the fetish (UM: 289, 294).

Linear media for McLuhan are 'hot', in the sense of having meaning prior to interpretation, while mosaic media are 'cool' in their need of depth interpretation. Most often for him the book, scientific discourse, film, the photograph and the newspaper tend to be Gutenberg age media (that is, visual, linear and hot), while television, advertising and, for example, the cartoon tend to be cool media. In practice McLuhan detects mosaic developments in most of the hot media too. Film can be either Gutenberg age material – as in narrative cinema – or electronic age stuff – as in Eisenstein – and, we will see below, in the star system. The novel tends to be linear narrative – but not in Joyce's *Ulysses* or *Finnegan's Wake*. *Ulysses* is more (electronic-culture) informational than narrative in nature: it is based in the 24 hour temporality of a newspaper deadline. *Finnegan's Wake* reverts to the tribalism of the oral culture: a *finn* is a tribe in Gaelic (1997: 326–30). The newspaper begins with Gutenberg-like dependence on the (discursive) linear and argued structure of editorial opinion. But speed-up in news delivery yields what is increasingly a mosaic medium. Indeed, McLuhan would argue that all sorts of Gutenberg media are now coming under the mosaic hegemony of informationalization.

What is a mosaic? According to the *Petit Robert*, a mosaic is – consider, for example, the classical mosaics of Pompei and Ravenna – a 'decorative assemblage'. It is originally a combination of small pieces of stone, glass, marble and clay, cemented together to make up a sort of design. The roots are from late Latin and shared, not with Moses, but with museum. Mosaics were constructed not by authors or genius-painters, but craftsmen, by '*ouvriers mosäistes*', who were '*carreleurs*' juxtaposing stones. Hence we can speak of wall and pavement mosaics, of mosaic rugs and leather mosaics. For André Malreaux, the mosaic is 'the mother of the vitrine'. The vitrine is most importantly the stained-glass window of churches, but also in department stores we see objects through vitrines. The church mosaic presents sequential events in simultaneity, and hence is difficult to read for the modern observer. Mosaics, in any case, work via not the 'light on' but the 'light through' principle of the electronic media (UM: 52–3). Impulses have a light-through character, while there is something static about light-on. The viewer does not receive impulses from it, but instead images. Impulses are a one-world, networked phenomenon. They are a basis for community. Indeed, in Benedict Anderson's (1989) *Imagined Communities*, stained glass windows featured as constitutive of community before the imagined communities of print media and nation-building. McLuhan's electronic communities should be understood as polar opposite to Anderson's imagined communities. Imagined communities are formed in the print age, with the unification of the nation-state, paradigmatically seen in (the linearity of) Napoleonic and Haussmann's France. Here schoolchildren learnt the same things at the same time every day. All read a national newspaper. National roads and urban boulevards enabled the movement of troops and messages. The imagined community is not the concrete community of the locality. You never meet the people in the imagined community, which is the nation. The imagined community is linear: it is monologic in terms of the passing of information. It is expansive. It is based on the extension of the social, indeed it signals the birth of the social, as Foucault (1998) noted, with the principle of social contractuality underlying a whole set of expansive social institutions of the nation-state. Its principle is the extension of social contractuality of individual rights-bearing citizens.

Contemporary electronic communities break with every aspect of the national and imagined communities. They are global at the same time as disruptive of all the imagined community's linearities. The long linear connections are fragmented into a set of shorter, non-linear networks. They are exploded. The temporal expansion and linearity of language, paralleled by the spatial expansion of the nation-state and the social is exploded into a set of more compressed but also more dialogic assemblages. The railways' national and continuous political space is displaced by the airport's global and discontinuous and less political (in the sense of institutional politics and the international expansion of the nation-state), indeed 'nomadic space' (UM: 36–8). The imagined communities' rights-bearing and national citizen gives way not to global citizens, but to 'the nomad', the wanderer who replaces the static and settled citizen. Citizenship rights are in sedentary cultures, they relate to settled and expansive cultures, to progressive cultures of meta-narratives. There is no sort of orderly progression in nomadic and electronic cultures (see Virilio, 1999a). There is instead an underlying nomadic movement of both tribal and global cultures. The mosaic of movement of tribal and global cultures makes impossible the expansion and betterment of Whig historiography. Human rights in this age are less citizens' rights than nomadic rights. There is in all this not sequence, but simultaneity of movement.

How *does* community work in the electronic age? McLuhan writes of the press, whose foregrounding of linear editorial 'point of view' is displaced now by the mosaic's 'exposure of multiple items in juxtaposition'. The newspaper editorial is discursive, based on point of view, on 'discursively redeemed validity claims'. Then the telegraph shortens the sentence, the radio shortens the news story. The press becomes less a representation then an extension, an additive, 'an approximation to the grapevine' (UM: 214). This takes its nth degree when the television no longer reports the war or even transmits a pro-war ideology, but the war happens on television, politics happens on television. The newspaper as a mosaic of recently breaking stories of all kinds is no longer representation, but pure information.

The advertisement becomes the bedrock of the press. In television, first comes the bad news, the news; and then comes the good news, the ad. The press takes on the 'function of communal cleansing' (UM: 207). Community works through in-depth involvement in iconic and mosaic images: not through tutelage or pedagogy of citizens. In the press the first items we turn to are what we know in order to 're-cognize' our experience. Newspapers no longer *represent* human association: they become *an 'aspect of* human association'. Newspapers are no longer pedagogical devices to produce citizens. They lead to participation in a sense much more cultural than political. As a citizen, one is a member of a superior instance, i.e. the state. To be a member of a culture, a form of life is a different matter. No longer at stake is a learning process or primarily cognition, but instead the recognition of our experience: the recognition of human association. Community in this is not the imagined community of 'progress and tutelage', but the community in terms of the codes of the *conscience collective*. This is more immediate than the abstract, imagined communities of the national state. It is more immediate in the sense that forms of life are immediate, that culture is immediate in a sense that institutional politics and the citizenship of the imagined community are not. Yet this immediacy is at the same time at-a-distance: via mediation through electronic technologies.

Crucial in this context is in-depth involvement. Future archaeologists would see 'ads as the richest and most faithful daily reflections that any society ever made of its entire range of activities' (UM: 232). The museums of the future, he noted, will see ads as the embodiment of human community in the electronic age. The semiotics of the advert consist of neither discourse nor narrative, but a graphic, mosaic, 'condensed and displaced form', opening this 'deep participation'. The Gutenberg age gives us the book, consumed under conditions of contemplation. In the electronic age we read the newspaper, watch television, browse on the Internet, under conditions of distraction. Deep participation takes place, paradoxically, under conditions of distraction. This recognition of communal codes is implicit and not fully conscious. The concentrated viewing and reading of the Gutenberg age is at the same time superficial in its distanciation from the object. The reader is superficially connected as a neutral and doubting subject. The distracted reception of electronic culture is at the same time immersed. There is suspension of disbelief. Reception is in a mode of dwelling. We consume television in the living room; we receive architecture and urbanism by living in it. In both cases immersion goes with distraction, just as distanciation with contemplation (Benjamin, 1974d).

This is also seen in the phenomenon of 'the star'. As narrative, cinema is linear. In the star phenomenon, the (linear) 'typographic' principle gives way to the 'graphic' principle. The star is graphically embodied as an icon. The icon incorporates community in the sense that individualistic linear narrative never can. Icons grew especially out of the Eastern Church. They were engravings and paintings of saints on woodcuts (*panneaux de bois*). They came from the Byzantine age, whose rulers, opposing excesses of priestly power, were indeed the first 'iconoclasts'. The icon for McLuhan is 'not a specialist fragment (like the connected fragments of linear culture) but

184

unified and complex compressed images ... that focus a large region of experience in tiny compass' (UM: 26). The icon is a sort of 'snapshot' of the collective unconscious. It compresses and concentrates simultaneously vast amounts of information. Movie stars are iconic. Here viewers are not so much citizens as *communicants*. The stars are public; yet the relation between the viewer, the public and the star is intensely private. The communication is transmitted from the private image of the star to the private self of the viewer. It has not the logic nor the definition of narrative. The star, the advert, the news item, the brand are 'the collective embodiments of the multitudinous private lives of subjects' (UM: 273). We exteriorize our sense, our sensuality in the star. Yet this is not individualized; it is somehow collective. With press photographers everywhere, the star is ubiquitous: to be seen not only in the movies, but also in newspapers, magazines, posters, television, adverts. Cinema as classical Hollywood narrative is a (clearly delineated) 'hot medium'. The star, like the modern newspaper, is a mosaic, a 'cool medium'.

In McLuhan community is based in pattern recognition, not in the nation-state but in fragmented smaller groupings, which are most often communities-at-a-distance, in a global *ecumène*. Central here is not the citizen, but the communicant. McLuhan's nomads are bad citizens. This is also a community of speed: speed as a set of interactions in simultaneity: actions, in not sequence, but simultaneity. Thus 'community is a series of ongoing date-lines', in which the 'electric media instantly and constantly create a total field of interacting events in which all men participate' (UM: 210, 248). There is an 'immediacy of participation in the experience of others'. Thus following your baseball team through a 160-plus game season, or following a soap opera has little do with the representation of classic narrative. It is not a representation of life, but an extension of it. And there is little, if any, time out.[6] There is 'instant all at once-ness', as 'speed creates a total and inclusive field of relations'. There is immediacy and depth at the same time. You don't read the codes. You sense them. You sense the patterns. And this field of impulses, this all-at-once mosaic is iterated again and again and again and again. Always new. Yet always repeated. As ephemeral, as useless, as yesterdays papers. But then there are today's papers. There is today's big match. The next number one hit. There is this summer's blockbuster movie.

For McLuhan the function of media as a technology is to store and expedite information (UM: 158). The storage and retrieval of information are functions played by all media, not just the computer. Woodcuts, for example, are modes of information storage. The alphabet is a 'visual' means of the storing and retrieval of information, as is the Cartesian map. So is the movie. The book and the library made enormous advances in such concentrated storage. Television and computers are non-visual means of such storage and retrieval. The media create messages out of information. The various media do things with information to create meaning, to create messages. Without media (and individuals) information is meaningless. The 'electric light', McLuhan writes, 'is pure information' (UM: x). The vitrine, in church stained-glass windows, is a frame through which light passes. Light as information takes on meaning as filtered through the stained glass. This is not 'light on' but 'light through'. Cool media do less work of mediation of such pure information than do 'hot media'. Cool media, the woodcut, print, mosaic, icon, ad, cartoon, television 'provide very little data about any moment in time or space of an object' (UM: 164).[7] Yet cool media motivate, they provide a pulse, an impulse. They provide a pulsion, a drive, for example, to piety and meditation. This is the crux of the 'light on' versus 'light through' distinction. 'Light on', in the novel and scientific experiment, presumes *reflection*: 'light through' foregrounds pulsion.

McLuhan's implicit semiotics finds its parallel in the classical semiotics of Peirce. Here the more abstract a sign is the more it represents; the more concrete and immediate a sign is, the more it motivates. The very concrete 'signal' or 'index' motivates. It does not represent but provides a pulsion. The intermediate icon or image both reflects and motivates. And the quite abstract symbol represents but motivates very little at all. Signification through 'semiosis' reflects, through 'mimesis', motivates. Pulsion and motivation work through a semiotics of sensation, in a one-world assemblage of desire. This is like Deleuze's and Guattari's (1983) 'body without organs'. The body is there. The organs have been externalized as the global central nervous system of the networks of information and communication. Antonin Artaud coined the term 'body without organs', that couldn't shit, couldn't fuck: there is no exit from this body. Artaud also wrote that theatre should not be the 'double of life' but should be life itself, like a 'police raid on a brothel' (Esslin, 1999). To the extent that the electronic media operate through pulsion and not through representation, the electronic media become technological *life*, become the pulsions of externalized desire. Thus the television 'viewer is a submarine, bombarded by atoms that reveal the outside as inside in an endless adventure of blurred images and mysterious contours'. The 'television viewer is the screen. He is bombarded with light impulses'; the television image, 'a ceaselessly forming contour of things limned by the scanning-finger' (UM: 313, 328). Gutenberg culture operates through the representations of the symbolic, or at best the imaginary. The electronic media for their part work through the pulsions of the *real*. In contemporary cultural studies, power is understood as exercised through the symbolic, resistance through the real. Yet in the information order, as we shall see below, domination itself is exercised pre-eminently through the real.

From Expansion to Implosion

McLuhan's reading of history, its focus on reversal and 'implosion', is as Gary Genosko (1999) notes, also featured in Jean Baudrillard. For McLuhan, millennia of slow explosion, of 'expansion' are followed by the all of a sudden 'implosion' of the electronic media of the second half of the twentieth century.

There is a spatial, temporal, social and semiotic expansion through differentiation, followed by this implosion. This implosion, this compression is at the same time a 'reversal', like Baudrillard's 'reversibility'. In McLuhan's beginning we were nomads and we are once again nomads in the media age. The linearity of expansion starts with the displacement of nomads by sedentary culture. Here the event-like and catastrophic temporality of nomads is displaced by the cyclical temporality of settled agricultural communities (Weber, 1980: 285 ff.). McLuhan takes the notion of 'implosion' from Lewis Mumford, who, prescient beyond belief, used it to understand ethnic immigration into the USA. The powers of assimilation here work up to a certain point. New immigrants can, up to a certain point, be accommodated into the melting pot. At a certain point there is saturation, there is 'overheating', and the result is multiculturalism, diasporas, hybridity, travelling, partly nomadic, cultures and individuals. Mumford (1974) here is forecasting the demise of the world system of nation-states and of Western Civilization. Mumford was implicitly forecasting Rem Koolhaas's generic city. This imploded city is not a city of Western Civilization, not a city of the nation-state and the modern world system. It is a transnational and multicultural city of a discontinuous world (dis)order. For Mumford too implosion meant a break with linearity and fragmentation.

McLuhan's reversal after so many centuries of expansion comes with exhaustion, with saturation, played-outness, with 'overheating'. This overheating comes partly from speed-up. Only with the telegraph, McLuhan notes, did the message begin to travel faster than the messenger does. The wheel is an accelerator, in the progression from pack animal to sledge to wheeled carriage and chariot. Acceleration and the increase in scope of power are linked. The Gutenberg revolution and mechanized phonetic writing – which was the original mechanization of the complex handicraft of scriptors – enhanced the storing and means of speedy retrieval of information, the spread of 'power that is knowledge' in the imperial, and budding, nation-state (UM: 171). Now states could have information on people for surveillance, and for the legitimation of punishment in legal-rational systems. But at a certain point speed-up outruns sequence, it outpaces linearity. The movement of causation becomes too slow. This is the point that of Virilio's (1997) 'escape velocity', when things start to happen so quickly that sequence fades into simultaneity. There develops an 'instant all at once-ness' as 'information comes to move at the speed of signals in the central nervous system' (UM: 104). Expansion also happens through functional differentiation, from 'the city state, the huddling together of tribal villagers' which is 'inclusive and integral' to the functional differentiation, that is, 'the separation and extension of human functions' in the 'specialist cities of the Roman Empire' (UM: 101). The movement is from countless centuries of slow expansion to all-at-once compression. Starting with 'the resonating tribal world', we move slowly to the expansion of 'Euclidean lineality and visuality', and then implode and compress again into a new tribal world.

McLuhan's imagery for the oral culture is of priests, of early Christianity, into which the overextended and exhausted Roman Empire imploded. He refers to 'hubris', the Greek idea in which creativity led to blindness. The Faustian expansion and creativity of the Gutenberg age of Phoenician-Roman-Euclidean linearity led to its own blindness, its own downfall. McLuhan thus favourably contrasts 'priestly power', based in pre-alphabetic writing in stone and brick, in the hieroglyph and stained-glass window, with the combination of alphabetic writing and papyrus of military power (UM: 39, 83). Priestly power is the stuff of the illuminated manuscript, which radiates impulses, and the scriptorium. Mechanized writing replaces the priestly scriptor of the monastic community. There was something interactive, dialogic among the priests – and participation in electronic communities is dialogic, in what McLuhan calls, not 'active' but 'reactive media'. The mediaeval classroom was a 'scriptorium with a commentary'. Manuscript writers left 'interlines' for interpretation and commentary in textbooks. These were 'scholastic regimes of oral disputation' (UM: 174).

This dialogic relation dovetails with Baudrillard's (1994b) idea of 'symbolic exchange'. Symbolic exchange breaks with the linearity of the symbolic and all regimes of value. Symbolic exchange is not a product but a process, a very much in-the-world process. When symbolic exchange stops there is reification, abstraction. This petrification of process emerges with the rise of the world religions, with the differentiation of a separate sacred and 'symbolic' realm. This is accompanied by the birth of linear temporality, as the symbolic stands as 'ought' to the 'is' of the profane. Whether metaphorically or prosaically, these abstract symbols 'stand for' things and processes in the prosaic world. So do 'values', so do what Baudrillard calls 'systems of values' (N. Gane, 1999). Thus Marxian use-value is a set of values conforming to a 'system of needs'. It puts together as equivalences systems of needs and systems of objects. So does exchange-value. Sign-value, for its part, works from an equivalence of signifier and signified that is itself derived from the relations between signs as values (Saussure, 1983). In each case we are dealing with abstraction, with linearity, with two-world notions of 'standing for'. In symbolic exchange there is no standing for. There is instead 'standing out' (ecstasis) into the excess, the agon of the potlatch. The potlatch as agon has little to do with the regimes of exchange-value competition. Along with exchange-value as a system of value, we have the reappearance of the petrified symbolic, this time as appearing in the space of 'lack' in the *individual* unconscious and guaranteeing the linearity of psycho-sexual development (Deleuze and Guatarri, 1983). With reversal (reversibility) this symbolic is externalized: as external organs we move back into the space of flows and the possibility once more of symbolic exchange.

If for McLuhan the result of implosion is a positive neo-tribalism, for Jean Baudrillard it is the neutralization of meaning and the impossibility of politics. For Baudrillard the lineal expansion of 'the social' has provoked Marxists and sociologists to speak in the *name* of the 'masses', while themselves occupying the same linearity, the same regime of value that fuels the expansion of the social. The Marxists and sociologists are thus operating in the old regime of linearity, while the imploded masses are historically in comparison to them, a vanguard. For Baudrillard this 'finality', this expansion of the social is confounded by the growth of the media. The media simulate the social. As the social outwardly expands, the media, through this simulation, at the same time 'inwardly bestialize' the social (Genosko, 1999: 94). Here the Marxists and sociologists have been deceived. It is not the social but the media that produces their beloved 'masses'. The social thus disappears as it loses meaning through being reabsorbed by the masses in its media simulation. The result has little to do with politics. Power is no longer at centre stage, as Baudrillard (1980) argues in *Forget Foucault*: the outcome instead is silence, indifference, inertia. If McLuhan's global village radiates and re-transmits the impulses, the flows, then Baudrillard's masses give you the black hole of absorption and death of the impulses and pulsions. Still Baudrillard, in his pessimism, leaves space for the re-eruption of symbolic exchange in his idea of semiurgy. This space is a space not of 'ologies', not of the distanciated study of, but a space of 'urgies', a space of work, of working with, an immanent plane of working and re-working. The information order signals a shift from 'metallurgy' to 'semiurgy'. Semiurgy's home is in the immaterial system of manipulable signs that appears in consumer capitalism between the 'materiality of objects' and the 'materiality of needs'. After the catastrophe of implosion, there is 'disappearance' of both objects and needs, leaving only the possibility in consumption of a radical semiurgy (Genosko, 1999: ch. 4).

Curiously both McLuhan and Baudrillard, and for that matter Huizinga and Garfinkel – discussed in Chapter 12 – seem to neutralize power. Baudrillard is the pessimist for whom the technoscape amputates the human sensorium: McLuhan, with Deleuze and Guattari, the optimist for whom the technoscape is the outering, the externalization of the sensorium. Baudrillard argues that, with the explosion and then implosion of linearity into a neutralizing compression, power itself disappears. McLuhan for his part remains in denial or at best blissful ignorance. The point I want to make, however, is that *power itself in the information order has become non-linear*. For McLuhan and Baudrillard power is a non-problem. Most of post-structuralism, from Foucault who locates power in discourse and Derrida who sees it in a metaphysics of presence, see power as mainly linear. Indeed critical theory – German as well as French – has seen power as basically linear. Critical theorists – whether from Frankfurt or Paris – situate themselves in a non-linear space from which they launch their critique of linearity. The information order changes all this. Power has changed. It has become itself informational. Power itself is discontinuous, mosaic and nomadic (Diken, 1999). It lies no longer in discourse but in the much shorter and more transient bits and fragments of information. For a thorough-going understanding of power in a non-linear age we turn to the work of Donna Haraway.

Towards a New Regime of Knowledge-Power: Donna Haraway

From Science to Technoscience: Forms of Laboratory Life

Haraway (1996: 9) speaks of a 'regime of technobiopower'. She speaks of a 'physical-semiotic field of technoscience'. The 'syntactical rules of techno-science' are everywhere, in this 'material-semiotic universe': 'we live inside of its material grammar'. 'We inhabit and are inhabited by the stories and explanations of technoscience.' In this sense we are responsible, 'accountable for it'. While at the same time we may be able to change it (Haraway, *Modest Witness* (hereafter MW), 1996, pp. xiv, 9). What is this technoscience she talks about? In the first instance it represents a sort of dis-autonomization of science. Once technology was by definition 'material' and science by definition 'semiotic'. Now science is 'semiotic-material'. Science once opera-ted in the realm of meaning, and technology in the world of material inter-ests. Now science dis-autonomizes into the realm of technology. At the same time, however, technology, so to speak, semioticizes, so that it is no longer recognizable as a purely material realm. Science has classically worked through the use of evidence backing up its facts: it worked through explana-tion and argument. Technoscience also works through the brute facticity of its products. Technoscience is effective, not only through the semiotics of discourse but also through brute material facticity.

Michel Foucault, like Haraway, is in an important sense a historian of the sciences. Comparison with Foucault's ideas of the 'episteme' and power is instructive. For Foucault discourses take their general shape in the context of the episteme to which they belong. He speaks in *Les Mots et les choses* of, for example, a Renaissance episteme, a classical one and a modern episteme. Foucault's (1966: 72) classical episteme is based in representation, in which words represent things. In his modern episteme, words, and implicitly knowl-edge, enter, as it were, into the physiology of things themselves. The organ-ism as a model – in biology and for society – is central to the modern episteme. Now power is no longer exercised just from above, or dualistically, but it circulates in the capillaries of society. In each case, however, power operates through discourse, be it clinical medicine or psychology or sexuality or jurisprudence. What Haraway is implying is that there is a new regime of power-knowledge that comes after the modern episteme. This emergent power-knowledge regime breaks with the organicism, the physiology of the modern episteme. It breaks with this for a *cybernetic* heuristic, one in which even organic (and other) systems are understood on the model of technologi-cal systems. Here organic systems become cybernetic systems of information management with military-like structures of command, control, intelligence and communication. Haraway's effectively postmodern episteme would govern not just contemporary biology but a whole number of realms.

The idea of an episteme implies a fundamental distinction between knowl-edge and power. In this sense the new paradigm of technological systems is really not an episteme at all. This is because knowledge is already fused with power in the technoscientific regime. Foucault's modern discourses are not material, but semiotic. They start semiotically from above, but then become material and constitute power relations as they circulate through the capillaries of society. Haraway describes a regime in which discourse is no longer king: one in which knowledge (science) is already fused with power (technology). Here the semiotic cannot circulate in the material, because the semiotic and the material are already fused. This is technoscience. The idea of episteme means also a place for the epistemological, for a separate realm of the epistemological. Haraway writes, however, in, and of, a post-epistemological age. Technoscience's collapse of science into technology signals a decline in the status of epistemology. Finally, for Haraway techno-science, unlike epistemology, does not function mainly as discourse. It presumes, as we shall see below, instead a modal change from the hegemony of structures of discourse to structures of information.

What are the figures of technoscience? They are the seed, the chip, the gene, the fetus, database, ecosystem. Figures of science, such as the cell, were natural categories. The figures of technoscience are fusions of the natural and the artifical. They are 'cyborg figures'. Indeed, the re-conceptualization of the organism as a technological system presumes a sort of cyborg episteme. The book at issue here is entitled *Modest Witness@Second_ Millennium: FemaleMan©_Meets OncoMouse™*. Central players in the new regime are featured in the title of Haraway's book, FemaleMan© and Onco-Mouse™. These are the figures that are the modest witness at the end of the second millennium. They are also what Haraway calls the 'wormholes' through which we enter the increasingly prevalent regime of technoscience and information-power. Let us try to understand this. What is a modest witness? Haraway takes the idea of 'modest witness' from Schapin and Schaffer's *Leviathan and the Air Pump: Hobbes, Boyle and the Experimental Way of Life*. Here we see the origins of the experimental way of life in which the witness's testimony in the face of scientific knowledge can establish crucial matters of fact (MW: 20). In Boyle's seventeenth century these witnesses were 'men of substance' whose 'narratives could be credited as mirrors of reality' (MW: 23). These witnesses could be trusted for their neutrality. Boyle, the father of Chemistry, drew these witnesses from the Royal Society of London for Improving Natural Knowledge, founded in 1667. The Royal Society listed the names of those men of substance attesting to the veracity of experimental reports (MW: 20, 23, 37). This was a not-quite modern age in which the laboratory was still seen as a theatre of persuasion. A fuller modernity was achieved once Boyle's iconic air pump could establish matters of fact irrespective of the human witnesses. There are two points here. First, there is a shift from the understanding of neutrality as contingent and social to its understanding as objective. Second, the witness had previously been human and now it was a thing.

Compare these proud witnesses of the emergence of science with Haraway's modest witnesses. Her 'mutated modest witnesses' establish truth in a regime of not science, but of technoscience. At issue is not the emergence of the 'experimental way of life', but the technological way of life. These witnesses are mutated in the sense of being somehow 'spliced'. The oncomouse results from spliced genes. Femaleman is spliced. Both are combinations of the artefactual and the natural. Because science has become technoscience, today's modest witness is necessarily also implicated in questions of power and ethics. Her 'retooled modest witness on the millennial borderlands' is involved in struggles. To be a witness now means also 'to call to account'.[8] It means to 'bear witness'. Thou shall not bear false witness says the Commandment. To bear witness is to testify, and such testifying is a public act. To bear true witness is to call to account. To bear witness to a nuclear or genocidal holocaust is to call others and oneself to account (MW: 20, 40, 68). Today's modest witness is responsible, must vouch for and is accountable for a technoscience whose importance lies much less in issues of cause than of consequences. Once knowledge is no longer distanciated but instead incarnated in the social and in technology there is a certain fusion of the cognitive and the normative. Knowledge now, as we saw in the discussion above of Garfinkel, comes to take the form, less of predicative judgements than accounts. Implicit in this is an accountability and responsibility in regard to others in a given local or global community. You give an account to make sense of what you do, and you are accountable for the consequences of what you do. Today's modest witness – who is so different from the neutral and immodest pure-scientific judge – bears witness to facts that are at the same time power. She bears witness to information that is trademarked, patented and accumulated as capital. She bears witness to configurations of information that themselves exercise power: keeping some people in and other people out. In informational capitalism it is facts that are trademarked, truths that are valorized.

Witnessed now is no longer the pure 'experimental way of life' of Boyle and the Royal Society, but 'the grammar of a mutated experimental way of life'. Much of this may take place in laboratories. Haraway takes indeed the term technoscience from Bruno Latour, with Steve Woolgar co-author of *Laboratory Life* (1979). For Latour, technoscience involves the mobilization of academic science in alliance with outside private and public sector institutions. Here the 'laboratory constitutes its inside by reaching out to its outside' (MW: 275). The implications of this extend to a much more general set of sociocultural changes in which more and more areas of everyday life are becoming like laboratory life. This is part of the dis-autonomization of science as technology into the realm of everyday life. With the increasing knowledge-intensivity of labour, more and more of the workforce is active in what are effectively laboratories. Whereas scientists have been active in 'pure' laboratories, technoscientists work in applied or R&D laboratories. The increasing design-intensivity of the economy means that more and more of the workforce are active in 'studios'. Whereas artists have been active in 'pure' studios, these new techno-artists are involved in design studios. It is as if these networks of laboratory (and studio) become everyday life are *halfway* lifted out, *halfway* autonomous, *halfway* between the pure and the profane.

They are thus a hybrid of the semiotic and the material. Here materiality corrupts the pure semiotics of art and science. Simultaneously, the pure materiality of economic life is corrupted by semiotics. Whereas pure science operated out of a linear logic of causation, the technoscientific networks operate out of a logic of 'additivity', a logic of the 'and', of what Deleuze calls the 'conjunction'. Truth is established thus through additivity: through building the networks, mobilizing the alliances. These are hybrid sites: hybrids of disembedded and embedded; immediate and yet generic.[9]

The problem, however, is that the external place for reflection and critique tends to disappear. The role of the witness, says Haraway (MW: 63), is not to represent knowledge, 'but to articulate the clusters of processes, objects' and figures and marks. It is, through this articulation to modify the boundaries. We, as modest witnesses, articulate and connect to the techno-scientific information order, not for a critical space but *as* an articulation. We occupy not a critical space of separate ontological substance, but are instead one more supplement, connected by one more articulation, one more 'and', one more conjunction to the global technoscientific information networks, linking to other laboratories, to other studios and to other sites. We thus participate in technoscientific 'lines of flight' (Deleuze and Parnet, 1987). We participate in the not causal but consequential logic of the 'and', of the discontinuous, non-lineal and halfway disembedded networks. Networks in which the experimental way of life is mutated away from the systematic doubt of pure science of the classic laboratories, and towards a sort of natural attitude of bracketing, of forms of life. Theses are hybrid spaces of doubt and the bracketing of doubt, where truth and profit are fused.

Economy: Accumulation and Intellectual Property

Biotechnology emerges, Haraway observes, when companies start taking molecular biology seriously. Biotechnology presumes an accumulation process. She, as does Marilyn Strathern (1999), views capitalist globalization as 'a semiotic-material production of some forms of life rather than others' (MW: 12, 287). Haraway sees 'biology itself' as a developing 'accumulation strategy', in which 'what accumulates is stranger than capital'. What accumulates indeed are 'proprietary forms of life'. In the information order, biological forms of life and information in general accumulate, in, for example, databases. In order to accumulate, these forms of life (from genetically modified food to oncomice) need to become proprietary, that is, they need to be patented or copyrighted (Franklin et al., 2000). For Marx too, without property, without a suitable regime of property law, capital could not accumulate.

Accumulation, by definition, must be of entities that are somehow abstract.[10] For Marx, not the concrete means of production, but abstract capital accumulated. What accumulates is somehow a congealed social relation. Hence again, not the material mean of production but capital are such a social relation. Tellingly, it is the semiotic, rather than the material that accumulates. What accumulates is proprietary, abstract and must be valorizable. Thus finance capital accumulates only to the extent that it is there to be valorized. The accumulation of capital is very much like Heidegger's 'standing reserve' in 'The Question Concerning Technology'. For Heidegger what is stockpiled in the standing reserve is the *Gestell* or frame. What is stockpiled are abstract frames. And it is only a standing reserve insofar as it is not an end in itself, but there only to be valorized, only as means. Ends do not accumulate. Only means, especially means of production.

For Marx, what accumulated was also already property. Now what accumulates is at the same time *intellectual* property. What accumulated primarily was the means of production as capital, as property. Now what accumulates is means of information. What used to get valorized was the means of production (as capital). Now what gets valorized is the prototype, and as intellectual property. What gets valorized are now prototypes and brands. Key to accumulation on an expanded scale is what Marx called 'department I' and 'department II'. Department I was the means of production; deparment II was consumer commodities. Most fundamental to total social capital was the accumulation in department I. At issue today is no longer the accumulation of means of production, but more so the accumulation of the, even more abstract finance capital. At the core of information capitalism is the accumulation of the prototype and brand. The prototype, in order for accumulation (and the brand) to be possible, must become proprietary. It must take the form of intellectual property. To realize surplus profits in the age of mass production you needed process innovation. Now in the age of flexible production, you need product innovation. You need more and more design intensive labour. Increased product innovation entails increased production of prototypes, which in turn must be patented or copyrighted in order to realize profits.

Technoscientific struggles very centrally concern objects, over whether and how objects or prototypes should be proprietary.[11] These are struggles over the boundaries between the proprietary and non-proprietary; and in the case of the proprietary, who shall have these intellectual property rights (Lury, 1993).[12] For Haraway the key to the new world order is the technologization of life, which is then 'enterprised up'. This is the semioticization and subsequent commodification of nature. To 'enterprise up' is to make nature into a proprietary technological-biological or material-semiotic object. Haraway starts with objects (and forms of life) that are natural and biological; they become at the same time technologies (as information) and finally they become proprietary as they are 'enterprised up'. This is a question of *intellectual* property: trademark, patent and copyright. Haraway is mainly interested in patent: in how patent law has been extended from industrial products to forms of life, to nature, to organisms.[13]

Haraway starts from Locke's notion of property, which is pre-eminently modern. For Locke, property rights begin from man having property in his person and by extension his labour. When an individual mixes his labour to make other property, it gives him rights in this property. Locke – and Marx drawing on Locke in *Theories of Surplus Value* – delineate two types of property. The first is the aforementioned, based on the mixing of labour of the individual. The second concerns a more general notion of rights stemming from a sort of enclosing of the commons. These second sorts of rights are more general than the first. Intellectual property rights follow from this first notion of rights. More traditional rights stem from the second type of property: for example, rights following from inheritance across the generations. Marx referred to the first type of rights as 'possession', the second as 'ownership'. Copyright, modelled on the first type of rights, is based on the rights not of the labourer but of the author in himself. Copyright law, emerging in England in 1710, is inscribed in the discourse of genius. In such an investment of intellectual labour, the assumption is that the author makes himself. Copyright connects the author to his work; it understands work not so much as product but instead as *oeuvre* (MW: 72; Lury, 1993; Coombe, 1998). Patent is inscribed not in a discourse of genius, but in a discourse of the 'progress of science and the useful arts'. Copyright is attributed to the author, patent to the inventor; copyright to the artist, patent to the scientist turned technologist. You copyright a great novel. You patent not a great scientific discovery, but the application of that discovery. Patent is not about the mixing of labour, but instead the mixing of *intellect* in a thing, in a useful thing. Hence patent protects not property, but intellectual property. In the US patent act of 1790, patent protected intellectual property in 'a machine, a process, a composition of matter' or an 'improvement' in the above (MW: 88). Copyright is inscribed in a discourse of genius and expression. You express your property in yourself in a work that is copyrighted, and you thus have rights in it. Patent is about not expression, but usefulness. It concerns the applied intellect. It is more a question of applied intellectual labour than 'pure' intellectual labour. We always associate the author (copyright) with a name. Only a very few patents are so associated with names. Copyright is about the creation of semiotic goods, about the creation of meanings, while patent is about the creation of utilities (or utility generators) as distinct from meanings. It is about material goods. These days, with the 'decline of the author', patent is often a stake less for individuals than for laboratories. While copyright is a stake not just for authors, but for *studios*. Thus labs are forever engaged in patent struggles, while say new media, design and advertising studios are engaged in battles over copyright.

Patent and copyright are vastly different from ordinary property. They both concern intellectual property. In normal property rights we invest labour in a good, in patent and copyright we invest intellectual labour in a prototype. The decisive property right in manufacturing society is property in the means of production. The decisive property right in the information society is connected to the means of design in laboratories and (digital media, media, architectural, advertising) studios. Laboratories (studios), Haraway writes, are 'world building spaces' (MW: 83). Rights in real property in the means of production are rights to exploit workers in a typical power relation. Rights in intellectual property are rights to *exclude* others from valorizing that object. Finally, with real property it is only labour (as variable capital) that creates surplus value, while in intellectual property it is the property itself that can create the surplus value, or at least realize surplus profits through monopoly.

After patent and copyright, the third main category of intellectual property rights concerns trademarks, as marks that mark 'the syntax of natural/ social/technical relations congealed in property'. Trademarks are 'syntactical (not semantic)' marks that mark 'a contingent but ultimately real entity' (MW: 7). In 1989 US legislation trademarks are 'distinctive marks, motto, device or emblem that a manufacturer ... affixes to goods so they may be vouched for' (MW: 84). Patent refers to intellectual labour inscribed in goods, and copyright to intellectual labour inscribed in meanings. Trademarks for their part affix semiotic marks, affix meanings to an *array* of goods. Trademark law assigns rights in marks that normally are already in the public realm. The meanings or goods marked by the marks do not have to be invented. They need neither author nor inventor. Yet the idiom of trademark is the secret of the brand. And branding is pivotal to accumulation and power in the information order. Indeed, a lot of intellectual labour now goes into the valorization of trademark in advertising campaigns and more generally in marketing.

Haraway is interested in patent. She is especially interested in how life becomes patented. She is interested in how living beings get patented to become 'proprietary forms of life', to become 'proprietary beings' (MW: 4, 43). Her above-mentioned 'wormholes' onto the technocultural world – the chip, gene, database, oncomouse, fetus, seed, ecosystem – are in most cases proprietary beings, whether copyrighted, patented or trademarked. Her hero is the oncomouse, who is first patented and then trademarked. There was an initial extension of patent law to some living organisms in the US Plant Patent Act of 1930, and later in the Plant Variety Protection Act of 1970. The patenting of biotechnological processes has been less controversial than that that of biotechnological beings. Stanford University and the University of California San Francisco, for example, were awarded the patent for the gene splicing technique, but not for organisms themselves until the 1980s. Thus a previously existing Patent and Trademark Office ruling, prohibiting the patenting of the genetically modified bacterium that breaks down petroleum, was overruled by a Supreme Court decision in 1980. Also patented in the 1980s, for example, were new beings such as a tomato spliced with a gene from a flounder, whose habitat was the bottom of cold seas. This new proprietary being could slow freezing processes. Haraway's genetically modified mouse was awarded a patent in 1988. This was the oncomouse, a 'site for operation of a transplanted tumour-producing gene'. This 'transgenic animal, containing an activated oncogene', promised a cure primarily for breast cancer. This genetically spliced mouse became the world's first patented animal. The patent was awarded to two genetic researchers in 1988 who gave it to their host university, Harvard. The latter, in turn, licensed it to Dupont. The oncomouse was marketed then as a research instrument by Dupont's New Life Science Products division.

This was advertised in *Science* magazine to an audience of researchers only (MW: 70, 79).

A parallel and major development in patent law underscores the extent to which pure science has been disautonomized in the direction of technoscience. The Patent and Trademarks Amendment of 1980 extends the award of title to non-profit organizations and to businesses whose research is funded by federal government. At the same time a number of molecular biologists have founded companies based on such tax-supported patents. Hence the inventors of the gene splicing process founded Genentech in 1976, one of the foremost and indeed the first biotechnological company. Genentech's first public stock offering was in 1980. In this context Genbank© has been awarded copyrights. Genbank contains the DNA sequence information that is the human genome database. A number of institutions in the world have such a database. One of these institutions – the Los Alamos National Laboratories – holds its copyright. Its 'mandate' is to make the database available 'for the progress of science and the advancement of industry' (MW: 74, 93).

At stake in all this is an implosion, a new indifference of the natural-material, on the one hand, and the semiotic, on the other. Patent was once about utilities, that is, about the natural-material. Once life enters its domain, patent is about utilities *and* meanings, about the natural *and* the cultural, the material *and* the semiotic. It becomes a subject of material and semiotic struggle, in the mass political protests in 1999 in Seattle against Western companies' patenting genes and seeds from the Third World. Copyright was at one point exclusively semiotic. Yet with the development of copyright of software and platforms the semiotic fuses with the utilitarian. Proprietary beings become also proprietary meanings. And vice versa. As life becomes informationalized (semioticized) in databases, it also becomes proprietary. This life as information becomes a 'specific proprietary circulation'. The information order, Haraway writes, citing Mariₗyn Strathern, comes to consist of 'globalized proprietary networks' (MW: 96). Thus politics and power take on the form of struggles over such intellectual property, over 'the reconfiguration' of 'objects' and 'boundaries'. The objects are semiotic-material and the boundaries concern, for example, *whose* intellectual property patented seeds from the South are. The boundaries divide the proprietary from the non-proprietary. Here struggles decide which of these pivotal semiotic-utilitarian objects should be which side of this boundary.

Struggles over property in technological forms of life bring to centre stage the question of *platforms*. Discourse on forms of life, whether in biology or philosophy, and corresponding roughly to the birth of sociology, were coterminous with the massive pervasion of manufacturing capitalism at the turn of the twentieth century and rise of the industrial working class. At centre stage was real property, and especially potentially movable and easily transferable and disposable real property in the manufacturing means of production. Here the platform at stake was real property in the means of production. Without this platform one did not gain entry to manufacturing capitalist forms of life, either as worker or bourgeois. Platforms are conditions of entry, are constitutional of any form of life. In technological forms of life, in, for example, information technology, the nature of the platform changes. The platform becomes material-semiotic and subject to the laws of intellectual property. Unlike in manufacturing capitalism, sometimes these platforms can become standards (Barry, 2001). The ownership of Ford Motor Company in manufacturing capitalism is the ownership of a platform that is not a standard. Intellectual property rights on Microsoft operating system have been monopoly rights in a platform that is a world-wide standard. Standards are not necessarily proprietary. A number of Internet standards are not proprietary. A number of platforms, for example, Java, are not standards. Or the Unix-based operating system for servers, which competes with Windows NT; Unix is neither a standard nor proprietary. The US mobile phone platforms are proprietary but there is as yet no standard. In Europe DSN is a standard and non-proprietary. Linux is also non-proprietary. Intellectual property rights regarding platforms are particularly central to technological forms of life. They are the constitutive rules without which the regulative rules are inoperative. In the absence of these platforms, we never get to enter the forms of life in which we deal with biotechnological and advanced new-media applications. We have no access to any sort of level playing field of trademarked brands. To be off these platforms is to be excluded from the global information order.

Biology as Technological System

Haraway has a basic argument that runs through all her work. This appears in her early 1976 book *Crystals, Fabrics and Fields: Metaphors of Organicism in Twentieth Century Molecular Biology* and continues in *Primate Visions* (1992), *Simian, Cyborgs and Women* (1991) and *Modest Witness*. The argument is that biology has moved from a heuristic of organic systems to one of technological systems. This is true, it seems, much more generally in the natural sciences and social sciences – this shift from an organicist to a cybernetic model. In sociology, for instance, the older organic systems theory of Durkheim and especially Parsons has been partly displaced by the cybernetic (and phenomenological) systems theory of Niklas Luhmann. This technologization of bioscience involves more than just this change from an organic to cybernetic model. It involves, as we mentioned, a disautonomization; a 'descent into the social'. Applied sociology had previously operated as 'social engineering' in the ethos of Popperian positivism. But what happens when meta-narratives turn biological? What happens with not just applied sociology but the technologization of science in applied biology? What happens when what is engineered is not just sociological forms of life but biological forms of life? It is such events that are experienced by Haraway's modest witness. And the Holocaust vocabulary of 'witnessing' is not inappropriate. Because at stake is not just the incursion into biology of a technological heuristic replacing an organicist one. It is the use of this heuristic in producing life, in, potentially, 'producing the human'.

Life, previously conceived as an organism, now is a technological system. Now the 'organism is an information system', the 'germ plasm is a data base' (MW: 97, 282). What does this mean? What is meant by life as an information system? In the first instance there is the cybernetic model of technological system of control, command, intelligence and communication. This is a military metaphor in which 'intelligence' involves information selection from the environment. These are 'autopoetic', or self-regulating systems. The rise of cybernetics is dated from the late 1950s; the idea of the cyborg as an 'enhanced man', a self-regulating man-machine system emerges in the early 1960s. In biological life, information is a property not just of system but of structure. Thus the biochemical genome is a 'structure of information', and the electronic genome database is a 'higher order structure of information' (MW: 99). Information and 'data' are the operative terms. In contemporary biology, there is an 'information management discourse' (MW: 148). And information is stored in human genome 'data' bases.[14] Biology and life was previously natural; now culture and nature implode. There is a semioticization of nature and of life. This semioticization is one in which neither narrative nor discourse, but instead information becomes the hegemonic signifier. This semioticization is of neither the symbolic nor the imaginary, but instead the real, in which life itself joins the database.

A genome is the 'totality of genetic information in an organism'. There is a frog genome, a mouse genome, the genome of a bacterium, the human genome. In each case the organism is considered as an information system, a system of genetic information. By genetic information is meant only nucleic acid. The genetic information in these information structures is not protein sequences or extra-nucleic DNA sequences, but only nucleic acid (MW: 245). Indeed, the icons of the genome project are images of DNA polynucleotide separation gels. Genetic information is data: it is 'nucleic acid sequence data'. Such sequence data is doing the coding. Linear codes of nucleic acid, in their sequencing, lead to protein sequencing, and thus to producing the organism. The informational unit is not the cell, but just the cell nucleus. Any genome's database consists of such genetic maps and sequences. The genome is the full set of genes in the cell nucleus contained on the chromosomes derived from each parent. On these twenty-six chromosomes are six billion base pairs of DNA, which represent copies from each parent of 50,000 to 100,000 genes. This is the 'chromosomic genetic complement'. The process of 'molecular inscription' goes from the DNA to the RNA and has protein sequences as end product. This is then a 'molecular inscription technology'; a 'writing practice' for 'materializing the text of life'; 'for producing the human' (MW: 148, 151 f.).

What sort of shape does this information take? The organism itself becomes a self-regulating information system. But the databases of the human genome project are not systems *per se*. They can be used for producing systems. But they are not systems. They are information structures; second order information structures. Organisms as systems are coded through structures. To the extent that systems are produced they are produced through structures. Structures are conditions of possibility of forms of life and of systems. The database is also a repository (Featherstone, 2000; Manovich, 2001). It is a repository for genetic map and sequence data. The operative term is 'bank'. Hence the US National Laboratories in Los Alamos, New Mexico use the name Gen*Bank* for their human genome database. The two other large public human genetic databases are the DNA Data Bank of Japan and the European Molecular Biology Laboratory. The 'semiotic-material definition', Haraway writes, 'of the human species is in these data bases'. The data must be collected and deposited: it is informational and physical (tissue, germ-plasm) data. Finally, these biological information structures are contained in a computer program. 'The new paradigmatic habitat for human life is the programme' (MW: 245, 313).

These databases are repositories for sequences and maps, and also potential structures for engineering new forms of life. In principle any naturally occurring genome can be experimentally redesigned. Such redesign can take place through splicing together two genomes – often an animal genome and a bacterium genome – as in the case of the oncomouse. Genetic redesign has further the capacity to occupy the future, the 'already written future'. Thus Elisabeth Beck-Gernsheim (1995) has written of middle class families being able to redesign their progeny in order to ensure their position in social stratification hierarchies. Here social-engineering functions of the welfare state may become biological-engineering functions of individuals. This can potentially lead to ever-greater levels of social inequality. These genetic databases contain structured accumulations of genetic information. These are 'frames' in Heidegger's sense: frames that can generate life. These frameworks are there only as a standing reserve in order to 'write the future'. Thus if power in previous forms of life were inscribed in capital accumulation, now they are also inscribed in information-accumulation, and moreover, genetic-information accumulation. Yet information and life is once again valorizable as capital.

Given these altered and threatening power relationships, technological forms of life also open up possibilities for radical political interventions. Such struggles, we noted above, take place around 'objects' and around 'boundaries'. They take place around 'boundary objects' (Callon, 1998). A boundary object is an object that has different meanings for different interests. The gene is such an (informational) 'boundary object'. It is a stake for example in struggles over biodiversity. This is the context of the Human Genome Diversity Project (HGDP), whose funding has been of the order of 5 per cent of the massive Human Genome Project. The genetic database of human nuclear DNA was developed as a 'reference composite for the species'. This reference or 'consensus' sequence, is 'the' human genome. This has been contested by the HGDP, in their concern about biodiversity information loss. The HGDP have taken a more 'populationist' direction in collecting tissue samples from some 700 indigenous groups. Yet indigenous groups have contested this 'genetic politics of difference'. An example of this is when blood from a Guyami woman in Panama containing potential leukaemia antibodies was the subject of a patent application from the US Secretary of Commerce. Here protests were raised of 'biopiracy' myths generated of 'bloodsucking Americans' and their trade in the circulation of body parts and tissues. These sorts of issues were tabled at the Earth Summit in Rio de Janeiro in 1993, establishing the Bio-diversity Convention (MW: 249–50, 312). In such power struggles gene and genome are circulating boundary objects. We are irrevocably in this world of circulating boundary objects, of human and non-human modes of practice. We are 'accountable' for this world. There is no space to step out for the distance and reflection of critique. We can reconfigure its objects and contest its boundaries. We can struggle over whether or not these objects will be proprietary or not, and if so whose property and what form of property. But critique must be interior to the information. There is no space outside of it, and no time out.

Conclusions

We then are irrevocably part and parcel of technological forms of life. Technological forms of life involve *à la* McLuhan, culture-at-a-distance, and *à la* Haraway, reproduction-at-a-distance. Technological forms of life are non-linear; they are discontinuous. They are networked. They are possessed with neither the organicism nor the holism of more traditional forms of life. Their networks always leave open the possibility of another link; leave open the possibility of a supplement. Technological forms of life can be more or less systemic. Structures don't reproduce. Systems do. Networks can be more or less reproductive. They are at the same time more or less open to not the reproduction, but the production of society and of culture, through the addition of another supplement. There is always a dangling conjunction. Platforms and standards are conditions of entry into technological forms of life; genetic databases are potentially such platforms. Technological forms of life are through and through informational. And the critique of information lies in the power of the 'and': in the power of the supplement to reconstitute the boundaries and reconfigure the objects. The critique of information lies in the supplement that can make its modest contribution to reconfiguring such material, human, biological and social forms of life. The modest witness is too modest to be the 'judge' of earlier critical theory. She can only be witness. The modest witness occupies neither the sphere of freedom of the judge, nor the sphere of necessity of the judged. She can only occupy the space of the 'and'. In an age of technological forms of life, the critique of information is the supplement.

Notes

1 I am indebted to Kevin Robins for this idea.
2 Talcott Parsons's systems theory had, as Garfinkel noted, predominantly positivist assumptions. Niklas Luhmann (1997) has given us more recently a phenomenological systems theory.

It is also a theory of information and communication. Luhmann's systems stand to their environment as the phenomenological subject to the object. Here a system observes its environment with an attitude, with an intentionality. Knowledge is thus neither objective nor relativist, but it is always for a system. In the absence of a system with an attitude towards its environment, knowledge can have no sense. This phenomenological systems theory is also a cybernetic theory of control and command within systems. Here the system observes and selects information from its environment in accordance to the command and control needs internal to it. It then processes this information in communications internal to the system and in this sense alters the system (Arnoldi, 2000). As in Garfinkel, in Luhmann we have an empiricist phenomenology of communications. Garfinkel and Luhmann proffer paradigmatic sociologies of the technological culture. The difference is that Luhmann's is a systems theory, in which the system is at the same time a social machine. There is in this sense in Luhmann a very important technological, indeed machinic dimension.

3 The non-linear causality of complexity theory is a different matter altogether. The information order and critique of information are characterized by non-linear causality.

4 I am speaking of teleports metaphorically here in terms of the terminals through which voice messages connecting dialoguing individuals at a distance are transmitted.

5 See discussion in Chapter 6 on 'media theory'.

6 I am indebted to Deirdre Boden for this idea that Harvey Molotch and she have developed in a long conversation with ethnomethodology.

7 Note here the distinction between 'information', on the one hand, and 'data', on the other. McLuhan would never have said that the light bulb is pure *data*. Pure information is meaningless. Data always has meaning.

8 This bears comparison with giving accounts in ethnomethodology. Account-giving in ethnomethodology also brings responsibility into questions of knowledge.

9 Indeed the 'generic' in the sense that I am using it in this book is not pure; it is halfway lifted out.

10 See Chapter 7.

11 These objects are, we shall see, boundary objects.

12 My discussions of intellectual property rights and the brand in this chapter have been strongly informed by collaborative work with Celia Lury. See Lury (1993, 1997, 1999) and Franklin, Lury and Stacey (2000).

13 Albeit 'spliced' organisms.

14 Thus the genome database, the book, the archive and the business systems built by oracle and IBM are locuses of information storage. So is the film and record library. Databases are also mechanisms, for information retrieval, manipulation and communication.

14

Conclusions: Communication, Code and The Crisis of Reproduction

Alasdair Scott is Creative Director of AMX Studios, one of London's leading new media companies. AMX is based in Soho. It carried out the first Web broadcast of a pop festival, the Phoenix Festival in 1996. The company has worked closely with the design and record industries. They have made enhanced CDs for a number of pop star clients. They have worked on advertising and marketing initiatives with Saatchi and Saatchi, and have worked with leading British retailer Tesco. They have designed business-to-consumer software for Barclays Bank, and have collaborated on projects for British Telecom, NewsCorp and Flextech, one of Europe's leading pay-TV broadcasters and content producers. AMX were recently acquired by Havas, the vast international advertising network, themselves part-owned by Vivendi who are at present involved in a takeover of Universal Studios. According to Scott, new media are comprised of three main elements: *'content'*, *'code'* and *'communications'*. For Scott *'content'* is the stuff that's sent down the pipes. It is the images, sounds, text, narratives, video-streaming, animation, discourse, enhancements, design, even the advertisements that are sent from one point to another. *'Code'* is the *'operationality'*, it is *'functionality'*. *'Code lets you *do* things'*. If content is the front end, code is what happens at the back end. It is what makes interactive media interactive. It is the nuts and bolts behind what is 'up there on the screen'. It is what is behind the interface; the interface's hind end. Deleuze and Guattari, in *Anti-Oedipus*, often write about 'code' and 'over-coding'. Al Scott's notion of code is quite opposite to Deleuze and Guattari. For the latter 'code' is semiotic, it is representational. For the new media practitioners, code is what destabilizes the semiotic; it puts representation into question.[1] *'Communications'* refers to the transportation of coded content from one point to another. The argument in this book is that content, code and communications are the three dimensions not just of new media, but of the information society more generally. They are the dimensions of information *and* the *critique* of information.

Communications

Communications is perhaps the most fundamental of our three terms. First-generation theories of information (Touraine, 1969; Bell, 1973) spoke simply of an information society, presumably primarily on a national level. Contemporary, second-generation theorists (e.g. Castells, 1996; Virilio, 1999a) speak of information and globalization as one and the same thing. What is it that connects these two main elements of contemporary social life – the global and the informational? It is *the communication*. Communication allows information to have 'global stretch'. Information on its own is static. Communication imparts to information a dynamic, a force: a source of energy. There is a basic velocity and long-distance stretch-out of communications that is at the basis of contemporary social life. The communication is the connecting link between the informational and the global. In this sense the communication and not information should perhaps be our basic unit of analysis. First-generation ICT development was fundamentally informational. The key sectors were semiconductors, software (operating system and applications) and computers. The second-generation, however, of the new economy is communicational. Hence the centrality of the Internet, of the net sector. Hence Cisco Systems, who make routers, the 'pipes' for Internet communications, for a time had a higher market capitalization than 'informational' Microsoft. Thus the rise of the new media. Here content and communications are as important as code, unlike the code-based information sector. First-generation ICTs were very much a California, a 'Silicon Valleys' affair. The second-generation is just as much a matter of, not so much the fresh and clean and semi-rural Silicon Valley, but of dirty and urban 'silicon *alleys*'. The original silicon alley was in downtown Manhattan, in proximity to and working with the older media – with television, design, publishing, cinema and the record industry. Silicon Valley was the 'I' of ICTs, the information. Silicon alleys have been the new *multi*media (Allen Scott, 2000). They are the multimedia convergence of information technology with the media. Silicon Valley grew in the Bay Area. Multimedia, for its part, spread to Los Angeles in conjunction with the film and recording industries. It spread to Europe. Once content was, if not 'king', at least rivalling code in importance, then the sector could thrive in the context of the various heterogenous European cultures.

If *multi*media (CD-ROMs, computer games) was a phenomenon of the mid nineteen nineties, the late nineties and beginning of the present millennium saw the development of '*new* media'. Indeed multimedia firms often in their lifetimes have transformed into new media firms.[2] The older multimedia firms did converge with old media and had the latter as their clients. They were largely '*content*' houses. They boasted *content* websites. Their strength was design. New media firms stay in their silicon alleys, but now not only or even primarily in juxtaposition with the old media, but in contact with the corporate headquarters of firms in *all* sectors. This is the context, not so much of Nasdaq or Neumarkt growth or crash, but the context in which all firms are becoming more or less Internet firms.[3] The old multimedia firms, at least those which had best survived, had become 'Internet solutions agencies'. Here they have moved from content to communications providing business to consumer marketing facilities and Intranets for firms from all sectors. The first generation of the information society gave us the major *information* firms – the generation of Intel, Microsoft and IBM. The second generation has produced the major *communications* firms, the growth of net sector firms like Cisco, Oracle, AOL, Netscape and Yahoo. These forms provide an infrastructure – a communications infrastructure for the Internet.

More significant in terms of ICT revenues at the turn of this century are mobile devices, especially mobile phones. Here Europe and Japan have been the leaders, the US the laggards, largely because they will not settle on a non-proprietary standard for platform. Thus we have seen the rise of such global giants as Vodafone, Nokia, Orange and Ericsson. This may be enhanced by WAP enabled hand-held devices, especially with the rise of 3G spectrum. These again are not information-sector but communications-sector developments. Consider also the rise of interactive television. Here the UK may play a leadership role, with at the time of writing some 5 million British households receiving their television through 'smart boxes'. Interactive cable television is also in the lead of providing broadband Internet access through cable modems.

The new economy is thus a *communications* economy. It is an economy less of accumulation of capital or information than one of flows. These flows are communications. They are communications in the broadest sense. Travel books talk for example about the quality of communications from a mainland to an island, that is, how often small planes and boats arrive and depart. Communications involve also the movement of goods and people. Theories of flows are thus at the same time theories of communication. And second-generation theories of the information society do presume the predominance of circulation. Circulation was not at all foregrounded by first-generation theorists such as Bell or Touraine who wrote at the end of the nineteen sixties and beginning of the nineteen seventies. But in 1989 both David Harvey's *Condition of Postmodernity* and Manuel Castells's *Informational City* proffer such a predominance of circulation for Harvey and 'flows' for Castells. What Harvey called 'flexible accumulation' is less a matter of accumulation than of circulation and especially the circulation of money (finance) capital. Harvey argues that in late capitalism finance-capital is hegemonic with respect to the productive capital. This circulation of invisibles becomes the governing principle in Harvey's post-modern condition.[5] It is the hegemony of volume two of Marx's *Capital* (circulation) over volume one. In the *Informational City* Castells wrote about the displacement of the logic of structures by the logic of flows. The idea of network in Castells's later *Network Society* and in Bruno Latour's actor-network theory presume the hegemony of flows. Networks are the sites through which the flows (of money, images, utterances, people, objects, communications, technology) navigate. Deleuze and Guattari also give us a theory, not of accumulation, but of circulation, of flows. For them most important are flows, 'pulsions' of desire and 'lines of flight'. These flows gain hegemony in the general 'de-territorialization' of structures and institutions. But there is never the pure indifference of flows. The de-territorialized flows wind up 'solidifying' in a group of new re-territorializations, some of which become infrastructure for the flows themselves. Networks and actor-networks are such re-territorializations. So are standards and platforms. So are international airports. The infrastructure more generally of the new net and communications sectors comprises such re-territorializations.

Communications are a question of culture-at-a-distance.[6] In the older manufacturing society, social relations took place in proximity. Relations were more diffuse, long-lasting: they were structured like narratives. The *social relation* was at the same time the social bond. Now in the information order, the social relation is displaced by the *communication*. The communication is intense, of short duration. Communications break with narrative for the brevity of the message. The older social relations took place in proximity; the 'communicational bond' is at a distance. Communications are about culture, not in proximity, but culture at a *distance*. Culture-at-a-distance involves either the communication coming from a distance or the people coming from a distance in order to meet face to face (Boden and Molotch, 1994). Intensity, brevity and the absence of narrative continuity are the governing principles (Simmel, 1971; Sennett, 1998). The communication and perhaps no longer the 'social act' becomes the contemporary unit of analysis. In theories of the manufacturing society from Weber, to Alfred Schutz to Talcott Parsons, the unit of analysis was the social act. In theories corresponding with the rise of the information order, the communication or the 'utterance' becomes the fundamental unit. This is true for Habermas (speech-act) and Foucault (discourse), Luhmann (communication) and Deleuze and Guattari (Deleuze, 1997) (the utterance). Once communication and flow are at centre stage rather than the social act and institution/structure, sociology may arguably begin progressively to be effaced by a general 'mediology' (Kittler, 1997; Debray, 2000).[7] This is the context of the massive rise in entrants in Media and Communications programmes throughout the world, not in just new universities, but by the most elite universities like Israel's Hebrew University of Jerusalem, Japan's Tokyo National University and Korea's Seoul National. At the moment most of these programmes teach what is effectively sociology of the media. But, especially with the input of information technology, they may be heading in the general direction of developing their own voice, their own logic of mediology. This involves, even at the most advanced level, working through media as much as working on media. Sociology had to do with the logic of the social that emerged fully in the mature industrial society and found its own voice in Durkheim and Weber. Mediology would have to do with the logic of media and of communications. It would come to maturity in the age of the flows. Durkheim's sociology was concerned by the anomie, the de-territorialization that occurred with the transition from feudalism to manufacturing capitalism. Mediology addresses the post-industrial 'anomie' of flows. Sociology deals with the re-territorializations of the social, of modern institutions and structures of industrial society. Mediology addresses the re-territorializations of the network society that come from the solidification of the flows.[8]

In 1987 John Urry and I published *The End of Organized Capitalism*, a book that dealt with the *dis*-organization of contemporary capitalism. This logic of disorganization is one of the *dis*-integration of institutions and organizations, of structures and systems. In 1994 we published *Economies of Signs and Space*. This book was about flows: about flows of money, tourists, immigrants, images, commodities, noxious substances and culture. *The End of Organized Capitalism* was about the disintegration, the de-territorialization of organized, manufacturing capitalism. *Economies of Signs and Space* was about the outcome of this; about the deterritorialized global information society. Manufacturing capitalism arises towards the end of a centuries-long (indeed millennia-spanning) process of differentiation: of structural differentiation and functional integration. It is the junction at which this differentiation of structures, systems, organizations and institutions reaches its high point, its summit. With the end of organized capitalism, this process of differentiation goes into reverse. It becomes a process of *in*differentiation, leading to a generalized indifference of the many kinds of increasingly digitized flows. It describes a process of the highest difference to one of generalized indifference. But at a certain point the indifference of flows starts solidifying in their own new territories, or should I say in their own new 'de-territories' (Rodowick, 1997).[9] These new (de-)territories are not new structures, institutions, organizations and organic-systems. They are instead such entities as platforms, brands, non-places, junkspace and cybernetic, open systems (Koolhaas, 2001). Nigel Thrift (Crang and Thrift, 2000) writes of cost-cutting through 'dis-intermediation' with the rise of the net sector, through the disintermediation of the bank, the bookshop and the record shop. Yet the flow-enhancing disintermediation leads to a set of re-intermediations. The deterritorializations lead to a set of reterritorializations. Embedded old intermediaries are displaced by disembedded new intermediaries.

What happens in the global information order is a generalized outsourcing. Things once done 'in-house' are now done miles, even continents away. The model for this is the vertically disintegrated firm. What was the old monopolistic, bureaucratic, hierarchical firm that integrated everything (purchasing, R&D, accounting, legal functions, marketing, sales, intermediate product manufacture) within the walls of the corporation, now subcontracts or out-sources all of these out-of-house. At the same time a lot of work is outsourced to independents and as home-work. When the array of privatized firms comprising formerly British Rail at the end of 2000 and the beginning of 2001 built in even greater irregularity to an already notoriously irregular service, passenger income took a steep drop. Passengers decided to commute less frequently to central London. A portion of this, the press suggested, was comprised of people who decided to work an extra day per week from home. Increased outsourcing is accompanied by an increase in density of networks of smaller firms. At issue is a *stretching* of productive relations. Work relations become a question of distanciated communication. They do so as they become simultaneously more informational. Heavy industry's means of production, primary materials and intermediate and final products are prohibitively expensive to shift at such distances. What happens though when the silicon chip replaces iron ore? How much does a service weigh? What is the weight of a unit of applications software?

This generalized outsourcing and stretching of productive relations is possible only in an era of 'lite capitalism', in a society in which for a large part we are 'living on thin air' (Leadbeater, 1999). Thus *communication* is the key term, the pivotal social fact for the global information order. The shift from a logic of structures to a logic of flows is made possible by the stretched relationships brought about by such generalized outsourcing. And this outsourcing is a *re*-territorialization. As the firm moves into the household, the family moves out. As the firm is outsourced into the household, the family is outsourced elsewhere. Hence we have not just the dissolution of the family but its reterritorialization. After divorce are weekend kids and long-distance partners – with the resulting communication links. Again, not diffuse, but intense relationships. Again there is a shift from the social relation to the communication, as family members stay in touch by email and every twelve-year-old gets a mobile phone for Christmas. Bargain flights from start-up airlines and Internet travel intermediators bring long-distance partners and family members together for brief, intense, yet regularly repeated encounters. These are long-lasting relations. But they have neither the continuity nor linearity of narrative. They are non-linear, discontinuous, yet long-lasting relationships. They comprise short bursts of intense intercommunication. These *long*-lasting relationships characterize both the 'outsourced family' and the networks of disintegrated small firms. Staff from the same small firms come together repeatedly over many years for short-term projects.

This is paralleled by an outsourcing of the welfare state and indeed more generally of the functions of the state. Britain outsources (or should we say 'in-sources') functions onto Scotland, Wales, Northern Ireland, onto the European Union, and onto subcontracting private and voluntary sector firms. There is an outsourcing of the *author* function onto teams of co-workers, an outsourcing of the expression function of formalist painting onto the installation of conceptual art. It is at this point that art becomes no longer a question of deep meaning and extended duration, but instead of operationality and brief duration. In this sense now art becomes communication. There is an outsourcing of the flux of inner experience onto the flows of images, media and information in the external world. The unconscious itself is outsourced into the world. Genes and memory are outsourced onto hardware, software and databases. Even reflexivity is outsourced, is externalized. It is no longer a reflection from the interior in an effective conversation within the self, but an externalized gloss on activities and events to others. Reflexivity becomes communicational. Reproduction is outsourced onto surrogates and others. With every deterritorialization there is a reterritorialization. The phenomenological essence thus of the global information order – at the root of both the global and the informational – is that which is the refusal of every essence: the communication.

Against Reproduction

What is accumulation? Things accumulate in piles, in heaps. For Marx (and implicitly in Heidegger's notion of technology) accumulation is of capital, and capital is a means. The accumulation of capital is the accumulation of means. The most important accumulation for Marx is the accumulation of means of production. In volumes two and three of *Das Kapital*, Marx left discussion of the individual capital to what he termed the 'total social capital' (*gesellschaftiches Gesamtkapital*) (*Das Kapital*, 1977, vol. 3: 172). This total social capital accumulated in two departments: of means of production and of consumption commodities. When Marx spoke of the accumulation of this total social capital he used the word 'accumulation' interchangeably with 'expanded reproduction'. Here means become functions and the total social capital is conceived as an organism. Accumulation is expanded reproduction. Yet what happens today with the new hegemony of circulation in which circulating money capital is partly detached from capital accumulation, so that, for example, a firm's market capitalization in the new sectors is partly disjointed from, and more problematically related to, the worth of its assets. What happens is not just a crisis and devaluation of accumulation but a crisis more generally of reproduction.

The idea of social reproduction and of the social as organism is the driving concept of sociology as originally and most forcefully conceived by Emile Durkheim. Philosophy 'paints its grey on grey', Hegel observed, only a very long time after the emergence and consolidation of a given ordering of human affairs. Thus the sort of theory of flows and communications, the sort of mediology to which this book is a contribution, comes a great number of decades, indeed nearly a century, after the first emergence of some sort of communications order.[10] The same is true of the notion of the social, emerging over a century after the fall of the *ancien régime* and the predominance of the *Gesellschaft*'s characteristic institutions, structures, organizations and systems. Durkheim's idea of the social (indeed the social itself) was comprised of 'facts'. Of 'social facts'. 'Society' now was a set of institutional social relations comprising national populations. 'Society' was no longer the sort of society we see on newspapers' 'society pages'. This came from society in its previous aristocratic sense, i.e. 'polite society'. As Benedict Anderson (1989) noted, the rise of the nation-state transforms the notion of society.

What is interesting here is that the social institutions of manufacturing capitalism arise not so much from a struggle of aristocrats and bourgeois. They arise instead alongside, and in excess of, the relationships of the *ancien régime*. Hardt and Negri (2000) suggest that it is not struggle or contradictions inside any given order that leads to a new order, but escape from or movement out of the earlier order. The same seems to happen in the transition from the social and the manufacturing order to the age of global information flows. The latter stems not from struggle or contradictions inside the former but *in excess* of the social. If the social, in Georges Bataille's (1991: 19–26) terms represents the 'restricted economy', the logic of flows is a question of the 'general economy'. At stake is the tension between, on the one hand, Durkheimian reproduction, and, on the other, Bataille's excess. Bataille, obsessed with anthropology, is rightly identified more strongly with conceptual art avant-gardes than with social science. But Bataille was a member of the Collège de Sociologie. He was consumed with Durkheim, and operated in the shadow of a Durkheimian *problematique*. Bataille's 'anti-Durkheim' disorder has no sense in the absence of Durkheimian order. Kant countered scepticism by presuming the existence of knowledge. He then asked how is knowledge (morality, aesthetic judgement) possible? Durkheim, as a neo-Kantian, noted we have society and asked more profoundly than anyone, what makes society possible? Bataille, who thrived on disorder, asked instead what makes society *im*possible?

Durkheim, as we know, was preoccupied with the problem of order, of reproduction. Order was guaranteed in traditional societies through 'mechanical solidarity', the solidarity of identical, undifferentiated parts with one another. Like a pile of bricks, whose mortar constitutes its conscience collective, and which needs re-pointing from time to time. With differentiation, solidarity had to become 'organic'. Institutions and individuals now were no longer like one another, yet they were interdependent on each other, like the organs of a body. Today we might ask, with Deleuze and Guattari, what happens when this social body is deterritorialized in the global information order? What happens when the social body loses, extrudes its organs? The social has been comprised of a set of subsystems – of institutions and organizations and structures. In each of these the frequency, intensity and depth of interactions and communications within each subsystem needed to be of a magnitude superior to those outside of the subsystem. The social exchanges of the institutions and organizations within a given society need to be of a greater magnitude than interchanges external to the society. What happens when neither of these holds true? What happens when the organs are not holding together any more – are fragmenting? What happens when they start exchanging exterior to – in excess of – the social as much or more than interior to it? What happens when the social body becomes effectively a body without organs?

What are the consequences for *culture* of the rise of this dis-informed information society? If the social is comprised of norms, culture is comprised of values and symbols. Norms are not values. They are rules. They need to be more or less 'followed' rather than somehow 'believed in'. Values and symbols have much greater duration than norms. The economy and the social are very closely bound together. This is true even though a crisis in the economy can lead to a refusal to rule-follow. But what about culture? For Durkheim culture was inscribed in a *conscience collective*. This is much more a collective consciousness than a collective conscience. More a collective ego, incorporating collective memory, than superegoic. Is this *conscience collective* part and parcel of society? Does it belong to the social? It would seem not. Social order for Durkheim is in traditional societies provided by both mechanical solidarity and conscience collective: in modern societies by both the interdependence of differentiated bodies and conscience collective. Cultural configurations like the Catholic religion and the French language and, say, Shakespeare overlap a number of social orders: feudal and industrial and informational. Talcott Parsons (1955) understood values in terms of 'pattern maintenance'; that is, the transmission of what underpins order from generation to generation. For Parsons thus norms are synchronic, values diachronic. Put another way, cultural is canonical in a way that society can never be. Or whereas societies are more or less finite, cultures are more or less universal. Although the symbolic is relatively autonomous as it were from the normative, it basically aids in the reproduction of economy and social orders. It is surely *not in excess of* either the social or the economic order. Durkheim's conscience collective becomes later the symbolic for both Lévi-Strauss and Jacques Lacan. In sociology there is a tradition of theorizing both on levels of social and psychic systems. Consider, for example, Parsons, who was a great Freudian, or the work of Niklas Luhmann. Indeed Freud was concerned with psychic order in a manner not a lot different than the concern of Durkheim and Weber for social order. For his part, Lacan with his individualization of the symbolic order is concerned with the reproduction of this psychic order in much the same sense as Durkheim and now Bourdieu address the reproduction of the social. For Lacan, the successful resolution of the Oedipus complex is at the same time the entry into language, into the symbolic. Language thus is at the same time 'law'. It is the 'law of the father'.

If the conscience collective, the symbolic order, is about reproduction then what indeed is in excess of the social? For Max Weber it is 'value'. Weber wanted us to separate fact from value: to separate social fact from more cultural, spiritual, hermeneutic value. This is, of course, the Kantian distinction between pure reason and practical reason. Pure reason is on 'the inside' alongside the knowable social and understandable according to the laws of nature and mathematics. In contradistinction, practical reason – ethics, freedom, God, the thing-in-itself, infinity – is on the outside. It is Heideggerian Being, where the sphere of freedom and ultimate meaning is in excess or on the outside as filtered through human beings who are operating in the realm of the same. This ethical and existential excess is the stuff of Max Weber's 'ethics of responsibility', and at the end of the day at bottom of Beck's risk society. Here excess is what is out of control. It is the unintended consequences. It is side effects. For Weber, the ethics of responsibility presumes already the end of meta-narratives, the decline of the Whig ideal. It is an understanding of the modern in terms of the multiplicity of gods and demons: of a modernity characterized by contingency. It is surely in this sense that our second, global and informational modernity is the risk society. And the key question becomes how do we deal with this? How do we deal with this responsibly? Weber was a secular animal, much more comfortable in the world of excess than Durkheim. Durkheim wanted a civil religion that was integral to the social. Weber is sceptical of religion. He is obsessed with the rise of the world religions yet was, himself, 'religiously unmusical'. He was aware of their extension, their dualistic extension, in the Enlightenment and Marxism. For Weber we must look to our ends and achieve the achievable while all the time taking responsibility for the side effects. We live in a world of risk and our conduct needs to take account of how whatever we do in this risk-environment will generate further contingency, further risks. This entails judgement. While Weber saw the risk generators among the political and aesthetic left with their ethic of ultimate ends, Ulrich Beck (1988) finds his risk generators among big capitalist industry and big science, whom he sees as involved in 'organized irresponsibility'. Both Weber as conservative and Beck as radical come to a similar conclusion: we need political institutions to deal with this uncertainty of risk, contingency and side effects.

But there is another side of the social's excess: another realm of contingency on its outskirts. If the first realm of risk of contingency – that of Weber and Kant – is ethical, existential, somehow and surely 'above' the social, 'above' the everyday, this second way into excess, contingency, risk, flux, happens somehow *below* the social. The social connects with its 'above' via the Cartesian point that connected mind and matter. It connects with its 'below' through what Bataille might have called the 'social anus'. Through this it not only excludes but *extrudes* its detritus. If God (along with freedom, the thing-itself and ethics) is in the realm of Kantian contingency, then this other realm of risk and contingency is diabolic. If high modernity is the other from above, then a very low modernity of contingency is the other from below. This is Durkheim's excess, far removed from the nobility of Weberian life-conduct. Durkheim's excess is 'the pathological', extruded so as to preserve 'the normal'. It is Durkheim's deviant, abjected so as to create a conscience collective of the same. It has nothing to do with judgement, still less with ethics. It is the rejection of aesthetics, though in it *art* plays a very important role. This is Battaille's space of not just contingency, but contingency via what is extruded from the social, what is abjected from the symbolic. The pimp, the prostitute, Walter Benjamin's 'rag picker', the homeless, the transsexual wear this face of the abject. In a Durkheimian vein, both national capital and social-democratic labour, in their corporatist interdependency, are the underpinnings of the social's organic solidarity. But Marx's and Bataille's lumpenproletariat, extruded from the social, were a different matter (Bois and Krauss, 1997).

If good, the good – though not the good life – is on the hither side of the social, then it is surely *evil*, the diabolic, that is on its nether side. On one side, *les fleurs du bon*: on the other *les fleurs du mal*. Disrupting the social metabolism, on the symbolic's nether side, is the viral, not just excess but *excess*. It is what Bataille (1991: 37–8) called *la part maudite* – the 'accursed share' in English. *Le maudit* is indeed accursed. According to *Le Peitit Robert* he is rejected or condemned by God. But he is at the same time *'repoussée de la société'*. *Les maudits* are *'les damnés'*. For a thing or person to be *'maudit'* is to be *'détestable, exécrable, haïssable'*. He is more colloquially *'fichu'*, *'sacré'*, *'sale'*, *'satané'*. *'Les Poètes maudits'* was the title of

Verlaine's famous essay of 1885. The lumpenproletarian and also the *bohème* is *maudit*. So are Walter Benjamin's disused objects, his cast-offs. Where are the *maudit* spaces? *'Maudire'* is *'maldire'* in its origins. The verb conjugates like *dire*. For a thing or person to be *maudit*, there must be some *mau-* or *maldir*-ing going on. Yet to *maldire* is, of course, not just to say badly about someone: it to say so with almost magical effects. It is the ultimate performative, whose effects are banishment. Is the disintegration of the social the work of the *part maudite*? Will the critique of information come from the *part maudite*? If freedom was once found in the lofty spheres of morality, value and infinity, is it now found in this diabolic space of excess?[11]

And it is also from that second, nether region of excess, of contingency that is found Freud's unconscious, his id instincts. At issue here is, of course, not the sex-drive, but the death-drive: not eros or the libidinal instincts but thanatos. The early Freud's constitutive dualism of the 'mental apparatus' counterposed ego and id. He even talked of two types of instinct: libidinal or id instincts and separate self-preservative instincts of the ego. In *Beyond the Pleasure Principle* in 1919 Freud introduced the death-drive. It is the death-drive that has to do with excess. The death-drive has to do with wastage, the sex-drive with reproduction. The death-drive with pathology, the sex-drive with normality. Both ego and id comprise the restricted economy. The death-drive makes possible the general economy. The *part maudite* indeed of life is death. To live is also at the same time to die. Life is also dissipation, decay, wastage, disorganization. The sex-drive tends to move us towards organization, the death-drive to flux, both in the individual personality and in the body of the social. In Lacanian analysis, the symbolic stands juxtaposed to the real. The symbolic abjects the schizophrenic into the real. The schizophrenic is uncomfortable in the realm of language. The real is given its logic by the principle of disorganization: of dissipation and disintegration. Here the repressed is not the oedipal father but rather the vengeful father (Zizek, 1989). *Totem and Taboo* was written in 1912–13 before the principle of the superego emerged in *The Ego and the Id* (1923). In *Totem and Taboo*, the horde of the brothers do not fantasize, but actually murder and devour the father. In *Totem and Taboo* it is not the *wish* to kill the father, but the *act* that is repressed. At stake is the actual act of killing the father by the horde, in violation of the taboo on their desire for the father's wives. The brothers linked libidinally, affectively to their leader, the original *primus inter pares* actually kill the father. Is this the original collective violence? Is this the origin of community?

Instinctual drives are forces. They comprise energy. The early Freud spoke of id and ego instincts, thus id and ego were drives, generators of energy. In the later Freud, the operations of the ego are derivable from libidinal instincts, i.e. erotogenic energy, erotogenic instinctual force. There is no independent energy generated from the ego. The id generates, the ego regulates. The point here is the centrality of libidinal energy. And it is libidinal energy that is ultimately grounded in the biological reproduction of the species. The death-drive is an independent source of energy. But it is a source that is based on the dissipation of energy. The logic of the id is the pleasure principle, of the ego the reality principle. For its part thanatos's logic is the 'nirvana principle', the total draining of sexual energy. Roland Barthes's orgasms are thus 'little deaths'. Pleasure and reality principles work through balanced semi-discharge of energy: thanatos through total discharge. It has to do with destruction and aggression as well as death. Turned inwards there is the disintegration of psychic apparatus and body: turned outwards the instinct becomes aggression/destruction.

Totem and Taboo's destructive father, the vengeful father, the sexually rapacious and leering father, is at the heart of the symbolic, of civilization. As well as repressed sexuality, he is at the heart of the 'discontents of civilization'. This father disobeyed the monogamy of oedipal reproduction and actually *had* all the women and was actually killed by the horde. The ego is derived from libidinal forces, the superego derives from this death/destruction-drive. The death-drive is thus at the heart of civilization, of what Derrida calls the archive. It is violent. The sex-drive and extended reproduction work best in sedentary peacetime. The death-drive connects to the movement of war. Ideology, economy, culture and society work on the inside of the social as reproductive organism. Violence and politics work on the outside. Yet there is this originary violence of any symbolic (Grosz, 1998). Indeed collective memory is based on repressed collective violence: not on its fantasy but on its reality. The repressed returns. The dead come back from the real to haunt us until they are properly buried in the symbolic. If the sex-drive and reproduction are what sustains the symbolic, the death-drive, with its expenditure and chronic production, is a matter for the real.

The point here is not just to point to the violence that is the condition of possibility of the organism. It is that the organism itself is in crisis; reproduction is in perhaps terminal crisis. At stake is not just the necessary presence of the flux and disintegration of the death-drive as the impenetrable basis on which the sex-drive and reproduction rests. It is the *crisis of reproduction itself*. It is the imminent impossibility of reproduction, in whose stead all we have is production: incessant production; the production of flux. Of flow. At stake are both psychic and social systems. This is at the crux of the conflict between the two main figures of late twentieth century French sociology, Alain Touraine and Pierre Bourdieu. Bourdieu's (1998) work has continually asked how society has reproduced itself. Touraine (1975, 1995) enquires instead into 'the *production* of society'. Touraine argues that in previous social arrangements – feudalism, industrial capitalism, communism – pivotal social processes were inscribed in a paradigm of reproduction. In the synchronic of any given previous form of society there was reproduction. Only in the diachronic, the transition from one mode of social life to another, was there significant change, was there production. It is only in the post-industrial societies, in globalized modernity, that the synchronic is no longer characterized by reproduction, but instead by chronic change and instability, by chronic innovation, in a word chronic *production*.

Thus Deleuze and Guattari have argued for chronic production in post-oedipal social arrangements. For them production (which is always at the same time 'desiring-production') is identified with the movement of becoming, reproduction with the stasis of being. Reproduction is oedipal, production anti-oedipal. Reproduction is the hegemony of the (psychic and social) symbolic: production the dominance of flows. From the standpoint of *Lebensphilosophie* or vitalism, reproduction paradoxically is life-destroying while production is life-enhancing. Thus the vitalism of Nietzsche, Bergson and Simmel (Deleuze) is polar opposite to the idea of 'life' of Durkheim. For Durkheim life is being. It is the reproduction of being. For the opponents of Durkheimian (and reproductive) positivism, *Lebensphilosophie* and later phenomenology, life is becoming. Life is flux. For Durkheim life is the normal to the exclusion of the pathological. Life has to do with risk reduction. For Nietzsche and Bergson life is a question of risk-*taking*. For organicist positivism life is involved in the normal's rejection (and abjection) of the pathological. For the philosophy of becoming, the ideology of the normal is a slave morality, while life is on the side of the pathological. Life, with David Cronenberg, is viral. Life goes on outside of the organism. The flux that shatters the symbolic is at the same time the destruction of reproduction by chronic production. It is also the violation of reproduction by waste, by expenditure, consumption (Bataille, 1991: 63 ff.). In either case reproduction enters into crisis: the symbolic is effaced.

From Meaning to Operationality: Conceptual Art as Critique of Information

Beings reproduce. At least social, animal and human beings reproduce. The social body as well as human and animal bodies reproduce. Deleuze and Guattari's 'body without organs' does not reproduce. Bodies need organs to reproduce themselves and their species. Without organs, bodies can only expend and produce, never reproduce. 'Being' in this sense involves reproduction, while 'becoming' is a question of production and expenditure. Being involves *meaning*. For Heidegger the meaning of Being needs to be filtered through beings, indeed through that very special human being that Heidegger calls *Dasein*. The reproduction of that collective being which we might call the social entails the transmission of meaning, of deep meanings from one generation to the next. Symbols have meaning, ideologies have meaning, discourses have meaning. Signifiers through their constitutive difference produce meaning. The reproduction of the social and the symbolic are dependent on meaning. But what happens when the symbolic is in fragments, when the social does not reproduce? What happens when meaning is not successfully transmitted over the generations, when signifiers refuse to signify? What happens when death, previously on the outside and constituting the existential meaning of life, is now on the inside and all amongst us?

What happens is a shift from a register of meaning to one of *operationality*. The organic systems of the national manufacturing order worked through meaning. The cybernetic and possibly open systems of the information age have to do instead with operationality. The question is not so much what does it mean but how does it work. Meaning and operationality are both 'logics of sense'. Logics of sense is what Pierre Bourdieu (1980) calls *'sens practique'*: ways that we orient ourselves in the world. This can be extended – as Henri Lefebvre (1986) does – to ways in which non-humans too orient themselves in the world. Today we – often in tandem with information and communication machines – orient ourselves in the world, in a logic of sense, a *sens practique* that owes perhaps less to meaning than operationality. We filter out the noise of the world as much through operationality as meaning. The social works through meaning: networks through operationality; the symbolic through meaning, the real through operationality. In his early work Manuel Castells referred to urban space as a 'regime of meaning'. But now in the network society this seems to change. The urban is somehow disembedded from the symbolic and re-inscribed in the real. Thus Rem Koolhaas and his architecture students from Harvard, drawing on years of frequent and lengthy research visits, have produced a volume of work-in-progress entitled *Lagos: or A Brief Description of What May Be the Most Radical Urban Condition on the Planet* (2000). Lagos is normally considered to be the worst example of urban disorganization: a chaos of shantytowns, poverty, dysfunction and corruption. Cities like Saõ Paulo seem positively Germanic in comparison to Lagos. Travellers are forewarned: don't go to Lagos. But Koolhaas and his students are looking for something else. They are interested in how Lagos *works*. How it functions. They make aerial and ground-level photographs of the movements of objects, vehicles and people in space. They look at informal markets: how electronic and microelectronic equipment in informal work units is repaired, reprogrammed and recirculated. Here an urban fabric, perhaps previously primarily a regime of meaning, is transformed into a regime of operationality. Indeed the urban itself may need rethinking in an age of flows. Flows don't *mean*. They *work*. They are operational.

Meaning is inscribed in an organic heuristic. Language is organic for Ferdinand de Saussure. Language is a signifying system. Language is a differentiated, organic system, having its own organicity, different from that of the Durkheimian social system. For the relationship of signifiers to signifieds or ideas, Saussure tells us to look at the formal relations of signifiers within the system. The signifier does not just map on to the signified outside of the system. But the latter depends on the differential relations of the former. The relations of the organs inside the system give us meaning. Meaning comes from that self-reproducing organic system that is language. But what happens when speaking disengages from the organic being of language, and re-engages in a logic of flow? What happens when speaking becomes *parole* without *langue*, becomes performance in the absence of competence. What happens with a new hegemony of flow, of flows of utterances?[12] We then ask less what words mean but instead what they do. How they perform.

Consider art. In 'modernist formalism', relations between elements in paintings or sculptures give us meaning. They can open up onto deeper existential meaning (see, for example, comments by Blaue Reiter artists, Picasso and many others). Contemporary art in contrast would involve not meaning but operationality. At issue is not the 'formalism' of modern art but instead *conceptual* art. Not the tradition of Picasso, Matisse, Braque and Pollock but Duchamp and the avant-gardes of the aftermath of the First World War. Conceptual art does not work through the materiality of the work of art (colour, texture, etc.) but through ideas. Modern art is mainly not conceptual art. Most contemporary art is conceptual. Conceptual art in the very strict sense is a late nineteen sixties phenomenon. There is a strong connection with minimalism – Sol Le Witt, Donald Judd. There is a connection with Pop Art – with Warhol and Richard Hamilton. The work of conceptual art is characteristically unfinished. This is not in any Romantic sense. Romanticism overvalues the position of the artist (author). Conceptual art devalues the artist's position. Indeed, it is left to the audience to finish the work, to complete it and thus make sense of it. But perhaps audience is the wrong word here. At issue is perhaps something more like the user. If classical and modern art involves duration, that is, lasting value across the generations, then conceptual art is to have the value-brevity of the communication. There was a very strong McLuhanite streak in late sixties conceptual art (Craig-Martin, 1999). In conceptual art what was the viewer becomes the user; interpretation becomes code. Formalist art works surely made sense in regard to the interpretation of the viewer: through meanings negotiated via artist and interpreting viewer. Conceptual art works more through the operationality of the viewer/user. As incomplete, the viewer must so to speak put together the last bits. The viewer becomes operational. He or she no longer interprets, but does. Thus conceptual art is so comfortable as installation, as three-dimensional spaces, that we not so much view or interpret, but use and inhabit.

If art is unfinished, it is at the same time accidental. In this sense Paul Virilio (1982) is right to imply we live in a culture of the accident. Not of the necessary or planned, but the accident. As accidental it is unintended. The work of art in this sense is an accidental byproduct of the idea. Art is a side effect. It is aleatory in John Cage's sense. The idea may be intended, the art not. At stake are not so much unintended *consequences* though. It is more an unintended means to an end. Yet the duality of means–ends language breaks down in the information order's age of immanence. Instrumental rationality entails an intending of the means. In conceptual art, the art is an unintended means on the way to a more or less contingent idea. If art is doubly contingent, a side effect of a side effect (the concept), then conceptual art does involve an anti-aesthetic (Foster, 1996). It is anything but Kant's 'finality without end' (*Zweckmässigkeit ohne Zweck*), and is surely not art for the sake of art. Aesthetic judgement and aestheticism disappear at the same time. Conceptual art is neither beautiful nor sublime. Both beauty and sublimity presume a sphere of freedom, as it were on the outside, that the work of art alludes to. With the disappearance of an outside, beauty and sublimity recede. Indeed aesthetic judgement becomes impossible. There is not sufficient time to judge. Nor is there sufficient distance, with the growing indifference between the judge and the judged. The judge too now stands in a position of operationality to the judged. Judgement presumes also a certain measure of law. Max Weber's understanding of modernity revolved very much around the differentiation of spheres, of what he called life-orders. Here a number of life spheres and disciplines take on their own autonomy. Art, sociology, linguistics, the economy, religion, ethics, sexuality become self-legislating, take on what Weber called an *Eigengesetzlichkeit*. With such self-legislation, judgement of activities in any sphere proceeds according to differentiated sphere-specific laws. But conceptual art and the information order tend to dissolve such differentiation into a general indifference. Its triumph of the pathological over the normal is also the violation of legislation and the sundering of the organicity of the spheres. Conceptual art is without either aesthetic or judgement. The critique of information is non-judgemental.

In Weberian differentiation every sector works within its own materiality. It works within a *problematique* of the differential combinations of its own particular elements. What the shift from the organic beings of these differentiated systems to open systems and flow gives us is *in*difference. It gives us not formalism but informe-alism. Each differentiated organic system works through the logic of materiality of its own elements. Now this differentiated materiality cedes to an undifferentiated ideality. The materiality of the signifier is displaced by the ideality of the signified. This idea without signifier is the unit of content of the information order. This idea works not through meaning, but operationality. Critique then works though operationality, through code. This is not instrumental rationality, but part of a logic which breaks with the dualism of instrumental versus substantive rationality, of exchange-value versus use-value, of a Kantian kingdom of means versus the kingdom of ends. At stake instead is a set of struggles in the medium of operationality, of code. At stake is a politics of reworking and re-inscribing code: a politics of access to, control over and ownership of code.

What are the 'concepts', the ideas involved in where art is an accidental by-product of concepts, of ideas. These are not Hegelian or Kantian ultimate ideas of reason (*Vernunft*). Conceptual art's ideas are not the Kantian ideas of freedom, God, infinity, morality and the thing-in-itself. They have little to do with the Hegelian idea of absolute reason. They are not even the concepts of the scientific (and positivist) understanding which subsume objects under subjects.[13] For conceptual art there is no difference between reason and the understanding. Conceptual art's indifferent ideas are accidents: they have the *in*significance of communications. They have little to do with discursive argument or even discourse. They are insignificant ideas: pure and very minor signifieds. They are so unformed as to resemble the ideas of the unconscious: the unconscious not as sexuality and reproduction, but its pathological, excremental *part maudite*. They are ideas without meaning, effective instead through operationality, as code. In conceptual art, art philosophizes, art thinks. But what kind of thinking, of thought, is at stake? Thought, and for that matter, critique, may be unconscious. Indeed Freud spoke of unconscious 'ideas' and André Breton of unconscious 'thought'. The stuff of the unconscious may have little to do with language, or even with the figural, but may be instead a mode of thought. This again is as far from Heidegger's '*Bauen, Wohnen, Denken*' as it is from Habermas's discursive legitimation of serious speech acts. Indeed, if discourse is comprised of serious speech acts, conceptual art's mode of thinking is decidedly *un*serious. This is thinking not in discrete segments, but as flow, as welded to desire. It is thought as shock: as Walter Benjamin's shock-experience (*Chokerlebnis*). Critique via shock-experience. For Benjamin, critique itself works via *Chokerlebnis* (Caygill, 1998). Gerhard Schulze (2001) is right. We live in an 'experience society', a shock-experience society. That does not mean we live in an irrational society. It does not mean that there is less thought than there once was. Indeed, critique is possible and critique works through thought. Only the thought and critique is inscribed in shock-experience. Benjamin, who knew Bataille, wrote, famously in his essay on surrealism that 'there is no room for that "penny in the slot" called "meaning"' (1997). Benjamin was a Critical Theorist. His colleague and sometimes friend Theodor Adorno gave us Critical Theory of manufacturing capitalism. Benjamin gives us the critique of information. The critique of information takes place through thought, through shock-experience, and via not meaning but operationality.

Sarat Maharaj (1999), art-theorist and curator, brings conceptual art to the centre of the critique of information. Maharaj is a Duchamp scholar. His Duchamp is inscribed in a lineage stretching from Bergson to Deleuze. The concept from Duchamp's critique that resurfaces in Deleuze's plane of immanence depends on a notion of thought that is ultimately Bergsonian. At issue is Bergson's image-ontology (in *Matter and Memory*) in which primordially is nothing but moving matter-images. There are no objects. There are no subjects, but there are only images. These images are at the same time material. These matter-images are in movement. There are moving and energy-generating matter-images in an environment of light.[14] In this beginning there is a generalized *indifference*. This is Bergson's primordial flux. But as the molten swirl of moving image-matter cools down there is differentiation. There is complexity. There is a solidification first into objects and subsequently into subjects. Only with such differentiation is thought and philosophy possible. Bergson and Deleuze want philosophy to be able to think its origin in indifference. In order, paradoxically, for philosophy to think indifference there must be the greatest amount of differentiation. This is the paradox of the information society: differentiation and in-differentiation at the same time. The simplest anarchic flux and the most complex differentiation at the same time. Homogeneity and heterogeneity simultaneously. The greatest rationality *and* the greatest irrationality. Such is the stuff of the information order and its critique.

Duchamp and conceptual art is constitutively reflexive. Formalist modern art, in the sense that it works through the logic of the aesthetic materials, already withdraws from representation into itself. Formalist art works from a logic of interior reflection that has nothing to do with the critique of information. Art must become conceptual in order for this to happen. Art must leave its specific difference to partake in a more general indifference. Taken inside the museum, Duchamp's urinal became suddenly reflexive. Glossing the figure of the urinal with the (false) discourse of 'R. Mutt' redoubled this. Formalist art is perhaps self-referential. Conceptual art is reflexive. It is critical. It is a reflexive critique of its own conditions of existence. Maharaj extends art as conceptual critique to the power relations of the institutions of production and circulation of art on a global scale. This critique is not through reasoned discourse or internal reflection, but a very externalized reflexivity of unfinished processes of art. This book has tried to begin to extend this sort of reflexive critique more generally to the global information and communications order. Here the most highly rational formulations and designs lead to the most irrational of consequences. Yet the information society is not irrational. It is highly rational and irrational at the same time. The 'idea' is the unit of content of the information order. And in the idea rationality and irrationality are juxtaposed in the highest tension. The point that this book has tried to make is that we can no longer step outside of the global communications flows to find a solid fulcrum for critique. There is no more outside. The critique of information is in the information itself.

Notes

1 This is clearly a semantic distinction and in no way undermines the force of Deleuze and Guattari's analyses. What the new media practitioners understand as code, the schizotheorists would see as 'lines of flight'.

2 These pages draw fundamentally on collaborative work with Andreas Wittel, Celia Lury, Deirdre Boden and Dan Shapiro on London's new media sector. The research project entitled 'Silicon Alleys' was part of the British Economic and Social Research Council's Virtual Society Programme. Programme Director has been Steve Woolgar. None of the above are to be blamed for this chapter and book's many shortcomings.

3 An ICM survey reported in The *Guardian* of 23 January 2001 found that 49 per cent of Britons had access to the Internet and 63 per cent of Britons owned mobile phones. Both figures were major increases on January 2000. The majority of mobile phone users said they used text messaging.

4 In January 2001, after the Nasdaq crash, the share-price to profits ratio of technology firms were still twice as high as other quoted firms. In June 2001, the market capitalization of Cisco, Oracle, Microsoft, Intel and AoL is still a multiple of their revenues.

5 As it is for Charles Leadbeater in *Living On Thin Air* (1999).

6 This notion came from discussions with Kevin Robins.

7 The idea of 'mediology' that I am speculatively discussing as a possible future departure does not draw on Debray's work. On 'mediology' also see Bourdieu (1998).

8 This is not to say that this sort of mediology might be addressed just as easily in sociology, geography or cultural studies programmes as in media studies.

9 Deleuze, drawing on Bergson, speaks of an original flux that later 'solidifies into objects and subjects'. This is fundamental to Deleuze's Bergsonian theory of cinema.

10 Posited by analysts such as Kittler (1997), McLuhan, Poster and Virilio to emerge in the years surrounding and just after the Second World War with the emergence of cinema, music

recording, the typewriter, with war as movement and later the first (1936) development of computers and television technology.

11 Maria Lakka (2000) has commented that a similar notion of freedom is found in the art avant-gardes of the 1920s.

12 See Guattari in Deleuze (1997).

13 They may, however, be like ideas formed in the Kantian imagination. I am grateful to Kostis Koukouzelis for this point.

14 See Rodowick (1997) and Flaxman (2000) on this.

Bibliography

Amin, Samir (1970) *L'Accumulation à l'échelle mondiale*. Paris: Editions anthropos.

Anderson, Benedict (1989) *Imagined Communities*, second edition. London: Verso.

Appadurai, A. (ed.) (1986) *The Social Life of Things: Commodities in Cultural Perspective*. Cambridge: Cambridge University Press.

Appadurai, A. (1996) *Modernity at Large: Cultural Dimensions of Globalization. Public Worlds*. Minneapolis: University of Minnesota Press.

Arnoldi, J. (2000) 'Niklas Luhmann's phenomenology of communications'. Unpublished paper. Goldsmiths College, London University.

Augé, M. (1995) *Non-Places*. London: Verso.

Barnes, B., Bloor, D. and Henry, J. (eds) (1996) *Scientific Knowledge: A Sociological Analysis*. Chicago: University of Chicago Press.

Barry, A. (2001) *Political Machines*. London: Athlone.

Barthes, R. (1993) *Camera Lucida*. New York: Vintage.

Bataille, G. (1991) *The Accursed Share*, Vol. 1. New York: Zone Books.

Baudrillard, J. (1976) *L'Échange symbolique et la mort*. Paris: Gallimard.

Baudrillard, J. (1978) *A l'ombre des majorités silencieuses ...* . Paris: Utopie.

Baudrillard, J. (1980) *Forget Foucault*. New York: Semiotext(e).

Baudrillard, J. (1981) *For a Critique of the Political Economy of the Sign*. St Louis: Telos Press.

Baudrillard, J. (1994a) *Simulacra and Simulation*. Ann Arbor, MI: University of Michigan Press.

Baudrillard, J. (1994b) *Symbolic Exchange and Death*. London: Sage.

Bauman, Z. (1991) *Modernity and Ambivalence*. Cambridge: Polity.

Bauman, Z. (1993) *Postmodern Ethics*. Oxford: Blackwell.

Beck, U. (1986) *Risikogesellschaft*. Frankfurt: Suhrkamp.

Beck, U. (1988) *Gegengift. Organisierte Unverantwortlichkeit*. Frankfurt: Suhrkamp.

Beck, U. (1992) *Risk Society*. London: Sage.

Beck, U. (2000) *The Brave New World of Work*. Cambridge: Polity.

Beck, U. and Beck-Gernsheim, E. (2001) *Individualization*. London: Sage.

Beck, U., Giddens, A., and Lash, S. (1994) *Reflexive Modernization*. Cambridge: Polity.

Beck-Gernsheim, Elisabeth (1995) *The Social Implications of Bio-Engineering*. New York: Humanities Press.

Bell, D. (1973) *The Coming of Post-Industrial Society*. London: Heinemann.

Bell, D. (1976) *The Cultural Contradictions of Capitalism*. London: Heinemann.

Bell, D. (2000) *The End of Ideology*. Cambridge, MA: Harvard University Press.

Benhabib, S. (1986) *Critique, Norm and Utopia*. New York: Columbia University Press.

Benhabib, S. (1992) *Situating the Self*. Cambridge: Polity.

Benhabib, S. (1996) *The Reluctant Modernism of Hannah Arendt*. Thousand Oaks, CA: Sage.

Benjamin, W. (1963) *Ursprung des deutschen Trauerspiels*. Frankfurt: Suhrkamp.

Benjamin, W. (1974a) 'Ursprung des deutschen Trauerspiels', in *Abhandlungen, Gesammelte Schriften*, Band I-1. Frankfurt: Suhrkamp. pp. 203–430.

Benjamin, W. (1974b) 'Charles Baudelaire. Ein Lyriker im Zeitalter des Hochkapitalismus', in *Abhandlungen, Gesammelte Schriften*, Band I-2. Frankfurt: Suhrkamp. pp. 431–690.

Benjamin, W. (1974c) 'Uber den Begriff der Geschichte', in *Abhandlungen, Gesammelte Schriften*, Band I-2. Frankfurt: Suhrkamp. pp. 693–703.

Benjamin, W. (1974d) 'L'oeuvre d'art a l'époque de sa réproduction mécanisée', *Abhandlungen, Gesammelte Schriften*, Band I-2. Frankfurt: Suhrkamp. pp. 709–39.

Benjamin, W. (1977a) 'Der Erzähler, Betrachtungen zum Werk Nikolai Leskows', in *Aufsätze, Essays, Vorträge, Gesammelte Schriften*, Band II-2. Frankfurt: Suhrkamp. pp. 438–65.

Benjamin, W. (1977b) *The Origin of German Tragic Drama*. London: Verso.

Benjamin, W. (1977c) 'Uber Sprache überhaupt und über die Sprache des Menschen', in *Aufsätze, Essays, Vorträge, Gesammelte Schriften*, Band II-1 Frankfurt: Suhrkamp.

Benjamin, W. (1997) 'Surrealism', in *One Way Street*. London: Verso. pp. 225–39.

Berger, Peter L. (1967) *The Sacred Canopy. Elements of a Sociological Theory of Religion*. New York: Anchor.

Berking, H. and Neckel, S. (1990) 'Die Politik der Lebenstile in einem Berliner Bezirk: Zu einigen Formen der nachtraditioneler Vergemeinschaftung', *Soziale Welt*, 7: 481–500.

Bhabha, H. (1990) 'The Third Space', in J. Rutherford (ed.), *Identity*. London: Lawrence & Wishart.

Bhabha, H. (1994) *The Location of Culture*. London: Routledge.

Boden, D. (1994) *The Business of Talk*. Cambridge: Polity.

Boden, D. (1998) 'The medium is reflexive'. Unpublished paper. Copenhagen Business School.

Boden, D. and Molotch, H. (1994) 'The compulsion of proximity', in R. Friedland and D. Boden (eds), *NowHere. Space, Time and Modernity*. Berkeley, CA: University of California Press.

Bois, Y.A. and Krauss, R. (1997) *Formless*. New York: Zone Books.

Boltanski, Luc and Thevenot, Laurent (1991) *De la justification. Les économies de la grandeur*. Paris: Gallimard.

Bourdieu, P. (1977) *Outline of a Theory of Practice*. Cambridge: Cambridge University Press.

Bourdieu, P. (1980) *Le Sens practique*. Paris: Éditions de minuit.

Bourdieu, P. (1984) *Distinction*. London: Routledge.

Bourdieu, P. (1998) *On Television and Journalism*. London: Pluto Press.

Buber, M. (1974) *I and Thou*. New York: Macmillan.

Callon, M. (1998) *The Laws of the Market*. Oxford: Blackwell.

Cassirer, Ernst (1995) *Philosophy of Symbolic Forms: Mythical Thought*, Vol. 2. New Haven, CT: Yale University Press.

Castells, M. (1989) *The Informational City*. Oxford: Blackwell.

Castells, M. (1996) *The Rise of the Network Society. The Information Age: Economy, Society and Culture*, Volume 1. Oxford: Blackwell.

Caygill, H. (1989) *The Art of Judgement*. Oxford: Blackwell.

Caygill, H. (1998) *Walter Benjamin: The Colour of Experience*. London: Routledge.

Clifford, James (1997) *Routes: Travel and Translation in the Late Twentieth Century*. Cambridge, MA: Harvard University Press.

Cohen, J. and Arato, A. (1992) *Civil Society and Political Theory*. Cambridge, MA: MIT Press.

Coombe, R. (1998) *The Cultural Life of Intellectual Properties*. Durham, NC: Duke University Press.

Craig-Martin, M. (1999) *Michael Craig-Martin and Sometimes a Cigar Is Just a Cigar*. Stuttgart: Verlag das Wunderhorn.

Crang, M. and Thrift, N. (2000) *Thinking Space: Critical Geographies*. London: Routledge.

Critchley, S. (1992) *The Ethics of Deconstruction: Derrida and Levinas*. Oxford: Blackwell.

Croker, A. (1992) *The Possessed Individual*. London: Macmillan.

De Landa, M. (1997) *A Thousand Years of Nonlinear History*. Cambridge, MA: MIT Press.

Debray, R. (2000) *Transmitting Culture*. New York: Columbia University Press.

Deleuze, G. (1997) *Negotiations*. New York: Columbia University Press.

Deleuze, G. and Parnet, Claire (1987) *Dialogues*. London: Athlone.

Deleuze, G. and Guattari, F. (1980) *Mille plateaux*. Paris: Editions de minuit.

Deleuze, G. and Guattari, F. (1983) *Anti-Oedipus*. London: Athlone.

Derrida, J. (1973). *Speech and Phenomenon. And Other Essays on Husserl's Theory of Signs*. Evanston, IL: Northwestern University Press.

Derrida, J. (1976) *Voix et phénomène*. Paris: Presses Universitaire de France.

Derrida, J. (1978a) '"Genesis and Structure" and Phenomenology', in *Writing and Difference*. London: Routledge. pp. 154–68.

Derrida, J. (1978b) 'Violence and metaphysics: an essay on the thought of Emmanuel Levinas', in *Writing and Difference*. London: Routledge. pp. 79–153.

Derrida, J. (1991) *Donner le temps, 1. La fausse monnaie*. Paris: Galilée.

Derrida, J. (1992) *Given Time, I. Counterfeit Money*. Chicago: University of Chicago Press.

Derrida, J. (1996) *Archive Fever*. Chicago, IL: University of Chicago Press.

Diken, B. (1999) 'Nomadic power'. Unpublished paper. Aarhus University: Aarhus.

Durkheim, E. (1947) *The Elementary Forms of Religious Life*. London: Allen & Unwin.

Durkheim, Emile and Mauss, Marcel (1963) *Primitive Classification*. London: Cohen & West.

Eco, U. (1984) *Semiotics and the Philosophy of Language*. London: Macmillan.

Eco, U. (1990) *Travels in Hyperreality: Essays*. New York: Harcourt Brace.

Esslin, M. (1999) *Antonin Artaud*. London: Calder.

Featherstone, M. (2000) 'Archiving Culture', *British Journal of Sociology*, JI.

Feenberg, Andrew (1993) *Critical Theory of Technology*. Oxford: Oxford University Press.

Ferreira, J. (1997) 'Judgement and modern social theory'. PhD Thesis, Lancaster University.

Flaxman, G. (ed.) (2000) *The Brain is the Screen. Deleuze and the Philosophy of Cinema*. Minneapolis: University of Minnesota Press.

Foster, Hal (1996) *The Return of the Real*. Cambridge, MA: The MIT Press.

Foucault, M. (1966) *Les Mots et les choses*. Paris: Gallimard.

Foucault, M. (1977) 'A preface to transgression', in *Language, Counter-Memory, Practice* (ed. David Bouchard). Oxford: Blackwell. pp. 29–52.

Foucault, M. (1984) 'What is Enlightenment?', in P. Rabinow (ed.), *The Foucault Reader*. New York: Pantheon.

Foucault, M. (1998) *The History of Sexuality*, Vol 1: *The Will to Knowledge*. Harmondsworth: Penguin.

Franklin, S., Lury, C. and Stacey, J. (2000) *Global Nature, Global Culture*. London: Sage.

Friedman, J. (1994) *Cultural Identity and Global Process*. London: Sage.

Frisby, D. (1985) *Fragments of Modernity*. Cambridge: Polity.

Gadamer, H-G. (1976) *Philosophical Hermeneutics*. Berkeley, CA: University of California Press.

Gadamer, H-G. (1986) *The Relevance of the Beautiful and Other Essays*. Cambridge: Cambridge University Press.

Gadamer, H-G. (1989) *Truth and Method*, second revised edition. London: Sheed and Ward.

Gadamer, H-G. (1990) *Wahrheit und Methode*, Band 1. Tübingen: J.C.B. Mohr.

Game, A. (1991) *Undoing the Social: Towards a Deconstructive Sociology*. Milton Keynes: Open University Press.

Game, A. (1995) 'Time, space and memory: with reference to Bachelard' in M. Featherstone, S. Lash and R. Robertson (eds), *Global Modernities*. London: Sage.

Gane, Mike (1991) *Baudrillard's Bestiary*. London: Routledge.

Gane, N. (1999) 'Weber and post-structuralism'. PhD Thesis, London Guildhall University.

Garfinkel, Harold (1952) 'The perception of the other: a study in social order'. PhD. Thesis, Harvard University, Cambridge, MA, 2 volumes.

Garfinkel, Harold (1967) *Studies in Ethnomethodology*. Cambridge: Polity.

Garver, N. (1973) Preface, to J. Derrida, *Speech and Phenomenon*. Evanston, IL: Northwestern University Press. pp. ix–xxx.

Gasché, Rodolphe (1986) *The Tain of the Mirror. Derrida and the Philosophy of Reflection*. Cambridge, MA: Harvard University Press.

Gehlen, A. (1962) *Das Mensch*. Frankfurt: Athenaüm.

Gell, A. (1998) *Art and Agency*. Oxford: Oxford University Press.

Gerschenkron, A. (1962) *Economic Backwardness in Historical Perspective*. Cambridge, MA: Belknap.

Giddens, Anthony (1990) *The Consequences of Modernity*. Cambridge: Polity.

Genosko, G. (1999) *McLuhan and Baudrillard*. London: Routledge.

Gilroy, Paul (1993) *The Black Atlantic*. London: Verso.

Gilroy, Paul (2000) *Between Camps*. London: Penguin.

Girard, M. and Stark, D. (2001) 'Distributed Intelligence and Organization of Diversity in New Media Projects', International Workshop, Socio-Economics of Space, University of Bonn, April.

Grosz, E. (1998) 'The time of violence: deconstruction and value', in S. Lash, A. Quick and R. Roberts (eds), *Time and Value*. Oxford: Blackwell. pp. 190–205.

Von Grunebaum, G.E. and Caillois, Roger (eds) (1967) *Dream and Human Societies*. Berkeley, CA: University of California Press.

Habermas, J. (1963) *Theorie und Praxis*. Neuweid: Luchterhand.

Habermas, J. (1971) *Knowledge and the Human Interests*. London: Heinemann.

Habermas, J. (1984) *The Theory of Communicative Action*, Vol. 1. Cambridge: Polity.

Habermas, J. (1987) *The Philosophical Discourse of Modernity*. Cambridge: Polity.

Hahm, C. (1994), 'Democracy and authority in the Post-Confucian context'. Paper for conference on the 21st Century and Democracy, Seoul, Korea, October. 1994.

Hall, Stuart (1999) 'Multiculture'. Paper delivered at Goldsmiths College, Colloquium on the Future of Political Culture, London, May.

Han, S-J. (1995) 'Media and mediations: the public sphere in Korea's democratic transition'. Conference on Korean Society II, Georgetown University, Washington, DC, May.

Haraway, D. (1976) *Crystals, Fabrics and Fields: Metaphors of Organicism in Twentieth Century Molecular Biology*. New Haven, CT: Yale University Press.

Haraway, D. (1991) *Simians, Cyborgs and Women*. London: Free Association Books.

Haraway, D. (1992) *Primate Visions*. London: Verso.

Haraway, D. (1996) *Modest Witness@Second_Millennium. FemaleMan©_Meets Oncomouse™*. London: Routledge.

Hardt, M. and Negri, A. (2000) *Empire*. Cambridge, MA: Harvard University Press.

Harvard Project on the City (2000) *Lagos Handbook*. Cambridge, Mass.

Harvey, David (1989) *The Condition of Post-Modernity*. Oxford: Blackwell.

Hegel, G.W.F. (1967) *The Philosophy of Right*. Oxford: Oxford University Press.

Hegel, G.W.F. (1970) *On Art, Religion and Philosophy*. New York: Harper Torchbooks.

Heidegger, M. (1971) 'The Thing'. *Poetry, Language, Thought*. New York: Harper & Row. pp. 163–86.

Heidegger, M. (1977) *The Question Concerning Technology and Other Essays*. New York: Harper & Row.

Heidegger, M. (1986) *Sein und Zeit*. 16. Aufl. Tubingen: Max Niemeyer Verlag.

Heidegger, M. (1994) 'Die Frage nach der Technik', in M. Heidegger, *Vorträge und Aufsätze*. Stuttgart: Verlag Günther Neske.

Hitzler, R. and Peters, H. (1998) *Inzenierung: Innere Sicherheit*. Frankfurt: Lesake + Budrich Verlag.

Holt, Richard (1989) *Sport and the British*. Oxford: Clarendon.

Honneth, A. (1995) *The Struggle for Recognition. The Moral Grammar of Social Conflicts*. Cambridge: Polity.

Horkheimer, M. and Adorno, T. (1997) *Dialectic of Enlightenment*. London: Verso.

Huizinga, J. (1971) *Homo Ludens*. Boston, MA: Beacon.

Husserl, E. (1975) *Experience and Judgement*. Evanston, IL: Northwestern University Press.

Husserl, E. (1987) *Cartesianische Meditationen*. Hamburg: Felix Meiner.

Husserl, E. (1991) *On the Phenomenology of the Consciousness of Internal Time*. Dordrecht: Kluwer.

Hutton, Will (1998) *The Stakeholding Society*. Cambridge: Polity.

International Labor Office (1996) *Multimedia Convergence and Labor Relations*. Geneva: International Labor Office.

Jay, M. (1993) *Downcast Eyes*. Berkeley, CA: University of California Press.

Jung, Hwa Yol. (1989) *The Question of Rationality and the Basic Grammar of Intercultural Texts*. Nigata: International University of Japan.

Jung, Werner (1990) *Georg Simmel zur Einführung*. Hamburg: Junius.

Kant, I. (1952) *The Critique of Judgement*. Oxford: Clarendon.

Kellner, D. (1994) *Media Culture*. London: Routledge.

Kittler, F. (1997) *Literature, Media, Information Systems*. Amsterdam: OPA.

Knorr-Cetina, K. (2000) 'Currency traders as epistemic communities', *American Journal of Sociology*, Vol. 65.

Koolhaas, Rem (2001) 'Junkspace'. Unpublished manuscript.

Koolhaas, Rem et al. (1997) *S, M, L, XL*. Cologne: Benedikt Taschen Verlag.

Laclau, E. (1990) *New Reflections on the Revolution of Our Time*. London: Verso.

Laclau, E. (ed.) (1994) *The Making of Political Identities*. London: Verso.

Laclau, E. and Mouffe, C. (1986) *Hegemony and Socialist Strategies*. London: Verso.

Lakka, M. (2000) 'Avant gardes and freedom. MA Dissertation', Goldsmiths College, London University.

Lash, S. (1990) *Sociology of Postmodernism*. London: Routledge.

Lash, S. (1999) *Another Modernity, A Different Rationality*. Oxford: Blackwell.

Lash, S. and Urry, J. (1987) *The End of Organized Capitalism*. Cambridge: Polity.

Lash, S. and Urry, J. (1994) *Economies of Signs and Space*. London: Sage.

Latour, Bruno (1993) *We Have Never Been Modern*. Hemel Hempstead: Harvester Wheatsheaf.

Latour, Bruno (1996) *Petite réflexion sur le culte moderne des dieux faitiches*. Le Plessis-Robinson: Synthélabo.

Latour, B. and Woolgar, S. (1979) *Laboratory Life*. Princeton, NJ: Princeton University Press.

Leadbeater, C. (1999) *Living on Thin Air*. Harmondsworth: Penguin.

Le Breton, D. (1997) *Du Silence*. Paris: Métailié.

Lefebvre, H. (1986) *La Production de l'espace*. Third edition. Paris: Éditions anthropos.

Lefebvre, H. (1991) *The Production of Space*. Oxford: Blackwell.

Leiss, W., Kline, S. and Jhally, S. (1990) *Social Communication in Advertising: Persons, Products and Images of Well-Being*. London: Routledge.

Levinas, E. (1973) *The Theory of Intuition in Husserl's Phenomenology*. Evanston, IL: Northwestern University Press.

Levinas, E. (1974) *Autrement qu'être ou au delà de l'essence*. Paris: Kluwer/Martinus Nijhoff.

Levinas, E. (1983) *Le Temps et l'autre*. Paris: Quadrige/Presses Universitaires de France.

Levinas, E. (1990) *De l'existence à l'existant*, second edition. Paris: Librairie Philosophique J. Vrin.

Libeskind, D. (2000) 'Technology and Memory'. Paper at conference Inhabiting Technology, London: Institute of Contemporary Arts, March.

Luhmann, Niklas (1997) *Die Gesellschaft der Gesellschaft*. Frankfurt: Suhrkamp.

Luke, Tim (1995) 'New world order or neo-world orders: power, politics and ideology in the informationalising Global Order', in M. Featherstone, S. Lash and R. Robertson (eds), *Global Modernities*. London: Sage.

Luke, Tim (1996) 'Identity, meaning and globalization: detraditionalization in postmodern space–time compression', in P. Heelas, S. Lash and P. Morris (eds), *Detraditionalization*. Oxford: Basil Blackwell, pp. 109–33.

Lury, C. (1993) *Cultural Rights*. London: Routledge.

Lury, C. (1997) *Prosthetic Culture*. London: Routledge.

Lury, C. (1999) 'Marking time with Nike: the Illusion of the durable', *Public Culture*, Vol. 11, 499–526.

Lutz, B. and Veltz, P. (1989) 'Maschinenbauer versus Informatiker – Gesellschaftliche Einflüsse auf die fertigungstechnische Entwicklung: Deutschland und Frankreich', in K. Duell and B. Lutz (eds), *Technikentwicklung und Arbeitsteilung im internationalen Vergleich*. Frankfurt: Campus. pp. 215–72.

Lyotard, J-F. (1991) *The Inhuman: Reflections on Time*. Cambridge: Polity.

Lyotard, J-F. (1994) *Lessons on the Analytic of the Sublime*. Stanford, CA: Stanford University Press.

MacIntyre, A. (1981) *After Virtue*. London: Duckworth.

Marx, Karl (1977) *Das Kapital. Kritik der politischen Ökonomie*. Frankfurt am Main: Verlag Marxistische Blätter.

McLuhan, M. (1993) *Understanding Media*. London: Routledge.

McLuhan, M. (1997) *Essential McLuhan* (eds E. McLuham and F. Zingrone). London: Routledge.

Mâle, Emile (1983) *Religious Art from the Twelfth to the Eighteenth Century*. Princeton, NJ: Princeton University Press.

Maharaj, S. (1999) 'Fatal natalities: the algebra of diaspora and difference after apartheid', *Strange, Photofile 57*, pp. 41–9.

Maharaj, S. (2000) *Sarat Maharaj: Works in Pre-gross*. London: Institute of International Visual Arts Paperback.

Manovich, L. (2001) *The Language of New Media*. Cambridge, MA: The MIT Press.

Manzini, Enzo (1989) *The Material of Invention*. London: Design Council.

Mauss, M. (1990) *The Gift*. London: Routledge.

Menninghaus, W. (1980) *Walter Benjamins Theorie der Sprachmagie*. Frankfurt: Suhrkamp.

Mink, Janis (1995) *Marcel Duchamp, 1887–1968. Art as Anti-Art*. Cologne: Benedikt Taschen.

Molotch, H. (1996) 'L.A. as design product: how art works in a regional economy', in Allen J. Scott and Edward Soja (eds), *The City: Los Angeles and Urban Theory at the End of the Twentieth Century*. Berkeley, CA: University of California Press. pp. 225–75.

Mumford, L. (1974) *The Pentagon of Power : The Myth of Machine*, Vol. 2. New York: Harcourt Brace.

Nancy, J-L. (1990) *Une Pensée finie*. Paris: Galilée.

Nancy, J-L. (1991) *The Inoperative Community*. Minneapolis: University of Minnesota Press.

Negroponte, N. (1995) *Being Digital*. London: Hodder & Stoughton.

Nietzsche, F. (1966) *Die Geburt der Tragödie*, in F. Nietzsche, *Werke in drei Bänden*, Band I. Munich: Carl Hanser Verlag. pp. 7–134.

Parsons, T. (1955) *The Social System*. New York: Free Press.

Parsons, T. (1968) *The Structure of Social Action*. New York: Free Press.

Patton, P. (ed.) (1996) *Deleuze: a Critical Reader*. Oxford: Blackwell.

Popper, K. (1972) *Objective Knowledge*. Oxford: Oxford University Press.

Poster, Mark (1990) *The Mode of Information*. Cambridge: Polity.

Poster, Mark (1995) *The Second Media Age*. Cambridge: Polity.

Rabinow, Paul (1999) *French DNA: Trouble in Purgatory*. Chicago: University of Chicago Press.

Ricoeur, P. (1981) 'Phenomenology and hermeneutics', in P. Ricoeur, *Hermeneutics and the Human Sciences*. Cambridge: Cambridge University Press.

Robins, Kevin (1996) *Into the Image: Culture and Politics in the Field of Vision*. London: Routledge.

Rodowick, D.N. (1997) *Gille Deleuze's Time Machine*. Durham, NC: Duke University Press.

Rose, G. (1981) *Hegel: Contra Sociology*. London: Athlone.

Rose, G. (1992) *The Broken Middle. Out of Our Ancient Society*. Oxford: Blackwell.

Santos, B. (1998) 'Time, baroque codes and canonization', in S. Lash, A. Quick and R. Roberts (eds), *Time and Value*. Oxford: Blackwell. pp. 244–61.

Sassen, S. (1991) *The Global City*. Princeton, NJ: Princeton University Press.

Saussure, F. de (1983) *Course in General Linguistics*. London: Gerald Duckworth.

Scarry, E. (1987) *The Body in Pain*. Oxford: Oxford University Press.

Schulze, G. (2001) *The Experience Society*. London: Sage.

Schutz, A. (1974) *Der sinnhafte Aufbau der sozialen Welt. Eine Einleitung in die verstehende Soziologie*. Frankfurt: Suhrkamp.

Scott, Allen J. (2000) *The Cultural Economy of Cities*. London: Sage.

Searle, J.R. (1969) *Speech Acts. An Essay in the Philosophy of Language*. Cambridge: Cambridge University Press.

Sennett, Richard (1998) *The Corrosion of Character*. New York: Norton.

Shields, Rob (1998) *Henri Lefebvre: Love and Struggle*. London: Routledge.

Silverstone, R. and Hirsch, Eric (eds) (1992) *Consuming Technologies*. London: Routledge.

Simmel, Georg (1971) 'The metropolis and mental life', in *Georg Simmel on Individuality and Social Forms* (D. Levine ed.) Chicago: University of Chicago Press. pp. 324–40.

Soja, Ed (1996) *Thirdspace*. Oxford: Blackwell.

Spivak, G. (1999) *A Critique of Post-Colonial Reason*. Cambridge, MA: Harvard University Press.

Srubar, I. (1988) *Kosmion*. Frankfurt: Suhrkamp.

Strathern, M. (1999) *Property, Substance and Effect*. London: Athlone.

Strange, Susan (1996) *The Retreat of the State*. Cambridge: Cambridge University Press.

Taussig, M. (1992) *Mimesis and Alterity: A Particular History of the Senses*. London: Routledge.

Thompson, John B. (1981) *Critical Hermeneutics*. Cambridge: Cambridge University Press.

Thompson, John B. (1990) *Ideology and Modern Culture: Critical Social Theory in the Era of Mass Communication*. Cambridge: Polity.

Thompson, John B. (1995) *The Media and Modernity: A Social Theory of the Media*. Cambridge: Polity.

Thompson, Michael (1979) *Rubbish Theory: The Creation and Destruction of Value*. Oxford: Oxford University Press.

Touraine, A. (1969) *La Société post-industrielle*. Paris: Denoel-Méditations.

Touraine, A. (1974) *The Post-Industrial Society*. New York: Wildwood Press.

Touraine, A. (1975) *Production de la société*. Paris: Editions du Seuil

Touraine, A. (1995) *Critique of Modernity*. Oxford: Blackwell.

Turkle, Sherry (1995) *Life on the Screen*. New York: Simon & Schuster.

Urry, John (2000) *Sociology Beyond Societies: Mobilities for the Twenty First Century*. London: Routledge.

Van Toorn, R. (1998) 'The society of "the and"'. Unpublished paper. Berlage Institute, Amsterdam.

Virilio, P. (1982) 'Exposer l'accident', *Traverses*, 6, *Les Rhetoriques de la Technologie*, pp. 36–41.

Virilio, P. (1984) *L'Horizon négatif*. Paris: Galilée.

Virilio, P. (1986) *Speed and Politics*. New York: Semiotext(e).

Virilio, P. (1987) 'L'image virtuelle mentale et instrumentale', *Traverses*, *44–5*, *Machines Virtuelles*, pp. 35–39.

Virilio, P. (1989) *War and Cinema*. London: Verso.

Virilio, P. (1990) *L'Inertie polaire*. Paris: Christian Bourgois.

Virilio, P. (1991) *L'Insécurité de la territoire*. Paris: Galilée.

Virilio, P. (1994a) *Bunker Archeology*. New York: Princeton Architectural Press.

Virilio, P. (1994b) *The Vision Machine*. London: British Film Institute.

Virilio, P. (1997) *Open Sky*. London: Verso.

Virilio, P. (1999a) *The Information Bomb*. London: Verso.

Virilio, P. (1999b) *Polar Inertia*. London: Sage.

Virilio, P. and Lotringer, S. (1983) *Pure War*. New York: Semiotext(e).

Walsh, W.H. (1975) *Kant's Critique of Metaphysics*. Edinburgh: Edinburgh University Press.

Weber, M. (1946) 'Politics as a vocation', in H. Gerth and C.W. Mills (eds), *From Max Weber*. Oxford: Oxford University Press. pp. 77–128.

Weber, M. (1963) *The Sociology of Religion*. Boston, MA: Beacon.

Weber, M. (1980) *Wirtschaft und Gesellschaft*. Tübingen: J.C.B. Mohr.

Webster, Frank (1995) *Theories of the Information Society*. London: Routledge.

Wiewiorka, M. (1991) *L'Espace du racisme*. Paris: Seuil.

Williamson, O. (1985) *The Economic Institutions of Capitalism*. New York: Free Press.

Wittel, A. (2000) 'Network sociality'. Unpublished paper. London University, Goldsmiths College.

Yar, M. (1999) 'Community and recognition'. PhD Thesis, Lancaster University.

Zizek, S. (1989) *The Sublime Object of Ideology*. London: Verso.

Zourabichvili, François (1994) *Deleuze, une philosophe de l'événement*. Paris: Presses Universitaires de France.

Index